THE CUTTING ROOM FLOOR

THE CUTTING ROOM FLOOR

LAURENT BOUZEREAU

A Citadel Press Book
Published by Carol Publishing Group

A Citadel Press Book
Published by Carol Publishing Group
Citadel Press is a registered trademark of Carol Communications,
Inc.
Editorial Offices: 600 Madison Avenue, New York, N.Y. 10022
Sales and Distribution Offices: 120 Enterprise Avenue, Secaucus,
N.J. 07094
In Canada: Canadian Manda Group, P.O. Box 920, Station U,
Toronto, Ontario M8Z 5P9
Queries regarding rights and permissions should be addressed to
Carol Publishing Group, 600 Madison Avenue, New York, N.Y.
10022

Carol Publishing Group books are available at special discounts for
bulk purchases, for sales promotions, fund raising, or educational
purposes. Special editions can be created to specifications. For
details, contact Special Sales Department, Carol Publishing Group,
120 Enterprise Avenue, Secaucus, N.J. 07094

Manufactured in the United States of America
10 9 8 7 6 5 4 3 2 1

Library of Congress Cataloging-in-Publication Data

Bouzereau, Laurent.
    The cutting room floor : movie scenes which never made it to
the movies / by Laurent Bouzereau.
        p.   cm.
    "A Citadel Press book."
    ISBN 0-8065-1491-4
    1. Motion pictures—Plots, themes, etc.   2. Motion pictures—
    Editing.   3. Motion pictures—Censorship.   I. Title.
PN1997.8.B64   1994
791.43'75—dc20   93-45401
                                                          CIP

CONTENTS

ACKNOWLEDGMENTS

I wish to thank the following people who helped me with this book:

My agent and friend Kay McCauley, at Citadel Press Allan J. Wilson and Alvin H. Marill, and at Carol Publishing Donald Davidson, Deborah Feingertz, Shirley Hinkamp, and Ben Petrone. I'm also grateful to my parents, Daniel and Micheline; my sisters, Cécile and Géraldine; and my family back in France.

And, in alphabetical order:

Merrick Bursuk, Jeff Cava, Stephanie Clayton, Jon Davison, Donna Dickman, Lynn Ehrensperger, Bob Gale, Noelle Hannon, Nicholas Hassitt, Vicki Hiatt, Deborah and Hall Hutchison, Perry Katz, William M. Kolb, Stephan and Cris Lapp, Van Ling, Andrew London, David Lowery, Don Mancini, Maitland McDonagh, John Pace, David Palmer, Jack Perez, Daniel Petrie Jr., Penny Shaw, Bud Smith, Kristen Valenti, Paul Verhoeven, the staffs of the Margaret Herrick Library and the following companies and studios: Amblin Entertainment, Columbia Pictures, Carolco, Lightstorm Entertainment, MGM/UA, Orion Pictures, Tri-Star Pictures, Twentieth Century Fox, Universal Pictures, Warner Bros., and my friends at Zaloom/Mayfield Productions.

I dedicate this book to my parents and my sisters.

INTRODUCTION

There's no such thing as the definitive version of a film.

Getting a film made is a challenge. Directors and producers have to fight against the Hollywood studios and their politics to get a project set up and approved. After months, sometimes years, in what studio executives refer to as "development hell" and during which a script is analyzed, changed, and rewritten a hundred times, a project is either put into turnaround (in other words put up for sale), shelved, abandoned, or "green-lighted" (meaning the camera can start rolling). But the battle continues on the set where filmmakers have to deal with strict budgets and with actors who often have more power than the director and the producers themselves. Once the film is "in the can," one should think troubles are over. In reality, the struggle has only just begun.

A film can be changed by a test audience, after a sneak preview, by the studios, by the rating board of the Motion Picture Association of America (MPAA), by the networks, by airline companies even! Delete a few frames and a whole sequence can lose its meaning; add one short scene and a director's vision, for better or worse, can be altered dramatically. Whoever gets the power of replacing, deleting, or adding images can mean for a movie the difference between life and death.

The Cutting Room Floor is about a group of films, arbitrarily selected, illustrating the different changes, or threats of changes, that can affect a director's original intentions. This book examines through these specific examples the wounds, bruises, fatal cuts, and sometimes miracle remedies that can improve or destroy a film. It is about not only what was cut, but also what was added and about changes in general. *The Cutting Room Floor* is about (in order of appearance):

- Alfred Hitchcock's *Suspicion, Topaz*, and *Spellbound*
- Robert Zemeckis's *Back to the Future I, II*, and *III*, and *Death Becomes Her*
- Ridley Scott's *Blade Runner*
- James Cameron's *The Abyss, Aliens*, and *Terminator 2*
- Steven Spielberg's *Close Encounters of the Third Kind* and *1941*
- John Boorman's *Exorcist II: The Heretic*
- Brian De Palma's *Dressed to Kill* and *Scarface*
- William Friedkin's *The Exorcist, Cruising*, and *To Live and Die in L.A.*
- Paul Verhoeven's *Basic Instinct*.

Preceding these titles is a brief history of the test-screening process, of the MPAA, and of other cutting measures.

This book is about the films you could have seen, the films you almost were never allowed to see. It's about a few frames left on the cutting room floor, or entire sequences that were thrown out and that miraculously, years after the initial release, reappeared. It also explores films that were vetoed by special interest groups—films that could have never made it to the editing room, or could have been changed before the director called "Action!"

A note to the reader: In some cases, scenes are described in great detail, shot by shot, even with retranscribed dialogue, to explain the changes that were made to some of the titles explored in this book. That way, you might be able to grab the videotapes of these films and see precisely what you could have seen and follow the processes through which the movies were changed. In other words, the logical companion to this book is your VCR. Also, you'll want to refer to the bibliography at the end of this book; it will explain why *The Cutting Room*

Floor is not about many other movies that were cut; in most cases, these have already been written about in excellent books that I hope you'll want to consult.

By the way, other titles that have deliberately been left out are being saved for *The Cutting Room Floor, Part 2.*

AN OVERVIEW OF HOLLYWOOD'S CUTTING MEASURES

SNEAK PREVIEWS

A shopping mall in the Valley. . . I think it was in Ventura, California, in 1990. . . I was on line for a sneak preview of *The Exorcist III*. Although the audience that had been recruited for this test screening was too young to have seen *The Exorcist* on the big screen when it came out in 1973, teenagers, mainly Hispanic-types, or jocks with, on their arms, girlfriends snapping bubble gum, seemed excited. *The Exorcist III* was written and directed by William Peter Blatty, based on his novel *Legion*. Blatty, the creator of the original *Exorcist* (he wrote both the novel and the script—for which he received an Oscar—and produced the film) was present at the preview and was surrounded by Joe Roth, then president of Twentieth Century Fox, and other executives from the studio. They stood in the back of the packed theater. A short speech: We were told that what we were about to see was a work-in-progress; at the end of the film, cards would be handed out to us, asking about our reactions to the picture. Did we like the film? What scenes did we like the most? Were there any scenes we did not like? Would we recommend this film to a friend? The screening started; the audience was tensed, expecting a big scare. Slowly, the audience seemed to be getting bored, restless, and ultimately annoyed by the movie. Although brilliantly acted by George C. Scott and Brad Dourif, cleverly directed, and intellectually stimulating, it was obvious that *The Exorcist III* was far too cerebral. Many left the theater before filling out their screening cards. I did my duty; my only criticism was over the ending, which I thought was confusing. As I departed, Blatty and the gang from Fox were hanging out, waiting for the verdict. I approached Blatty, interrupted his discussion, and told him how much I liked the film. Unfortunately, the film was in trouble. *The Exorcist III* was not what audiences expected. It was not *The Exorcist*. The studio knew that word of mouth would be bad and decided to release the film without showing it to the press. The opening weekend was incredible; *The Exorcist III* was number one—by the way, the ending had been changed and worked! But by the following week, *The Exorcist III* was already history.

In his 1950 book, *Hollywood Looks at Its Audience: A Report of Film Audience Research*, Leo A. Handel, then probably the only full-time audience-research director employed by a major motion picture company, studied the different methods to analyze public opinion, surveys, and sneak previews, how they could guide filmmakers, producers, and studios in choosing material and stars, and how they could help the marketing of a film. Another pioneer in that field was Dr. George Gallup. During Hollywood's golden age, his company, Audience Research, Inc. (ARI), was used by RKO, Columbia Pictures, and producing giants like David O. Selznick and Samuel Goldwyn. Among ARI's services was the "want-to-see" poll, designed to foretell audience reaction to a proposed film project. Armed with a synopsis and photos, interviewers in approximately one-hundred cities and towns, ranging in size from New York City to Waukee, Iowa (pop. 473!), would ask people: Would you like to see this movie? How much? Why? When the question "What do you think of Ingrid Bergman and Humphrey Bogart together in a movie called *Casablanca*?" was asked, for instance, women and men responded positively to the idea, and ARI's figures indicated accurately that *Casablanca* would do outstanding business. On the other hand, ARI had been wrong in predicting that *How Green Was My Valley* would not be successful because of Walter Pidgeon; there was more to a film than its stars, and in that particular case, ARI had not taken in consideration John Ford's directing.

Once a film was completed in a rough cut, ARI organized test screenings. Gallup had developed a test known as "televoting." Each audience member received a matchbox-sized electrical device which fit in the palm of a hand and was wired to a control box in the rear of the theater. Before the film started, instructions were given on how to use the gadget. If the film played well, the audience would turn a little dial over to the right, toward a wee light marked "Like" or way down to "Like very much." Over to the left were "Dull" and "Very dull." The reactions were charted on a graph.

Other devices were created by Gallup's competitors. Paul F' Lazarsfeld of Columbia University and Frank Stanton of Columbia Broadcasting System developed the Lazarsfeld-Stanton Program Analyzer. Viewers would have a green button in one hand and a red one in the other, both connected to a battery of pens resting on a moving tape of paper. If they liked the film, they pressed green, and red if they didn't. If they felt indifferent, they didn't press either button. There was also the Schwerin System, which relied not on a mechanical device but questionnaires that were filled out at certain intervals while the movie was being shown. In all these cases, if the movie scored very low, it was released quickly, without much advertising. If the results were good, plans for the publicity campaigns were made accordingly. ARI also provided another service called "audience penetration," which disclosed the number of people who had learned about the picture through publicity. Based on the results, the campaigns could be altered.

In the 1950s however, because of the growth of television, the public started staying away from movie theaters. Bigger movies had to be made to bring audiences back. With the development of cable TV and home video, risks of box-office failure multiplied, and sneak previews inevitably became an important step in the filmmaking process. Today, a man named Joe Farrell, with his company, National Research Group, established in 1978, is a leader in the preview field. Audience testing is truly a science, and while it might sometimes drive creative directors crazy, this system has changed the fate of many movies for the better. Today, most movies, even by the greatest directors, go through test screenings and are inevitably changed one way or another.

Stanley Kubrick is a director whose work was highly influenced by test screenings. *Dr. Strangelove* (1964), his satire about the atomic bomb starring George C. Scott and Peter Sellers (playing three different roles), initially had a different ending. A large part of the film takes place in the war room at the Pentagon; at the end of the picture, Russians and Americans originally threw cream pies at each other, and finally, Peter Bull, who played the Russian ambassador, and Peter Sellers, as the President of the United States, sat pie-covered on the floor making custard castles while singing "For he's a jolly good fellow," the "he" being Strangelove, also played by Sellers. The sequence took about two weeks to shoot and required at least 2,000 pies laced with shaving cream (real custard gets rock hard too fast). After the first day of shooting, an additional shot, taking place before the battle with the pies began, was needed; the whole set had to be cleaned up, and when a lady of the wardrobe department showed up at the dry cleaner's with all the costumes covered with shaving cream, the owner commented, "I get it; this is for *Candid Camera!*" And all that trouble for nothing. After test-screening the film, Kubrick realized that although the scene was funny, it simply did not fit into the story and decided to cut it. "It was too farcical and not consistent with the satiric tone of the rest of the film." While filming the sequence, however, another ending with Strangelove miraculously rising from his wheelchair was conceived; this became the last image in the war room.

Kubrick's *2001: A Space Odyssey* (1968) was originally 160 minutes. With a two-year production schedule, the director did not finish editing the film until eight days before the first press preview. Any reflection on his cutting could not be reached until Kubrick saw the film with an audience and the critics. "I had not had the opportunity to see the film complete with music, sound effects, etc., until about a week before it opened," Kubrick said, "and it does take a few runnings to decide finally how long things should be, especially scenes

which do not have narrative advancement as their guideline."
He realized that the first part of the film was a bit too long. "I
have never seen an audience so restless," he recalled. "The
unreceptiveness of the audience that night, I think, can be
attributed in part to the fact that it was made up largely of
people between thirty-five and sixty, who were unresponsive
to a film that departed so radically from established conven-
tions of filmmaking such as a strong narrative line." When *2001*
came out, Kubrick explained that 90 percent of the audience
that went to see the film was between thirty-five and sixty.
The preview audience and the paying audience were at two
ends of the moviegoing scale, which explains why the film
played poorly at the first screening. Kubrick did not realize
this until later and decided to cut his film. "I just felt as I looked
at it and looked at it that I could see places where I could
tighten-up, and I took out nineteen minutes," Kubrick declared,
"I didn't believe that the trims made a crucial difference. I
think it just affected some marginal people. The people who
like it [the film], like it no matter what its length, and the same
holds true for the people who hate it."

Kubrick trimmed down the opening sequence entitled "The
Dawn of Man," scenes on the moon, and those in Discovery 1,
which showed in more detail the routine life aboard the spaceship. To explain the action more clearly, Kubrick added two
titles: "Jupiter Mission, 18 Months Later" and "Jupiter Beyond
the Infinite."

Kubrick went as far as recutting *The Shining* (1980) after
the film had already been released. If you saw it the week it
opened and decided to go again the second week, you might
have thought you were imagining things. Kubrick eliminated a
scene at the end during which Shelley Duvall is recuperating
at a hospital and receives the visit from Barry Nelson, the manager of the Overlook Hotel where Jack Nicholson, Duvall's husband, lost his mind—and his life. "I decided the scene was
unnecessary," Kubrick said after he noticed that audiences felt
it threw off the excitement reached during the film's climax.

Orson Welles, on the other hand, was less lucky with the test-
screening process. In fact, many of his projects were recut,

some even aborted after shooting began. His career—as well as his relationship with RKO Pictures—was forever changed after *The Magnificent Ambersons* (1942) tested badly and was cut down and altered dramatically. At the time of the sneak preview, Welles was in Brazil making "a cultural interchange" film entitled *It's All True* for RKO Pictures, which incidentally was never completed by Welles himself. (The footage, thought to be lost but then discovered by Welles colleague Richard Wilson in the vaults of Paramount Pictures in 1985, was finally released in 1993 and was included in a documentary also entitled *It's All True*.) "About forty-five minutes were cut out— the whole heart of the picture, really—for which the first part had been a preparation," Welles said about *Ambersons*. "The closing sequence in the hospital was written and directed by somebody else. It bears no relation to my script." Most of the cuts and some additional scenes were in fact directed by Robert Wise, who edited *Citizen Kane* (1941) and *Ambersons*. "We had a picture with major problems, and I feel all of us tried sincerely to keep the best of Welles's concept and still lick the problems," Wise asserted. "Since *Ambersons* has become something of a classic, I think it's now apparent we didn't 'mutilate' Orson's film." No prints of Welles's original cut supposedly survive.

Francis Coppola test-screened *Apocalypse Now* (1979) on Friday, May 11, 1979, at the Mann's Bruin Theater in Westwood, California. Tickets were $7.50, with all proceeds going to benefit the Pacific Film Archive of the University of California at Berkeley. With a questionnaire came a letter from Coppola himself explaining to the test audience that what they were about to see was a work-in-progress:

> I must say something about myself. I was and probably still am a theater director. For me this means I need the opportunity to show my work as close to its final form as I intend it so I can judge how it affects my audience. Therefore, I have prepared some questions I would like answered as a director asking his audience for their response. In a real sense, it is my invitation to you to

help me finish the film. Please understand that I will not take your responses literally and put them into effect, but rather I am asking for your opinions, and I will use those opinions in finally forming my own decisions on the film. It is the way I collaborated with hundreds of fellow artists who have worked with me on this film, and it is the way I would like to collaborate with my audience. This questionnaire is as much part of the making of *Apocalypse Now* as any of the others, and I thank you for your serious consideration of each question asked.

Apocalypse Now was released with two different endings; the 35mm prints showed the destruction of Marlon Brando's camp and explosions over the credits, while the 70mm version ended in a more ambiguous way, less violently, without explosions or end credits.

The initial ending of Adrian Lyne's *Fatal Attraction* (1987) was reshot after a sneak preview. Originally, Glenn Close killed herself, and Michael Douglas, who had had an affair with her, was arrested for her murder. Anne Archer, who played Douglas's wife, while looking up the number of her husband's lawyer, found a cassette tape in which Close disclosed the fact that she was going to kill herself. Archer ran out of the house with the evidence and the film ended with a flashback showing Close slashing her throat in her bathroom while listening to *Madame Butterfly*. "I adored the ending," Adrian Lyne said. "It was totally horrifying. She's got him from the grave!" The film was test-screened with that particular ending in Los Angeles, San Francisco, and Seattle. "I could feel the film go flat," the director noted. "And the audience was so with the movie until that point that it felt dramatically unsatisfying at the end. So we decided to make a change, only and purely for dramatic reasons." A new ending was shot and cost Paramount Pictures $1.3 million. In the released version, Glenn Close stalks Michael Douglas and his family at their house in the country. After a gruesome and shocking struggle between Douglas and Close in a bathtub, directly inspired by Henri-Georges Clouzot's 1954 classic *Les Diaboliques*, Anne Archer shoots the mad woman. In Tokyo however, where the original version played in three theaters, the suicide/hara-kiri-ritual ending appealed to the Japanese sensibilities.

To kill or not to kill the dog. . .

Daniel Petrie, Jr., is synonymous with success. He wrote *Beverly Hills Cop* (1984) and *The Big Easy* (1987), cowrote and produced *Shoot To Kill* (1988), cowrote and executive-produced *Turner & Hooch* (1989), and cowrote and directed *Toy Soldiers* (1991). His experience on *Turner & Hooch*, a comedy in which Tom Hanks plays a cop who teams up with the only witness to a crime—a drooling, slobbering junkyard dog named Hooch—and the way test audiences influenced the ending, is as perfect—and comical—an example to explain how the system works today. Petrie noted:

> We had three problems with the ending. In the script, our intention was always that Hooch dies but he has a puppy, and the family is left with a Hooch puppy at the end. In the script, the character played by Reginald VelJohnson [Hanks's partner] gets killed, and the combination proved to be too dark for the level of comedy that the movie was playing at. So, Roger Spottiswoode [the director] decided to recut the movie so that that character wouldn't get killed; we had to shoot an additional scene with Reggie coming back at the end of the story. We also shot a version in which Hooch lived and several others with little puppies for the tag of the movie. Here is what we found: First of all, having Reggie VelJohnson live worked perfectly well. But the ending whether Hooch lived or died was extremely controversial for the preview audiences that we showed it to. We did a back-to-back screening where the only difference was the last reel. One audience saw Hooch die at the end; the other saw the ending in which Hooch lived. There were focus groups afterwards in addition to cards, and the audience who had seen the ending in which the dog dies was extremely passionate. Some people argued vehemently that it was a betrayal to kill the dog at the end, that it

was horrible. Nobody cared about people getting killed, but the dog, now that was a real problem. A human being dying is something so horrendous that people don't engage their emotions as readily as they do the experience of losing a pet. [Incidentally, test audiences resented the fact that Kathleen Turner killed a dog in *The War of the Roses*, made a pâté out of it, and served it to her husband Michael Douglas. While this scene was kept, Danny DeVito, who costarred in and directed the film, added a shot of the dog, showing that it had in fact not been killed.]

Anyway, other people who had seen the print with Hooch dying at the end thought that the movie would have had no emotional content if we had *not* killed the dog. In the preview where the dog lived, by contrast, there was no passion; people would say oh, yeah, it was a cute movie. No one disliked it, but no one liked it as much as the people who had liked the other ending. The marketing and distribution people at Touchstone Pictures argued passionately for the ending in which the dog lived. They felt that that would be much better for the success of the movie. Roger and I made the case that we thought that it was a better film with the original ending. And Jeffrey Katzenberg [the head of the studio] was listening to all these arguments. He had the right to decide, and he said, "In the absence of compelling evidence that I would be doing a disservice to my shareholders, I have to side with the filmmakers." The ending that we always intended stood. But we still had a problem with the puppies at the end. The puppies were cute but inanimate. They didn't have any sort of personality to them. We decided that the thing to do was to have a more chaotic tag that would have a larger puppy, show that it had obviously torn up the house, and then reveal the puppy at the end. That proved to work very well. But that was our fourth attempt!

You do expect to learn things from sneak previews. You don't know quite what you're learning until you've had a chance to see the cards and digest the results. But you do a get a sense on how the movie plays. Sometimes your test audience is attentive but not enthusiastic, and you're surprised when they score the film quite high. Other times, the audience seems enthusiastic in the room, but when they come to mark their card, they don't score the film very high, and you're puzzled why that should be. Sometimes the film improves from screening to screening and the scores don't change and you wonder why that is. Sometimes you get some very specific piece of information that you can change and solve. On *Toy Soldiers*, for example, there was a line that I thought would work. At the end of the movie, our hero, played by Sean Astin, is about to hide in the basement when he hears a voice ask "Where is Arnold?" It's a kid who's gotten lost while the other kids have hidden. So Sean grabs the kid and hides him in a dumbwaiter saying, "Don't worry, Arnold's alright. He is downstairs. You hide here, don't say a word." Then he closes the door and says, "Who the fuck is Arnold?" We thought that would be very funny. In fact, the crew was going to make a tee shirt for the film that said: "Who the fuck is Arnold?" because they thought that was the funniest line. At our first preview, the audience seemed to really, really like the film. We had great scores, but on maybe a third of the cards there was a comment: "Liked the movie, but who was Arnold? What was that about? Where is Arnold? Was that guy Arnold?" They didn't get it at all. It wasn't received as a joke. People seemed to be bothered by the fact that we were trying to make a joke at a tense moment, although other little jokes that we had at tense moments worked out well. Who knows? But the thing that we thought would be the funniest line in the movie we immediately cut out. It was a specific thing; the preview audience helped us.

Ultimately, you want the film to work for the audience that it's intended for. So certainly you try to be a little bit governed by what that audience wants.

Research companies don't deliberately set out to find people that are uneducated. But they do recruit people at theaters where the film will be shown or at a nearby mall. It has to be an area where no film people live, but it has to be close enough so that studio executives can go to the screenings. They seek to recruit a random sample of people and read them a synopsis of the film: "Would you like two tickets for a new film with Tom Hanks, in which he teams up with a snarling junkyard dog?" In other words, the audience is self-selected. They attempt to recruit an audience that's equally male and female and divided more equally between age groups. Sometimes they will recruit younger people, sometimes not, but they will always attempt to choose people who are over twelve and under fifty. Depending on the neighborhood, they might attract different ethnic groups as well. The perception of a movie can be very much determined by the scores it gets at a sneak preview, whether it's regarded as a film in trouble or a film that has the potential of being successful.

Many European films are made without regard to whether or not they're going to make money or are made for so little money that they will make a profit by appealing to a small segment of the audience. Films like that should not be previewed, unless the director wants it. Movies like *Reservoir Dogs* [1992] or *Bad Lieutenant* [1992] should be as unconventional and as challenging as the director or the writer wish them to be. Most American films, however, are made for a lot of money and need to find a wide audience and acceptance in video stores or on television, and then be able to be played all over the world in order to see a return. So I would say if you're going to remake *La Femme Nikita* [1990], for instance, in America with a star, a star director, and a big budget, and spend a lot to market it, then it's perfectly appropriate in my view to use any tool you can to try to make it as pleasing to audiences as possible to make that money back. [*La Femme Nikita* was remade in 1993 as *Point of No Return* by John Badham, starring Bridget Fonda.] That's not to say that every movie should have a happy ending, like in the case of *Turner & Hooch*, which was extremely successful for the studio, even with a dark moment at the end.

One of the funniest cards I received was on *Toy Soldiers*. It said: "It's bad, it's awesome, it rules!" I went to a recruited-audience screening at Paramount for *Beverly Hills Cop*. It was extraordinarily successful. I remember my wife nudged me; she was irritated because people were excited and making too much noise. I told her: "Honey, this is a good thing!"

THE MPAA

Before a film faces the critics and the public, it must receive a rating. Films are submitted to the Motion Picture Association of America (MPAA). In some cases, the rating can limit dramatically the audience and commerciality of a film. The movie industry, however, could not function without the MPAA.

The Motion Picture Producers and Distributors of America (MPPDA) was created in 1922 by the Hollywood studios, and Will H. Hays, Postmaster General of the United States and chairman of the Republican National Committee, was chosen as the head. The studios hoped to ward off local and state censorship by policing themselves. A series of scandals in Hollywood precipitated the creation of the MPPDA. One of them involved Roscoe (Fatty) Arbuckle, who was accused of the rape and death of a minor actress, Virginia Rappe. Although Fatty was acquitted, three of the movies he had completed prior to his arrest were never released, and his earlier pictures were removed from circulation. Another scandal swirled around the murder of director William Desmond Taylor and put in jeopardy the careers of two actresses, Mabel Normand and Mary Miles Minter, involved in the case. Also controversial was the death of silent movie idol Wallace Reid, who died while trying to cure himself from drug addiction.

On April 18, 1922, six days after Fatty was acquitted, the organization was created. Two years later, a self-regulatory policy known as "The Code" was established, and Hays appointed Col. Jason Joy, a former war department public-relations man, to review scripts and advise on possible objections. Although still not legally enforced, a second code was established in 1927 with a list of "Don'ts and Be Carefuls," basically rules on profanity, nudity, drugs, perversion, sexual-related themes (i.e. venereal diseases, childbirth, children's sex organs), white slavery, miscegenation, ridicule of the church, and offenses against the nation, race, or creed.

On March 31, 1930, a production code was written by Martin Quigley, publisher of the *Motion Picture Herald*, and Rev. Daniel A. Lord, a clergyman from St. Louis. In April 1934, the Legion of Decency was formed by a committee of Catholic bishops, whose goal was to warn the public as to which movies to avoid. This movement received support from other non-Catholic groups as well. As a result, Hays created the Production Code Administration Office, and Joseph Breen was put in charge of enforcing the code. Another influencial and powerful figure on the board was Geoffrey M. Shurlock, the administrator of the industry's Code. At last, Hays had the power to enforce the regulations, and before cameras began to roll, scripts had to be approved; before films came out, advertising had to be submitted for approval as well. A studio violating the Code could be fined $25,000, and no picture without the Production Code seal could basically get a theatrical release.

The Code had three general principles:

1. No picture shall be produced which will lower the moral standards of those who see it. Hence the sympathy of the audience should never be thrown to the side of crime, wrongdoing, evil, or sin.

2. Correct standards of life, subject only to the requirements of drama and entertainment, shall be presented.

3. Law, natural or human, shall not be ridiculed, nor shall sympathy be created for its violation.

Howard Hughes was responsible for the first violation of the Code, when in 1943, without the seal, he released *The Outlaw*, starring a provocative Jane Russell. During the shooting and before the release of "the movie that couldn't be stopped,"

Hughes simply refused to execute any of the changes suggested by Joseph Breen. *The Outlaw* was subsequently banned in many cities. Religious groups urged the public to boycott the film. The billboards showing Russell's ample cleavage prompted local police to prepare warrants for the arrest of Hughes and of publicity chief Russell Birdwell until the director finally complied.

Two years later, Will Hays retired, and Eric Johnston took over; the MPPDA was now called the MPAA. An example of a film that caused problems for the Code was Elia Kazan's *A Streetcar Named Desire* (1951). The themes explored in the Tennessee Williams play (namely rape and homosexuality) were prohibited under the Code's rules, and changes were applied to the story for the screen adaptation. Also, under the pressure from Catholic organizations, some sequences had to be cut out before the film got released. Without consulting Elia Kazan, producer Charles Feldman had about four minutes of film taken out. Incidentally, this footage was found in a film vault in Van Nuys, California, by Michael Arick, an expert in film restoration, and thanks to his efforts, *A Streetcar Named Desire* was rereleased in 1993 with the footage that had originally been deleted.

The rules of the Code were maintained and generally followed until Otto Preminger refused to delete some of the dialogue in *The Moon Is Blue* (1953), a sex comedy about a woman who innocently discusses her virginity. In 1956, the Code was slightly revised, although it was still strict over sex, blasphemy, and obscenity.

Kirk Douglas, who produced *Spartacus* (1960) in addition to starring in it, hired Dalton Trumbo to write the script. Trumbo had been one of "The Hollywood Ten," was sent to jail for refusing to disclose whether he was a communist to Senator Joseph McCarthy's infamous House Un-American Activities Committee, and had been unable to find work in Hollywood for a decade. The Code Administration had a whole set of problems with *Spartacus*. The film, ultimately directed by Stanley Kubrick—Anthony Mann originally was the director— was violent and dealt with critical issues like suicide, but most of all, the story also hinted at the fact that General Crassus

(Laurence Olivier) was homosexual and was attracted to Antoninus (Tony Curtis), a slave. Homosexuality was taboo and perceived as "sexual perversion" under the Code's rules. Geoffrey Shurlock, in his correspondence to Universal Pictures and upon reading the script, determined that some of Crassus's dialogue during the scene in which Antoninus bathes him suggested that he was sexually attracted to women and men. "This flavor should be completely removed. Any suggestion that Crassus finds a sexual attraction in Antoninus will have to be avoided." Shurlock also suggested that "the reason for Antoninus's frantic escape should be something other than the fact that he is repelled by Crassus's suggestive approach to him." *Spartacus* was restored in 1991 by Robert A. Harris and James C. Katz for Universal Pictures, adding about six minutes of deleted footage, including the controversial scene between Tony Curtis and Laurence Olivier, with actor Anthony Hopkins dubbing Olivier's dialogue. Today, the film can be seen as it was originally intended.

William Wyler encountered a similar situation when he decided to adapt to the screen Lillian Hellman's lesbian-themed *The Children's Hour*. The play opened on Broadway in 1934 amid rumors of possible police interference owing to the nature of the subject matter. The first screen adaptation of it changed the story entirely; instead of a woman discovering she's in love with another, the plot involved two women in love with the same man. Furthermore, in a letter to producer Samuel Goldwyn dated July 31, 1935, Joseph Breen instructed, aside from the fact that all possible suggestion of lesbian-ism had to be removed, that the title of the play could not be used and that no reference be made directly, or indirectly, in either advertising or exploitation of the picture, to the stage play. In the *Variety* review of *These Three* (as Goldwyn had the movie retitled) of March 25, 1936, the credit block read: "Screenplay by Lillian Hellman (from her current Broadway play *The Children's Hour*, but the legit source is not to be exploited.)" In 1961, director William Wyler remade *These Three* as *The Children's Hour*, with Audrey Hepburn, Shirley MacLaine, and James Garner in for Miriam Hopkins, Merle Oberon, and Joel McCrea. This time he did not hide what the story was about, despite Geoffrey Shurlock's warning that he could not initially approve the script under the regulation of the Code, which read "sex perversion or any inference of it is forbidden." Shurlock said, however, that he "found nothing in the treatment of this subject in the script itself that would seem to be offensive."

Alfred Hitchcock repeatedly explored homosexuality in his films and was warned by the Code on that issue on several occasions. Regarding *Rebecca* (1940), Joseph Breen wrote:

> It will be essential that there be no suggestion what-ever of a perverted relationship between Mrs. Danvers [the character portrayed by Judith Anderson] and Rebec-ca. If any possible hint of this creeps into this scene [Breen is referring to a scene in which Mrs. Danvers apparently reveals her infatuation with the late Rebecca], we will of course not be able to approve the picture. Specifically, we have in mind Mrs. Danvers's description of Rebecca's physical attributes and her handling of the various garments, particularly the nightgown.

To Hitchcock and David O. Selznick's credit (Selznick produced the film), that scene did creep in and most of the ambiguity of Mrs. Danvers's character was maintained. The same issue came up again with *Suspicion* (1941). Breen observed:

> The character of Phyllis Swinghurst [a guest at a din-ner party] seems suggestive of lesbianism and hence is entirely unacceptable. It will be necessary to remove this flavor entirely. In this connection, we call your attention to the stage directions showing that she is dressed in a manish suit, and also the following dialogue:
> JOHNNIE [the character portrayed by Cary Grant]:   It's too complicated, old boy.
> PHYLLIS: Don't call me old boy.
> JOHNNIE: All right then—young fellow.

While that dialogue was removed, the character still appears dressed like a man.

Rope (1948) also proved to be a problem. The Code people pointed out that they thought there was a possible flavor in some of the dialogue that a homosexual relationship existed between Brandon (John Dall) and Philip (Farley Granger). This was of course heightened somewhat by the fact that there was some degree of similarity between these two characters and 1920s "thrill killers" Leopold and Loeb, convicted of murdering a young boy for the sake of killing. That "flavor" however is still present in *Rope*.

When Stanley Kubrick and his producer James B. Harris decided to buy the film rights to Vladimir Nabokov's controversial novel *Lolita*, they asked Geoffrey Shurlock if the subject matter of the story, an elderly man having an affair with a twelve-year-old girl, would fall into the area of "sex perversion" prohibited by the Code. "They [Kubrick and Harris] countered with the suggestion that they would treat the novel so that the man was married to the girl in some state like Kentucky or Tennesse where such is legal," Shurlock wrote in his notes on September 11, 1958. "I agreed that this seemed to remove the element of perversion if this were a legal marriage. However, if the girl looked like a child, the effect might still be offensive to the point where we would not want to approve the picture." Kubrick and Harris maintained vehemently that the treatment of the story would not deal offensively with a sexual relationship "but with the humor that arose from the problems of a mature man married to a gum-chewing teenager." The Code was extremely concerned about the project. "The novel itself seems to have aroused so much resentment and revulsion in so many quarters," Shurlock wrote in his notes dated March 18, 1959. "On account of its depravity; we felt there was a danger that no matter how well the rewrite was handled, a great deal of damage might be done to the industry and to the Code even before the picture was released."

When Nabokov adapted his novel to the screen, despite the Code's fair warnings, he decided to remain faithful to his story: Lolita and Professor Humphrey were not to be married. After reviewing the script, Shurlock thought the basic story was approvable, provided that the girl was portrayed as being not less than fifteen years old. The casting of Sue Lyon as Lolita definitely met with that requirement. "The only important scene that we find unapprovable," Shurlock wrote in a letter to Martin Quigley dated January 20, 1961, "is the seduction scene. Our only suggestion at the moment is that the seduction must be done by suggestion, without any pointed dialogue, and certainly not on a bed." Of course, the purpose of that scene would be defeated if it took place anywhere else but on a bed. "Wouldn't it be more offensive if we implied that such a thing happened on the floor or some other place?" Harris argued. The producer assured Shurlock that for that scene Lolita would wear a heavy flannel, long-sleeved, high-neck, full-length nightgown and Humphrey (James Mason) pajamas and a bathrobe. "Needless to say," Harris told the Code, "the necessary expositional point of the seduction (Lolita seduces Humphrey) will be made by implication only and in the most tasteful manner possible." Harris finally concluded, "We are never forgetting for one minute how crucial this scene is in relation to censorship, but we ask that you try to realize how crucial this scene is relative to our story." Although Kubrick always said that he would have wanted the film to be more provocative, the storyline remained intact. Under pressure from the Legion of Decency, an "Over 18" tag line ran with the ads for the film.

In 1966, Jack Valenti replaced Eric Johnston as president of the MPAA and of the Association of Motion Picture and Television Producers (AMPTP), after serving as special assistant to President Lyndon B. Johnson. Along with Valenti's new position came two difficult movies. "The first issue was the film *Who's Afraid of Virginia Woolf?* [directed by Mike Nichols, starring Elizabeth Taylor and Richard Burton], in which for the first time on the screen the word 'screw' and the phrase 'hump the hostess' were heard," Jack Valenti declared. The other one was the daring *Blow Up*, directed by Michelangelo Antonioni and starring Vanessa Redgrave. Geoffrey Shurlock wanted the nudity to be taken out, but MGM declined and released the film without the seal through a quickly formed subsidiary distributor.

With the United States Supreme Court upholding in April 1968 the constitutional power of states and cities to prevent the exposure of children to books and films that could not be denied to adults, Valenti realized that the old system had become obsolete. "I knew that the mix of new social currents, the irresistible force of creators determined to make 'their' films (full of wild candor, groused some social critics), and the possible intrusion of government into the movie arena demanded my immediate action."

Valenti began discussing a movie-rating system with two organizations: the National Association of Theatre Owners (NATO) and the committee of the International Film Importers and Distributors of America (IFIDA). For five months, he met as well with actors, writers, directors, producers, unions, film critics, religious groups, and the heads of the MPAA member companies. On November 1, 1968, the voluntary film-rating system of the motion picture industry was born. The board would rate not only films but also trailers, print ads, radio and TV spots, and press kits.

There were four categories:

- G for General Audience. All ages admitted.
- M for Mature Audiences. Parental guidance suggested (this label was later changed to PG for Parental Guidance suggested.)
- R for Restricted. Those under 16 (later raised to 17) must be accompanied by parent or guardian.
- X for No one under 16 (later raised to 17) admitted.

"We would no longer 'approve or disapprove' the content of a film," Valenti declared, "but rather would rate movies for parents who could then make an informed decision on whether their children should attend." In July 1974, Jack Valenti named Richard Heffner as chairman of the Code and Rating Administration (known as CARA [In 1977 the Code and Rating Administration became the Classification and Rating Administration.]) and successor to Dr. Aaron Stern, a New York psychiatrist. Heffner had so far divided his time between an academic life, teaching American history, and the mass media, working, among other activities, as a radio newsman, as first general manager of New York's Channel 13 (which Heffner helped acquire) and as the producer of *The Open Mind*, a weekly public-affairs television series. Heffner was chosen because he had no personal affiliation with the film industry and because of his lifelong involvement with American social history in relation to the media. "I am not an industry censor," Heffner said. "It must never have one. And, as a former member of the national board of directors of the American Civil Liberties Union, I would never be one. I am simply chairman of a film-rating board composed of six other disinterested persons [parents] whose sole aim and concern is as reasonably, as evenhandedly, as consistently, and as intelligently as possible to classify the hundreds of films that voluntarily come before us each year."

The board is still in effect today, and if a producer is displeased with his film's rating, there is always a rating appeals board comprised of theater owners, studio executives, and independent distributors who help the MPAA reach a final verdict. The MPAA has two strong objectives. The first one is to allow creative filmmakers to construct their movies the way they want. The second is to give parents accurate information to guide their children.

"I don't make R movies, I make PG movies," Steven Spielberg declared in 1982. At the time, Spielberg was angry at the R rating given to *Poltergeist*, which he produced. The appeals board overturned the R and finally *Poltergeist* received a PG. The MPAA had been criticized for giving a PG to Spielberg's *Jaws*. The rating board was challenged again in 1984 over the PG rating of Spielberg's *Indiana Jones and the Temple of Doom* and Joe Dante's *Gremlins* (which Spielberg executive-produced). Both films were considered too violent for children by many parents. The controversy led to the creation of a new PG-13 rating on July 1, 1984 ("Parents strongly cautioned. Some material may be inappropriate for pre-teenagers"). Incidentally, three scenes in *Indiana Jones and the Temple of Doom* were trimmed by the British censors. U.K. viewers did not see a hand entering a man's chest and pulling out his heart, and the scene during which the same victim is lowered down in a pit of lava was altered, as was the death of a villain being crushed after fighting Indiana Jones on a conveyor belt and ending up as a large blood stain.

The X rating created in 1968 was a problem: Getting an X effectively meant no advertising in most newspapers, on television, or on the radio. Many shopping malls refused to show any films that had been labeled X. Basically, it meant a very short life on the big screen, and it was perceived as synonymous with pornography. However, some X-rated films, like Brian De Palma's *Greetings* (1968) and Bernardo Bertolucci's *Last Tango in Paris* (1973), were well received. John Schlesinger's initially X-rated *Midnight Cowboy* (1969), starring Jon Voight and Dustin Hoffman, even received Academy Awards for Best Picture, Director, and Screenplay Adaptation (Waldo Salt); the X was revised and changed to an R when *Midnight Cowboy* was rereleased a year after the Oscars. But usually, filmmakers were forced to avoid the X and had to cut out controversial shots of violence or sex from their films, change even strong language. In 1971, for example, Stanley Kubrick received an X for his masterpiece *A Clockwork Orange* because of explicit sexual material in a fast-motion *ménage à trois* between Malcom McDowell and two women. Another problematic shot took place during the aversion-therapy sequence where footage of a gang rape is projected for McDowell. A few frames (a total of thirty seconds) were substituted by Kubrick, several months after the film was released. The director had initially refused to trim his film to avoid the X. He ultimately changed his mind in view of broadening the booking of the film, even though he knew that under the MPAA rules, in order to be rerated, a film had to be withdrawn from circulation for at least sixty days before a new R-rated version could become publicly effective.

On July 25, 1990, an open letter to Jack Valenti was published in the film trades, signed by directors such as Francis Coppola, Jonathan Demme, Ron Howard, Spike Lee, Barry Levinson, Sydney Pollack, and Rob Reiner, who stated that their artistic freedom was being compromised "by an outdated and unfair rating system whose practices have and will continue to result in the *de facto* censorship of their work." The group complained that the X rating resulted in massive and arbitrary corporate censorship. "We therefore strongly suggest that a new rating of 'A' or 'M' be incorporated into the system to indicate that a film contains strong adult themes or images and that minors are not to view them." Filmmakers were supported by many critics, producers, and distributors who agreed that there was a stigma attached to the X rating.

The opportunity to take action occured that same year when Philip Kaufman's *Henry and June*, about the controversial life of Henry Miller, received an X. Universal Pictures decided to appeal for an R. The appeal was dropped when the MPAA announced the creation of a new NC-17 rating ("No one under 17 admitted. Adult themes and material not appropriate for children or adolescents"). Basically, NC-17 films would be evaluated as X-rated films were in the past. Major studios still hesitate to release movies slapped with an NC-17, because most theaters located in shopping malls refuse to play them.

Ironically, when Warner Bros. decided to rerelease the director's cut of *The Wild Bunch* (directed by Sam Peckinpah) in 1993, the same version that had received an R in 1969 was given an NC-17. "In the last decade, there has been a public outrage about violence. . . and the judgment of the ratings board," Jack Valenti declared on this issue, "which is comprised of parents, is that the degree, the intensity, and the persistence of violence is beyond the ken of young children." Aside from the titles explored in this book, other movies like Adrian Lyne's *9 1/2 Weeks* (1986), Alan Parker's *Angel Heart* (1987), or Louis Malle's *Damage* (1992) had to be cut to avoid the X or the NC-17. For the most part, the uncut versions are eventually released on video.

TV AND OTHER CUTS

Film history is full of movies that were cut by or because of the studios and not necessarily with the collaboration of the filmmakers: Erich von Stroheim's *Greed* (1924) was reduced from an initial nine hours to two hours twenty minutes. Von Stroheim had tried to recut the film himself without pay; his contract specified his services were required only as a director. He had done the film for Goldwyn, but during the spring of 1924, the company merged with Metro. Louis B. Mayer was put in charge of production, and his name was added to the company to form Metro-Goldwyn-Mayer. Working with Mayer was his new young production manager, Irving Thalberg. Eventually, *Greed* was taken away from its egomaniacal director and recut. What was left of the negative was destroyed to squeeze from it the small amount of silver it contained!

There are the famous cases of George Cukor's *A Star Is Born* (1954), starring Judy Garland and James Mason, and Joseph L. Mankiewicz's *Cleopatra* (1963), starring Elizabeth Taylor and Richard Burton. Both films were cut down and dramatically altered after their initial release. David Lean was forced by producer Sam Spiegel to cut twelve minutes of *Lawrence of Arabia* (1962); Spiegel himself also deleted an additional eight minutes of footage. In fact, Lean agreed that twenty minutes of film needed to be trimmed; what he regretted was that entire sequences were deleted. Luckily, in 1988, with the support of Columbia Pictures; Dawn Steel (who was then the head of the studio), Steven Spielberg, Martin Scorsese, producer Jon Davison, David Lean; and Anne V. Coates (who had edited the film), *Lawrence of Arabia* was restored by Robert A. Harris and Jim Painten. The restored film features additional footage, including, among other scenes, shots of slaughtered Arabs in a village, a scene explaining that Lawrence (Peter O'Toole) was an expert cartographer, and the controversial one during which Lawrence is sodomized by a sadistic Turk (José Ferrer).

United Artists was set to release Michael Cimino's epic western *Heaven's Gate* in November 1980. After a disastrous press screening, the film was literally pulled out of distribution. The director recut the film, trimming it from 225 minutes to 145 minutes, and added a voiceover narration by lead actor Kris Kristofferson. The film was sneak-previewed to a largely working-class audience that was told it would be seeing a thriller entitled *Thief*, starring James Caan, which included several strongly violent scenes designed to appeal to a blue-collar audience. Finally, *Heaven's Gate* was released again in April 1981. While the uncut version has reached a dubious cult status, *Heaven's Gate* remains infamous as being the film that brought down United Artists.

Terry Gilliam's *Brazil* (1985) was judged unreleasable by Universal Pictures. After a much publicized battle between the director and Sidney J. Sheinberg, president and chief operating officer of MCA, Inc., and after *Brazil* received Best Picture, Best Director, and Best Screenplay awards from the Los Angeles Film Critics Association, the film finally came out in the U.S. in a shorter version than the one seen in Europe.

There's also the home video market. You're asking yourself, what can be cut out from a film for home video release? Simple. Films shot in the widescreen format have to be altered to fit on a small screen. A technique known as "pan and scan" was developed to keep the main action intact, but that process fails on epic movies; up to 43 percent of an original image can be lost if a widescreen movie is shown in pan and scan on video. With the laserdisc market, many films are presented in the "letterbox format" with black bars at the top and the bottom of the screen. Unfortunately, most consumers still prefer pan and scan versions for their home viewing.

Then, there's of course the airline version. Don't expect to see any violence or sex at thirty-thousand feet! Logically, scenes showing crashes of any kind are prohibited as well. Do you remember Dustin Hoffman's monologue in *Rain Man* about crash statistics? Airlines wanted that scene out except for Qantas, whose perfect safety record was noted by Dustin!

Perhaps the cuts most dreaded by directors are the ones applied to their films by the television networks. With the ever-growing concern—from government officials, viewers . . . and, of course, sponsors—over sex and violence on television and how they might influence viewers, more than ever feature films have to be watered down dramatically before they can reach the small screen. The studio has to recut the film according to a television list called "standards and practices" that indicates what is unacceptable. While in production, some scenes are shot twice, one for the theatrical version using strong language, one for the TV version, using softer dialogue. Network versions are often different from later ones, once the films go into syndication for maximum profit. The extent of the cutting will depend on the time at which the film is shown, bearing in mind that there must always be enough time allowed for commercials.

While violence, sex, and profanity are usually cut out, other scenes that did not exist in the original theatrical version of a film are sometimes added. Francis Coppola for instance re-edited entirely *The Godfather* and *The Godfather Part II* for television, with Barry Malkin, who was editor on both films; the flashbacks were deleted, and the story was presented in chronological order. While some of the material that was judged too intense for television was cut out, there were many additional sequences never seen before. Thanks to television, Coppola was able to have his dream of seeing both films as one come true. *The Godfather: The Complete Novel for Television* was shown on NBC, which paid Paramount Pictures $15 million for it, in November 1977.

The case of David Lynch and *Dune* was a different experience altogether. The film premiered on KTLA Channel 5 in Los Angeles in 1988, with fifty minutes worth of additional footage. An artist named Jaroslav Gebr designed a series of graphic stills outlining the history and geography of the universe created by Frank Herbert, the author of the novel. This new material was written by Francesca Turner in the form of a voiceover narration. The new footage was assembled by Harry Tapelman, MCA TV special-projects vice president, using the original editor's script as a guideline. "We added some of David Lynch's original footage not in the theatrical movie to give the picture a straight-line continuity," Tapelman told *Daily Variety*. "In the theatrical version, Lynch tried to pour a quart of milk into a pint. We did lots of recutting within the picture, shortened the long walks and long exits, and reconstituted some of the battle scenes to make them more abrasive. Lynch couldn't see the forest for the trees." The TV version runs 187 minutes

14 seconds, while the theatrical version was 140 minutes. The TV version might have gained footage, but it lost writer/director David Lynch; the credits read "An Alan Smithee Film," Smithee being the pseudonym used by the Directors Guild of America when a director wants his or her name removed from a film. The script was attributed to Judas Booth, also a pseudonym. Chris Willman of the *Los Angeles Times* speculated that the name might have been a composite of Judas Iscariot and assassin John Wilkes Booth.

Sometimes, additional footage is shot and new subplots are created especially for the network versions, as in the cases of *Earthquake* (1974) and *Two Minute Warning* (1976).

Filmmakers are worried about all of the above. But if that's all they have to worry about they can consider themselves lucky; many controversial films were threatened with censorship because their content was offensive to minority groups. Religious groups tried to stop the 1988 release of Martin Scorsese's *The Last Temptation of Christ*, based on the 1951 novel by Nikos Kazantzakis. As a result, some theaters did not show the film, newspapers refused to advertise it, and picket lines were formed outside movie houses and at Universal studios to protest against the film. Several countries—including Israel—declined its showing, and a firebomb was placed in a theater in Paris.

As mentioned earlier and on the brighter side, studios, with the help of obsessive/compulsive film archivists, have put in a real—reel?—effort to restore some great celluloid treasures. Movies that had originally been cut by the board of ratings, trimmed by studio heads, amputated after sneak previews, or simply banned are reappearing in their original form. Merian C. Cooper and Ernest Schoedsack's *King Kong*, Frank Capra's *Lost Horizons*, Victor Fleming's *The Wizard of Oz*, Walt Disney's *Fantasia*, William Dieterle's *The Devil and Daniel Webster*, George Cukor's *A Star Is Born*, Bernardo Bertolucci's *1900*, Michael Cimino's *Heaven's Gate*, Sergio Leone's *Once Upon a Time in America*, and many more were either rereleased with additional footage restored or are available on home video as they had originally been intended. Another example: initially released in 1977, Martin Scorsese's musical love story *New York, New York*, set in the forties, got a second chance in 1981 with additional footage. The most significant new material included a sequence with a drunken Robert De Niro making a scene and being thrown out of a nightclub, as well as the notorious film-within-the-film "Happy Endings" sequence, an incredible musical number in which Liza Minnelli as an usherette fantasizes about stardom. While the film had received initially a cool reception, this new version established *New York, New York* as a masterpiece.

ALFRED HITCHCOCK'S *SUSPICION,*
TOPAZ, AND *SPELLBOUND*

"Well, I'm not too pleased with the way *Suspicion* ends," Alfred Hitchcock told French director François Truffaut in the early 1960s in an interview for the book *Hitchcock/Truffaut*. Written by Samson Raphaelson, Joan Harrison, and Alma Reville, Hitchcock's wife, *Suspicion* (1941) was based on the novel *Before the Fact* by Francis Iles (aka Anthony Berkeley). It starred Joan Fontaine, in her second film with Hitchcock following *Rebecca*, and Cary Grant, in the first of the three movies he'd do with the Master of Suspense, the other two being *Notorious* and *North by Northwest*.

The story of the novel told of a woman who gradually realizes that her husband is a murderer and who, out of love for him, allows herself to be killed by him. In the film, the woman, Lina McLaidlaw (Fontaine), suspects her husband, Johnnie Aysgarth (Grant), of planning her murder after discovering he is a gambler and might have killed his best friend Beaky (Nigel Bruce) for money. One night, Johnnie brings her a glass of milk; Lina thinks he's trying to poison her and believes he got the idea from Isobel Sedbusk (Auriol Lee), a mystery writer. In a final confrontation, Lina discovers that she was wrong all along. Johnnie still wants to break up, but in the end, it seems Lina might be able to convince him otherwise.

Originally, Hitchcock had something else in mind. "The scene I wanted, but it was never shot, was for Cary Grant to bring her a glass of milk that's been poisoned," Hitchcock told Truffaut, "and Joan Fontaine has just finished a letter to her mother: 'Dear Mother, I'm desperately in love with him, but I don't want to live because he's a killer. Though I'd rather die, I think society should be protected from him.' Then Cary Grant comes in with the fatal glass, and she says, 'Will you mail this letter to Mother for me, dear?' She drinks the milk and dies. Fade out and fade in on one short shot: Cary Grant, whistling cheerfully, walks over to the mailbox and pops the letter in."

Ironically, Hitchcock's negative comments on the ending of *Suspicion* are quite contradictory with what he had to say to Beth Twiggar of the *New York Herald Tribune* at the time the film was released. "All through *Suspicion*, belief piles up in the wife's mind and the audience's that the husband is a murderer. The written novel had time for soliloquy and brooding. So when the husband is proved actually to be a murderer, it is psychologically right and proper. But that conclusion wouldn't do in a film or a short story. Build him as a killer with all the tricks of the trade and then say yes, he is a killer, and the audience would ask a weary 'So what?' Aesthetically, the novel's outcome is perfect. In a picture it would be simply flat. No, it's got to have a twist." Maybe Hitchcock had forgotten or changed his initial intentions by the time he spoke to Truffaut (and claimed he would have liked a dark ending for *Suspicion*), or simply had lied to reporter Twiggar when the film was released to avoid revealing he'd had to compromise over his initial vision.

"I knew as soon as I read *Before the Fact* that there'd have to be a different ending," Hitchcock continued. "I asked myself the question I always ask before going to work on a picture: Is it worth making? Obviously, the answer was yes. The story had such definite psychological value and such richness of character in a fast-moving plot that it struck me as well worth a public showing—even with a different finish." Hitchcock admitted at the time that Hollywood tried to avoid at all cost unhappy endings. The director mentioned exceptions such as *Wuthering Heights* and *Gone With the Wind*; both films were based on well-known novels, and therefore the filmmakers had to be faithful to them. Hitchcock also mentioned in his *Herald Tribune* interview that Bette Davis was one of the very few actresses audiences expected to see suffer on the screen and they went to her films knowing in advance they had sad endings.

"In *Suspicion*, we had a story that led naturally to an unhappy finale," Hitchcock said. "But the play [Hitchcock meant the novel] itself was unknown, so that we did not have an audience predisposed to a sorrowful closing. Cary Grant is familiar as a light comedian, and Joan Fontaine is remembered mainly as the heroine of the happily ending *Rebecca*. It is doubtful that those two would be accepted as figures of tragedy." Indeed, a movie in which Cary Grant turned out to be a killer would have been accepted neither by the audience nor by RKO, the studio that produced the film. "One of RKO's producers had screened the picture," Hitchcock told Truffaut, "and he found that many of the scenes gave the impression that Cary Grant was a killer. So he simply went ahead and ordered that all these indications be deleted; the cut version only ran fifty minutes. Fortunately, the head of RKO realized that the result was ludicrous, and they allowed me to put the whole thing back together." But there was another reason why Hitchcock couldn't have the hero of the story be a murderer. "Supposing we had made the husband a murderer," he explained in regard to the novel, "then we'd have had the Hays Office to deal with. The Code demands that a murderer face punishment by law. All right. The man poisons his wife, and it's psychologically right and aesthetic as all get out. But it will take an anticlimactic reel or two to turn him over to justice. That's no good."

There was another ending, aside from the one mentioned by Hitchcock to Truffaut, that had been written but was never shot either (according to Hitchcock he discussed as many as twenty different endings for *Suspicion*!). In it, Lina confronted Johnnie with her suspicion that he was a killer and discovered he was only a gambler. Their confrontation was basically the same as the one in the original draft of the script. The next morning she found a note: "Lina—Please tell Melbeck [Johnnie's former employer] I'll pay him back his money. It may take some time. As for you—I owe you a greater debt. I'll try to find some way to pay that debt, and if I do, we'll see each other again." Lina later found out that Johnnie had changed his name and, on the outbreak of war, had joined the air force. She went to see him and learned he was a war hero. The script ended with Lina watching him get aboard his plane (which Johnnie had baptized "Monkey Face" after the nickname he had given Lina) with tears in her eyes.

In fact, this is the first ending that was filmed: After a dinner party at Isobel Sedbusk's, Lina asks Johnnie to leave her alone; he's quite annoyed and feels rejected. At night, she's convinced he's going to murder her. In the morning, she says she's leaving for her mother's. Johnnie decides to drive her. He takes a shortcut, and suddenly the passenger's door— which Johnnie had announced needed to be fixed—flies open. Lina screams. We cut to Lina in bed; she passed out during the near-fatal incident. Isobel, the mystery writer, is by her side. She casually mentions that Johnnie asked her about a certain type of poison which, if used on a victim, would be untraceable. Later, Johnnie brings Lina a glass of milk. She drinks it although she believes it's been poisoned. She then confronts Johnnie; he understands his wife thinks he's a murderer. He tells her he's just like a child; he's made the wrong choices but never killed and would never kill anyone for money. Lina understands that the milk was not poisoned. Johnnie and Lina realize that their love is strong and decide to make a fresh start.

Hitchcock had a very low tolerance for many of his collaborators, but he respected his audience. He said he always took the audience into account and that he did not make movies to please himself but to satisfy viewers. "A good film," Hitchcock declared, "is that which absorbs the audience's attention and enables them to come out of the theater and say, 'The dinner, the baby-sitter, the price of admission—that was all worth it."

Suspicion, which was then titled, like the novel, *Before the Fact*, was screened—with the above-mentioned ending, for a preview audience at the United Artists Theater in Pasadena, California, on June 13, 1941. The cards handed to the test audience had six questions:

1. How did you like the picture?
   (a) Excellent ☐ (b) Very Good ☐ (c) Fair ☐ (d) Poor ☐

2. Was the action in the picture entirely clear? If not, where was it confusing?

3. Was the dialogue entirely clear?

4. Did any parts seem too long? If so, what parts?

5. Did you like the ending?

6. Have you any other suggestions?

About eighty cards were filled out. The audience seemed to have enjoyed the premise of the film, but most of all, people loved the chemistry between Cary Grant and Joan Fontaine. The following comments from one member of the audience sum up the feedback provided by the persons who marked the film either "Excellent" or "Very Good":

> Excellent. With a superb cast and director, this picture is unquestionably one of the best I have seen in recent times. *Rebecca* stands out in my mind as the last film of the caliber of *Before the Fact*. Every scene of *Before the Fact* was enjoyable; every scene added to the feeling of questioning, bewilderment, and tenderness of the audience. To deplete any section of the picture, I believe, would lessen the emotional tension and subsequently lessen the impact of the final scene. I can only add further praises for the fine performances of Cary Grant and Joan Fontaine and the matchless direction of Alfred Hitchcock, the three best in their respective places.

At the same time, several cards reported that the beginning was too long, that too many characters were introduced too late in the picture in order to build up the guilt of the husband, and that basically it was the acting that saved the picture. One member of the audience had this to say about the character played by Joan Fontaine: "It was a mistake to put two such good actors in a picture that was ridiculous from start to finish. The heroine was portrayed as an immature, driveling sentimentalist with no conception of real love—just a sex-starved intellectualist grabbing the first man who showed an interest in her."

Another card: "Frankly, why pictures can't be made with high ideals and morals when you had such fine actors and actresses. The acting and speaking was [sic] fine but so poor story and plot. It was a picture that does not make one feel good in any way for having seen it."

Other negative comments were, to say the least, quite colorful:

"Why must Cary Grant wear collars that make him look like a clown? A goiter?"

"It seems as if *Monkey Face* would have been a better title."

"Absolutely a waste of time to see anything with so low ideals."

"Junk the picture. Get a good cowboy story."

Another member of the audience made some insightful remarks on how the film was perceived from a puritanical standpoint:

> The picture started out as a light comedy, and then changed too abruptly to the possible tragic. The audience was not prepared for it. In other words, most of the last half of the picture seemed wasted as far as the audience was concerned. The applause showed that. Many in the audience even continued to laugh at the more tragic scenes later. That is about all that you could expect them to do. Perhaps the trouble lay to the fact that the audience did not entirely understand the husband and wife early enough in the picture. Remember very few families have experienced that type of marriage, and their adjustment to it in the picture was too choppy. Too much was asked of the audience to follow this rather disconnected last half. *Wuthering Heights* is a good example of completeness in contrast to this picture."

There were also many positive comments—although most of them were short and not very insightful—but the one unanimous criticism was of the ending. Aside from one member of the test audience who wrote: "Any ending would have suited me, for I was at a loss to conceive any possible ending, short of an asylum for the heroine." Most cards showed that the resolution of the picture did not work. Here are some of the most interesting comments on the ending of *Suspicion:*

"Up till the last scene everyone thought Cary Grant was the murderer, so why confuse the entire audience by changing the impression. He should admit trying to murder her, then after confessing, attempt to murder her. She should then either kill him in self defense, or she should escape and should be killed during the pursuit."

"More significance would be attached to Johnnie's last promise to reform if he announced that he had been writing novels and finally one was accepted."

"It is the typical happy 'Hollywood' ending that is not particularly true to life. I'm getting tired of seeing happy endings. I don't want to see sad ones either. Hollywood is supposed to be the city of miracles. Let's see a new ending."

"At the ending where he promises not to bet or gamble again, I believe that if they show a scene of them both at a racetrack it would have been much better. This is entirely my opinion."

"A person doesn't change over so quickly from a playboy to a serious-minded man."

The following statement was by far the most negative comment on the ending of the film:

It was very difficult to understand in many places. Especially after Joan Fontaine drinks what she thinks is the death potion. And how the audience laughed! You violated the first big principle of every human—preservation of life at any cost. Here a woman willingly drinks the supposed poison her husband offers, proclaiming love for her would-be murderer. The whole premise is utterly fantastic and unbelievable. What sane woman would act that way? Pictures, after all, should have some relation to everyday living. Did you think Cary Grant's promise to reform at all convincing? I don't think it fooled anyone but the wishy-washy Joan Fontaine. Just scrap the picture and give Joan and Cary another lease on life.

In general, the audience felt many things went unexplained. In the film, Nigel Bruce portrayed the character of Beaky, Johnnie's best friend. It is established early on that Beaky should not drink, that it could kill him. Later, Beaky dies in Paris in the company of an Englishman after drinking a glass of brandy. "You never explain why the brandy affected the friend, nor who was with him in Paris when he died," one card complained. "Although he [Johnnie] claims he was not in Paris (he was at the races) and didn't kill Beaky, no other explanation re: Englishman. Is this another lie?" Another member of the audience wrote: "Who on earth killed Beaky and why? Who was the Englishman with Beaky in Paris? Was it murder or suicide?"

Ten days after the first sneak preview, *Suspicion* was screened again, this time at the Academy Theater in Inglewood, California. A total of 144 cards was received: forty-seven members of the test audience wrote *Suspicion* was "Excellent," seventy "Very Good," nineteen "Fair," and eight "Poor." The other questions received mixed to positive reactions.

Was the action of the picture entirely clear?

(50)   Clear

(26)   No answer

(27)   Confusing

(20)   First part confusing

(8)   Car-riding confusing [this refers to the near-fatal incident during which Joan Fontaine almost falls from the car. Incidentally, a card at the Pasadena preview said: "I wondered if the wife dreamed the auto accident or if it really happened."]

(9)   Ending confusing

(12)   Did-he-kill-Beaky confusing

Most members of the test screening found the dialogue entirely clear (although some thought that Nigel Bruce's thick British accent was at times difficult to understand), sixty-four people did not think any parts were too long (thirty-nine did, while thirty-one persons did not answer that particular question). Among other suggestions, someone noted: "Too much time spent on inconsequentials such as pouring tea." Another person wrote: "Too suspenseful!" Someone else remarked that Cary Grant looked rather phony while saying in the last scene "Oh, my darling." Another card said: "It would have been lovely if it were in color." [Interestingly, Turner Home Entertainment released in 1989 a colorized version of *Suspicion*!] One angry viewer said: "I don't think RKO will make any money out of it. And it won't do Cary Grant any good." [Actually, many viewers seem to think Grant was best when doing comedic roles.] Another member of the audience thought the whole film was too morbid.

The ending received the following rating: seventy-nine members of the audience liked it, fifty-four didn't, and eleven did not answer. Here is a complete breakdown of the comments received by the fifty-four people who did not like the ending of *Suspicion*.

Did you like the ending?

(27) [just said] "No!"

(1) Why didn't he commit murder just to be different?

(1) Not particularly. Bit too sudden and not dramatic enough for entire scene.

(1) Ending should show whether or not he reformed.

(1) Too many details not cleared up. If you are going to leave the verdict up to the customers, you should have made it more definite as to whether he killed Beaky or not. Personally, I believe he was supposed to have done it and was only covering up to his wife as he had done on various occasions. If he is innocent, it is too much of a letdown.

(9) Not clear. Did he kill Beaky?

(1) Have it more romantic.

(4) Too abrupt. Kept wondering whether or not he was lying, whether or not he was a murderer.

(1) Seems story is not quite finished.

(1)   Not too exciting.

(3)   Ending letdown.

(1)   Build up too big and then too-big letdown.

(1)   For length of time developing plot, ending too rapid.

(1)   All wasn't explained about Paris and why he wanted to find out about poison.

(1)   Rather poor attempt on Lina's part to be noble.

One person simply wrote: "God, that Hitchcock!"

Fifty-four was too large a number not to be ignored. "Toward the end of the film, Grant brings Miss Fontaine a glass of milk which she believes is poisoned," Hitchcock told the *New York Herald Tribune*. "It seemed logical to me that she should drink it and put him to test. If he wished to kill his devoted wife, then she might well want to die. If he didn't, fine and good; her suspicion would clear away, and we'd have our happy ending. We shot that finish. She drained the glass and waited for death. Nothing happened, except an unavoidable and dull exposition of her spouse's innocence. Trial audience booed it, and I don't blame them. They pronounced the girl stupid to willfully drink her possible destruction. With that dictum I personally do not agree. But I did agree that the necessary half-reel of explanation following the wife's survival was really deadly."

Suspicion had to be changed, and a new ending was delivered on July 18, 1941. The film was completed in August for a November release. This is how the final ending was rearranged:

Lina and Johnnie come back from the dinner party at Isobel's. They have an argument. Lina faints. When she awakens, Isobel is at her side. Isobel casually mentions that Johnnie has inquired about the poison. Johnnie brings Lina a glass of milk. We cut to the next morning; a close-up of the still full glass of milk clearly establishes that Lina did not drink it. She announces she's going to see her mother for a few days. Johnnie says he'll drive her. In the car, he takes a shortcut along a winding cliffside road, and the door on Lina's side suddenly opens. Lina screams and Johnnie stops the car. The couple has a final confrontation. This time, it's clear that Johnnie was not with Beaky at the time of his death, although the identity of the Englishman who was with him is never revealed. Johnnie didn't go to Paris; he went to Liverpool to see if he could borrow some money from his wife's life insurance. (In the first ending, Johnnie said he had gone to the races, using Beaky's money.) We also find out that Johnnie was curious about the poison because he wanted to kill himself. (In the original ending, Johnnie said he had inquired about the poison because, as Isobel suspected it herself, he wanted to steal the idea to write a mystery novel.) Lina forgives Johnnie, blames herself for suspecting him, and begs him to give their love a second chance. (In the previous ending, Lina told Johnnie she would borrow money from her mother to pay back Melbeck.) He refuses at first, but then turns back and drives home.

Suspicion was generally well received, although, despite Hitchcock's efforts to try to deliver a satisfactory ending for the film, the climax was still weak. "Hitchcock does a superb job in creating and sustaining an enormously absorbing mood," Rose Pelswick of the *New York Journal-American* wrote in her review. "Up until, that is, the last few minutes when, for some reason or other, someone or other tacked an unconvincingly contrived happy ending." *PM* critic Cecelia Ager found that "It [the film] offers so much to be grateful for that its hasty compromise ending must be rejected more in sorrow than in anger. No matter how it ends, it gives plenty."

"A satisfactory ending could be accomplished by either having the wife drink the glass of milk, which we are led to believe is poisoned, and finding that it is not—indeed the whole thing nothing but her suspicion," suggested *The Hollywood Reporter* in its review of September 18, 1941, apparently unaware that that particular ending had been shot and tested. "Or the film must have an artistic, unhappy ending," the critic went on, "with both principals dying, which it must be admitted, would make the film probably financially unprofitable. But certainly the melodramatic and tawdry ending as it now stands will completely throw and stupefy an audience and kill any possible word-of-mouth build up."

Maybe Hitchcock should have followed his initial instinct and ended *Suspicion* with Cary Grant really being a killer. Unfortunately, neither Hollywood nor audiences were ready for a downbeat ending. But, may Hitchcock rest in peace, come to think of it, they still aren't. . . .

Topaz (1969) is another Hitchcock film whose ending was highly influenced by sneak previews. Based on a novel by Leon Uris, it had a plot that even Hitchcock himself had trouble summarizing. Basically, as Donald Spoto described it in *The Dark Side of Genius*, the film was "about espionage among the French, Cubans, Russians, and Americans at the time of the 1962 missile crisis." Hitchcock described *Topaz* as "the ridiculous picture in which the French spoke English."

The film was shown to a test audience on Friday, August 22, 1969, at the St. Francis Theater in San Francisco. Present at the screening were Lew Wasserman, head of MCA, Universal's parent company, and his wife; Samuel Taylor, who had written the script, and his wife; and Peggy Robertson, Hitchcock's assistant, and Alma Reville, his wife. Hitchcock himself had decided not to go. "Another thing I'm afraid of," he once declared, "is going to see any of my pictures with an audience present. I only tried that once, with *To Catch a Thief*, and I was a wreck. I'm scared of seeing the mistakes I might have made."

The screening started on a positive note when the audience applauded at Hitchcock's name. The public seemed to have the right reactions, even to laugh when it was expected. It was noticed that the audience laughed at his trademark cameo appearance in the film only when he stood up (the director is seen pushed in a wheelchair; he stands up to shake someone's hand); it seemed the audience didn't see him earlier. Several people left when André Devereaux (Frederick Stafford), the hero of the story, is packing and having a discussion with his wife Nicole (Dany Robin). Although the screening report mentioned that the people who left had gone to "the powder room" and seemed to return later, Hitchcock ordered his editor to trim the scene. (About four lines of dialogue were taken out.)

Based on the audience feedback, Hitchcock cut down other minor scenes, eliminated a shot here and there, and extended, for example, a sequence with Kusenov (Per-Axel Arosenius), a Soviet defector to the U.S. In the scene, Kusenov is having coffee and is shown relaxed, almost cynical, which plays in contrast with the way he behaved at the beginning of the picture. The audience applauded that humorous scene, and Hitchcock extended the beginning of it by showing Kusenov serving coffee. The scene in which Rico Parra (John Vernon), a Cuban leader, shoots Juanita de Cordoba (Karin Dor), a spy for the Americans and Devereaux's mistress, was ambiguous; no one could tell that Parra had a gun, and Hitchcock inserted a shot of Parra holding the weapon. The sequence with Dubois (Roscoe Lee Browne) in New York, during which he steals secret documents from Rico Parra, was suspenseful and was received with applause from the test audience.

Unfortunately, the audience hated the ending that had Devereaux agreeing to have a duel with Granville (played by French actor Michel Piccoli), a spy for the Russians who's also having an affair with Nicole, Devereaux's wife. The duel is to take place in an empty stadium near Paris. (The scene was indeed shot near Paris, although parts of it were reshot during the editing process at a stadium in the U.S. Several close-ups shot on a soundstage at Universal studios were also added.) But just as the duel is about to begin, Granville is shot in the back by a hitman sent by the Russians who have no need for him anymore. André is reunited with Nicole. The last shot is of a newspaper headline announcing the end of the missile crisis. Someone throws the newspaper on a bench; the camera then pans from the newspaper to the Arc de Triomphe in Paris.

"Laugh on first shot of duel," the screening report said. "Titter continued and chatter throughout. Man in front of Peggy [Robertson] said something about 'Every five years you see a duel in a picture.' " As a result, *Topaz* received only scattered applause at the end.

Hitchcock was upset with the audience's reaction to his ending. He had discovered through research that a duel had taken place in Paris, five years prior to the production of *Topaz*. According to François Truffaut, Hitchcock felt that young Americans could not accept the idea of chivalrous behavior and the concept of a duel. In his eyes, the youth of America had become cynical and could not understand that it made sense that André Devereaux would accept the duel even though if he lost, he would get killed, and if he won, he would have to escape from France and hide in Spain.

The second ending that was shot takes place at the Paris airport. Devereaux and Nicole, on their way to America, see Granville boarding a plane to Russia. Granville salutes them and wishes them bon voyage. The dialogue between André and Nicole goes as follows:

NICOLE: How can they let him get away like this?

ANDRÉ: I told you, my love, he doesn't miss a trick.
They have nothing against him. Anyway,
that's the end of Topaz.

The last shot showing the newspaper headline and the Arc de Triomphe is the same as in the initial ending.

Well, that ending was not the end for *Topaz*. Although Hitchcock argued that this version showed that "spying is arduous and difficult but seldom fatal," he also felt that it was too sophisticated and too cynical. It was historically correct that spies had been allowed to get away, but it just didn't have the sharpness that an ending ought to have. This ending however was in the first release prints that were shown in Europe.

After the first sneak preview, Hitchcock made the following suggestion for a new ending: "As the doors of the conference room close [Hitchcock is referring to the scene in which Granville has been exposed at the French Foreign Office and is ordered by his superior to leave the room], hold on the closed doors for one foot [of film], then make a four-foot dissolve to the newspaper headline. The reprise of the Russian march music from the main credits should sneak in just as Granville hears the words of the French diplomat and then rise over the newspaper shot in Paris and through the end titles." This solution, it seems, was by far the best and the most simple. It didn't require additional shooting, but at the same time, the audience wouldn't know what happened to Granville.

Notes from Peggy Robertson reveal that Hitchcock then began thinking of an ending in which Granville killed himself and for which he could use shots from the second ending: After the camera has moved up to a close-up of Granville being exposed in the French Foreign Office, you immediately cut to the exterior of Granville's secret house, in the Impasse de la Visitation. The camera dollies in toward the front door. There is a pause, and then a loud muffled revolver shot indicating that Granville has killed himself. From there we will cut to Devereaux and his wife mounting the ramp into the Pan Am plane bound to Washington. From there, we go to the *Herald Tribune* banner headline announcing the missile crisis is over. The paper is thrown down, and the cast list appears over the Avenue de Triomphe [there's actually no such avenue in Paris], and the accompanying music is a reprise of the Soviet march that we heard at the beginning of the picture.

By now, going back to Paris to shoot a brief scene with Michel Piccoli, who played Jacques Granville, going inside his house to kill himself, was out of the question. Piccoli was not available, and Hitchcock had to convey the same idea using whatever footage he had shot during principal photography. The problem was that there wasn't one single scene with Piccoli entering his house; the two characters that were seen entering or exiting the house were Nicole, Granville's mistress, and Henri Jarré (Philippe Noiret), a spy and Granville's accomplice. Noiret and Piccoli looked quite different, even from a distance. For one thing, Noiret had a cane. Therefore, Hitchcock only used the end of the shot of Noiret walking in and closing the door behind him. We then have a freeze-frame on the house, and as we zoom in on the front door (through an optical process), we hear the gunshot offscreen, indicating that Granville has killed himself. This is followed by quick flashbacks (the Mendozas, a couple who spied for the Americans, in jail; Jarré lying dead on top of a car; Juanita being shot by Parra; Devereaux looking pensive aboard the plane after he's escaped from Cuba and heard of Juanita's death) overimposed by the *Herald Tribune* headline announcing the end of the missile crisis. As in the two other endings, someone throws the newspaper on a bench, and the camera pans to the Arc de Triomphe. In that ending, we never find out what happens to Nicole and André, despite the fact that, all along, Hitchcock had wanted to indicate that the couple got back together in the end.

Whatever happened to the duel sequence in *Topaz* was a mystery until Australian director Richard Franklin (*Psycho II*), who knew Hitchcock, discovered that the infamous scene had been kept in Hitchcock's garage and had been given to the Academy of Motion Picture Arts and Sciences by Patricia Hitchcock, the director's daughter, after her parents' death. Although it was never restored in the film, it can be seen, along with the ending at the airport, in the laserdisc version of *Topaz*.

Topaz, unlike *Suspicion*, was a box-office failure. The critics hated the film and judged the ending anticlimactic, and so did Hitchcock himself, who feared his inability to finish *Topaz* symbolized the end of his career. In fact, what Hitchcock couldn't finish was making films. After *Topaz*, Hitchcock directed *Frenzy* (1972) and *Family Plot* (1976). Until the day he died, Hitchcock worked on projects and refused to admit that his career would one day be over. That's an ending even the toughest audience would have rated "Excellent."

The most regretfully lost scene from a Hitchcock film was not cut out as a result of a test screening. It is not the ending that the director had originally planned for *Vertigo* (1958) and which showed Jimmy Stewart coming back to Barbara Bel Geddes after Kim Novak's death. It is not the original ending from *Strangers on a Train* (1951) either. The release of the latter film was delayed to allow Hitchcock to add one last scene on a train with a man recognizing Farley Granger, who plays Guy Haines, a famous tennis player. Remember, that's how the film begins. . .with Robert Walker as Bruno Anthony, a psychotic killer, recognizing Guy, later carrying out his plan to kill Guy's wife, and framing the tennis champion for the murder. Originally, the film ended with Ruth Roman, Guy's girlfriend, finding out over the phone that the real killer was stopped. She hangs up, and her sister, played by Patricia Hitchcock, hugs her. Ruth Roman's dialogue was: "He says he looks funny in his tennis clothes." That last line was taken out, and the other ending with Granger and Ruth Roman on the train was tagged on. When the stranger—a priest—recognizes Guy, the couple simply walks away. Incidentally, when that ending was added, a scene at the beginning of the film between Farley Granger and Robert Walker was trimmed down. The two men are on a train, and the original print of the film had them ordering food to a waiter. Bruno orders lamb chops, French fries, and chocolate ice cream; Guy orders a hamburger and a cup of coffee. Considering that food was an important element in Hitchcock's life and films, that scene definitely lost some of its significance when these lines were deleted.

The gem, the lost treasure, the one scene that was cut out and shouldn't have been is the dream sequence designed by surrealist Spanish artist Salvador Dali for Hitchcock's *Spellbound* (1945), which David O. Selznick, the producer of the film, decided to amputate.

In *Spellbound*, Gregory Peck plays John Ballantine, a man framed for murder. Ingrid Bergman is Constance Peterson, a psychologist, who believes he's innocent. With the aid of a colleague, Doctor Brulov (Michael Chekhov), she analyzes one of John's dreams, hoping to find clues in his subconscious that will lead to solving the murder case. In the script written by Ben Hecht, that scene was just straight dialogue, but Hitchcock wanted to convey the dream "with great visual sharpness and clarity, sharper than the film itself." He wanted to break the traditional dream sequences that were usually filmed "with swirling smoke, slightly out of focus." Selznick, Mr. *Gone With the Wind*, was as much a control freak as Hitchcock himself. Although he was responsible for bringing the British director to America (Hitchcock's first film in the U.S. was *Rebecca*, which Selznick produced), the collaboration

between these two film geniuses was tumultuous and difficult. Selznick thought, for instance, that Hitchcock wanted
Dali to design the *Spellbound* dream for publicity purposes
only, whereas in fact the director genuinely liked the artist's
work. Dali had coauthored with director Luis Buñuel such
avant-garde classics as *Un Chien Andalou* (1929) and *L'Age
d'Or* (1930). Hitchcock thought Dali's work was similar to that
of the Italian painter Giorgio de Chirico, who, like Dali, had
"the same quality, the long shadows, the infinity of distance,
and the converging lines of perspective."

Selznick, Hitchcock, and Dali met in the summer of 1944.
Dali said he would submit five drawings and, if Hitchcock
liked his ideas, he would execute oil paintings of his sketches.
The artist asked for $5,000 ($1,000 per painting) as well as
total creative control. Dali received $4,000 and delivered his
five drawings; their filmic rendition was estimated to cost
$150,000. Hitchcock had to reassure Selznick that he would
use miniatures and therefore reduce the cost to $20,000. Dali
was a fair player and later even offered to do additional drawings at no cost. The Spanish artist wanted his work for his
first American film to be perfect. Joseph Breen of the Code
administration office was a bit concerned about the sets and
the gigantic (phallic) pillars being maybe a bit too sexually
explicit. He pointed out in a letter to the filmmakers that the
woman (a patient of Constance Peterson, played by actress
Rhonda Fleming) in the dream had to be more covered than it
seemed she would be in the script. There was also a moment
in the dream sequence in which Constance was dancing and
suggested a symbol of sexual intercourse. Selznick's own psychiatrist, May Romm, was hired as technical adviser and was
particularly concerned about objects that might have sexual
connotations and might prevent the endorsement of the film
by the psychiatric profession. Selznick removed everything
that was questionable in order to satisfy everyone.

Dali liked Hitchcock because, like himself, he was mysterious. With that in mind, Dali did not want to put any limitation
on his own imagination. Originally, Dali wanted to have fifteen
gigantic pianos hanging from the ceiling above a ballroom.
Instead of using dancers, Dali planned to have life-size cutout

silhouettes arranged in such a way to create a strange perspective that gave the illusion that they disappeared in the distance. But when Dali showed up on the set in Culver City, he was in for a big surprise; tiny pianos had been used and were surrounded by forty little people! Extras, not cardboard silhouettes, were dancing underneath. The set designer had arranged sophisticated projectors to create contorted shadows. Hitchcock, who had originally wanted to shoot the scene out-of-doors, had been forced by Selznick to film on a soundstage. Dali thought the whole thing looked silly and wrong, and that his vision had been betrayed, but he never knew that Hitchcock himself had come up with the idea to use little people and tiny pianos. The director had created a similar illusion using little people for a surreal scene in paradise in *The Blackguard* (1924), on which he had served as art director and screenwriter.

The dream was set to open up with one hundred human eyes glaring down at Gregory Peck from black velvet drapes, which were to have been tied in the shape of bats. Dali explained to *PM* reporter Frederick C. Othman, who visited the set, that this scene was to merge gradually into a landscape with one enormous tree on the left of the screen and a cloud that looked vaguely "like the GOP elephant," as the reporter put it. Peck was set to be in the middle of this, about the size of a tin soldier. "And pretty soon," the reporter carried on, "there's an enormous pair of pliers (yep, I said pliers) chasing him up the side of a pyramid. These pliers are fifteen times taller than Peck, and they cast enormous black shadows as they cross the horizon and pursue our hero up the pyramid, which seems to be cracking, as if the foundation had been lifted." In the final cut of the dream sequence, the image of pliers cutting up the eyes was reminiscent of the famous razor blade slashing an eyeball in *Un Chien Andalou*. Other images, like the crooked wheel, a faceless man, strange and distorted perspectives definitely were recognizable as typical of Dali's style as well.

The next image starred Ingrid Bergman. The idea was to convey that, in the patient's mind, she became a statue. A plaster cast was made of the actress's body. For her costume,

Hitchcock selected a blond wig, a white sarong-like gown, and a gold necklace with an arrow. A scene was filmed with the body of the statue flying away, revealing Bergman underneath. That shot was then run in reverse to give the illusion that Ingrid Bergman turned into a statue when Gregory Peck reached out to her. Then, Dali wanted the statue to start to decay, and when she moved, the plaster cracked and two thousand black ants crawled out of the crack. "He [Dali] wanted me to have those—those things crawling out of my face," Bergman said. "But that was too much. I even squirm when I think of it." Dali found this particular segment very symbolic. "[Symbolic] Of what?" Frederick C. Othman asked Bergman. "I do not know," the actress replied. Of that sequence, Hitchcock said, "You might call this scene ants in your countenance." Ultimately, this idea was discarded.

In another scene, Peck and the man he thinks he killed play cards at a table with shapely female legs, in front of Dali's wall of eyeballs. Dali's landscapes served as a backdrop—painted in black and white, like the rest of the sets—for specially built replicas of a cracked house and an anthropomorphic precipice.

Selznick hated the sequence. It was fifteen minutes long, and he thought it lacked imagination! "The more I look at the dream sequence in *Spellbound*, the worse I feel it to be," Selznick wrote in one of his famous memos. "It is not Dali's fault, for his work is much finer and much better for the purpose than I ever thought it would be. It is the photography, setups, lighting, et cetera, all of which are completely lacking in imagination and all of which are about what you would expect from Monogram [a Poverty Row company that specialized in low-budget films]. I think we need a whole new shake on this sequence, and I would like to get Bill Menzies [the noted production designer] to come over and lay it out and shoot it. We must bear in mind that Peck will be required for the day or two that will be required for shooting. Also Miss Bergman."

Peck's voiceover narration explaining the dream was trimmed down, and along with his speech went the images. Selznick wanted to remove everything that was strictly visual, while trying to keep the clues that ultimately revealed the plot.

As stated in his memo, Selznick brought in William Cameron Menzies and art director James Basevi to work on the sequence, after consulting with Hitchcock and Dali, who had agreed—did they have a choice?—changes should be applied. Menzies did additional shooting which cost another $4,000. Selznick still hated the sequence. The art department came in, trimming the sequence some more. The sequence never lived up to Selznick's expectations, but at least it was shorter.

Here are a few images from the dream sequence that survived:

In the first one, Gregory Peck, playing cards in a large gambling house, is surrounded by drapes with eyes painted on them; a man is cutting up the drapes with a large pair of scissors. Then, a girl, lightly dressed, comes around and kisses everyone. Although Peck says the girl looked a lot like Constance (Ingrid Bergman), that role was played by Rhonda Fleming, a patient of Constance's, who is introduced at the beginning of the film. That line of narration may have been initially intended for the scene in which Bergman turned into a statue. Since Bergman's bits for the dream sequence were entirely cut out, Selznick might have thought it simpler not to refer to Constance's patient at all, but to refer to Bergman at least once in the sequence—although it's Rhonda Fleming running around. There's also a short bit at a gambling table with a man without a face (the actor is wearing a thick stocking over his face that hides his features). The next scene takes place on a roof; a man wearing skis goes over it, and the faceless man is revealed, hiding behind a chimney, holding a wheel, which he drops. The last brief image shows Peck running down a slope with the shadow of giant wings coming after him.

To Hitchcock and Dali's chagrin, the dream sequence was never shown as they had initially wanted it to be. It is brief and the symbolism that's left conveys the clues to the mystery heavy-handedly, without great inspiration or conviction. Even Ingrid Bergman declared that the original sequence was more interesting and belonged in a museum. "There were so many wonderful things in it," the actress said. "It was such a pity [that the scene was cut down]. It could have been really sensational."

"It is typical of a Selznick production that the dream sequence—only a flash in the final release footage, but of high importance to the plot—is designed by none less than Salvador Dali," Jack D. Grant wrote in the *Hollywood Reporter*. "The effect is exactly what was wanted, arresting and imaginative." Another reviewer called the dream sequence "highly fantastic but most interesting." A critic in *Cue*, though, was less enthusiastic about the truncated version of the sequence:

> In *Spellbound*, however, the dream sequence was scissored to a tiny fraction of [its] original length, and discussed rather than shown. That is a serious fault in any motion picture. Accordingly, the involved dreams, which were an integral part of the story's original psychotic plot pattern, have been stripped of their important visual impact, and the result is a picture superficially psychoanalytic in design, actually weak in Freudian fact. Which is not to say, however, that the slick and suspenseful handling of the tightly constructed 'murder mystery' will not prove substantially and profitably popular.

Spellbound illustrates perfectly how a producer can—and will—alter a director's vision. Aside from recutting the dream sequence, Selznick deleted another fourteen minutes after a sneak preview. Luckily, not much later in his career, Hitchcock received total creative control on his films; he was 100 percent responsible for his successes. . .as well as for his failures. Rather than allowing anyone else control his career and his choices, Hitchcock only trusted himself. . .and us, his audience.

CUTS BECOME YOUR FILMS

ROBERT ZEMECKIS'S *BACK TO THE FUTURE* TRILOGY AND *DEATH BECOMES HER*

What bigger cut could there be than to remove an actor entirely from a film, or worse even, to have an actor replaced after shooting has begun? Did you know, for instance, that Eric Stoltz was replaced by Michael J. Fox after a third of *Back to the Future* (1985) had already been shot? *Back to the Future* is the fantasy comedy adventure presented by Steven Spielberg, directed by Robert Zemeckis, and produced by Bob Gale and Neal Canton, from an original screenplay by Zemeckis and Gale, with Steven Spielberg, Kathleen Kennedy, and Frank Marshall serving as executive producers. The story focuses on Marty McFly (Michael J. Fox), who travels from the eighties back to the fifties when he gets behind the wheel of a nuclear-powered DeLorean invented by an eccentric scientist named Doc Brown (Christopher Lloyd). In 1955, Marty walks through his hometown and meets Lorraine (Lea Thompson) and George (Crispin Glover), two teenagers who will become his parents. Having tampered with history, Marty has to solve a number of challenging problems before he can get back to the future. *Back to the Future* was an enormous success and was followed by two sequels.

Coscreenwriter Bob Gale: "Bob Zemeckis put the picture together and felt that we made a mistake in the casting of Eric Stoltz. He ran the footage to Frank Marshall, Kathleen Kennedy, Steven Spielberg, and myself, and we all agreed that the movie didn't seem to be working with Eric.

"We'd done some scenes in the fifties: the skateboard chase, some clocktower stuff. We were shooting the scene in the parking lot of the shopping mall when we decided to make a change.

"It was tough. Bob Zemeckis was the director and felt it was his decision and that it was his place to be the one to tell Eric. He accepted it very well. We had gotten the feeling on a couple of occasions that perhaps he felt uncomfortable doing some of the things that weren't natural to him. Eric is a very intense actor; he's more introverted than Michael J. Fox, but he is certainly a good actor, which is why we cast him originally. We felt he could do some of the things that weren't natural to him, but it didn't come across on the screen the way we had imagined it.

"The fact is that Michael J. Fox had been our first choice for the role. It was absolutely impossible for him to do the picture because of his TV series *Family Ties*. Kathleen Kennedy went to her friend, Gary David Goldberg, the producer of the show. He read the script and said, 'This is a perfect movie for Michael, but I can't let him see it because he'll want to do it so badly that I'll end up being the jerk who tells him he can't do it.' They needed Michael for the TV series, especially because Meredith Baxter Birney, who played his mom, was pregnant at the time and wasn't going to be able to be in every show. They had rewritten the series so that Michael had a much bigger role, and it was absolutely critical that they had him. We had so much trouble casting the lead character for *Back to the Future* that we had to push back the starting date twice and even had an open casting call, trying to discover somebody. So by the time we decided we had made a mistake, Meredith Baxter Birney had had her baby, she was back on the show, and we again went to Gary David Goldberg, who, this time, said 'All right, if you guys agree that *Family Ties* is in first position, I'll let Michael read the script, and if he really wants to do it, he can do it as long as his first commitment is to the TV show.' So Michael read the script, and he got aboard.

"The only things that we salvaged from the Eric Stoltz shoot were some reaction shots, some coverage with Christopher Lloyd. Of course, none of the shots with Eric could be used.

The fact is that we shot the scenes the same way that they'd been shot before. There might have been a few angles on the skateboard chase that we did differently. We shot the scene when Marty first comes to Doc Brown's house and Doc is wearing the brainwaves machine on his head, with both Eric and Michael. In that sequence, there are a couple of shots with Christopher Lloyd that were from the first shoot. It used to drive Michael crazy when people would say, last time we did such and such. Of course, everybody knew how it had been shot the first time, except for Michael. You know that David Lean shot one week of *Lawrence of Arabia* with Albert Finney as Lawrence and decided that he wasn't right and shot down the set. That's one case that not many people know about. There are other cases where an actor dies, like Natalie Wood in *Brainstorm* and Brandon Lee in *The Crow*."

Film history is full of stories of test screenings jeopardizing the fate of a picture; the case of the *Back to the Future* trilogy, however, is fascinating in that the sneak previews played an important step in the success of the three movies.

Bob Gale: "The first time we sneak-previewed *Back to the Future* was in San Jose; after that screening, we cut about six minutes out. For that first preview, we had no studio executives there; it was truly a filmmaker's sneak, and we got a feeling on where the movie was playing long. There were perhaps overkill or unecessary things. Bob Zemeckis and I have a tendancy in our screenplays to overexplain things with the expectation that the audience will get it the first time, and that we won't have to repeat ourselves. But just in case they don't, we cover ourselves.

"In the case of *Back to the Future*, we found out that they did get it. There was a scene for instance in which Doc Brown in 1955 is going through a suitcase that Marty put in the trunk of the DeLorean when he left from the shopping center. Doc Brown doesn't know what a hairdryer is. He says, 'A hairdryer? Don't they have towels in the future?' He is also amazed that there is cotton underwear in the future, because he thought all the clothes in the future would be disposable paper garments. Then he finds a *Playboy* magazine; he looks at the pinups and says, 'Well now the future is finally starting to look good.' It's a funny scene but we didn't need it; it was just some jokes, and jokes are fairly easy to cut out when they don't advance the story, the plot, or the characters. So we cut that out just for pacing.

"In the version we previewed, we also realized that the scene during which Lorraine is attacked in the car was too long. Originally, George McFly [who eventually saves her and needed to time his arrival] couldn't figure what time it was and had to go into a phone booth to call the time and temperature. One of the nasty kids, who earlier kicked George in the ass, slid a stick in the door of the phone booth and trapped him in there. The school disciplinarian eventually helped him out, and George arrived right on time to save Lorraine. We realized that the audience just wanted to see what was going to happen to Lorraine and didn't like being away from her as long as we were. So we cut out the stuff with George.

"A very strange phenomenon happened during the first preview of *Back to the Future* that never, never happened again. In 1985, when we made the film, nobody knew what it was. Nobody had heard of it; there had not been much publicity on it, so the audience that saw the film at the first preview was completely cold. They had absolutely no idea what the movie was about, that it was even about time travel. So, in the scene at the mall parking lot, when Doc Brown puts his dog in the DeLorean for the first time-travel experiment and when the car disappears, there was a hush from the audience. They were very uncomfortable because they were worried the dog would get killed. That's something that never happened again because once the publicity started, everybody knew before they bought their ticket that the movie was about a DeLorean time machine. When they saw Doc putting the dog in the machine, the audience knew that it was a time machine, even though Marty McFly didn't. But that first audience took about forty minutes to understand where the movie was going, and that happened in the scene in the diner when Marty first sees George, his father, as a young man.

"Once that scene started, there was a sort of sigh of relief from the audience; okay, now we understand what that long setup was for; that's his dad. This is really neat. He is meeting his dad when he was a kid. Then, the audience was completely with the movie the whole way. During that first preview, we were thankful that we didn't have the studio there with us, because we knew that once the publicity campaigns kicked in for the movie, those things were not going to be issues. Had there been someone from the studio, they might have said, it took the audience forty minutes to understand what was going on with the movie. Maybe you guys should cut some stuff out of there. The sneak preview, however, told us that the joke about Uncle Joey, for instance, paid off about an hour later when you see the little baby in the playpen. The audience remembered that setup. [At the beginning of the film, we find out that Uncle Joey is in jail; when Marty meets him as a baby in 1955 and looks at him in his playpen, he tells him he better get used to being behind bars!] Again, that was something that we could have easily cut out, but we got such a huge laugh that we knew it worked.

"We test-screened the film a second time at the Hitchcock Theater on the Universal Studios lot. The Universal executives were present. The sneak was extremely successful, and Sidney Sheinberg, the president of MCA, was so elated with how well it played to an audience that he decided to advance our release date by six weeks.

"In *Back to the Future Part II* [1989], we did make some changes after we screened it. The big controversial thing we changed had to do with Biff [the villain played by Thomas F. Wilson] altering his past after he stole the DeLorean. When he returns the DeLorean to the future, he breaks his cane, staggers out of the car, and falls down in the street. In the release version of the movie, we cut away, and you don't know why he's fallen down; you figure that the shock of time travel was just too much for the old guy and maybe he's having a heart attack or something. In the script and the way that the scene was shot, Biff falls to the street, and then he fades out of existence. Of course, the reason why he would fade out is because he's altered his own past; the future that he's returned to is a future in which he no longer has the same function, and therefore he is erased from existence. Now that's a great idea and a great special effect, but it was something that audiences were really confused by. It was one of those ideas that made sense only the second time you saw the movie, but the first time, you didn't understand that at all. The whole rationale of erasing yourself from existence, which we made a big deal out of in the first film, was forgotten four years later when audiences went to see the sequel. I would say 90 percent of the audience did not understand why Biff disappeared. The majority ruled, and we felt that we had lost a large portion of the audience; you never want to confuse the audience, so we cut it out.

"We put the trailer for *Back to the Future Part III* (1990) at the end of part two, and the test audience did not like it at all. Unfortunately, there was nothing we could do about it. It had always been our intention to let the audience know that yes, we're leaving you hanging here, but we got the other movie in the can, and you're going to see it real soon. We showed that trailer out of a reaction that Bob Zemeckis and I had when we walked out of *The Empire Strikes Back*; we were pissed off at the fact that Han Solo [Harrison Ford] was left in carbon freeze, that the movie was ending with Darth Vader still at large and that we didn't know if there was going to be another film. So we thought to ourselves that if we're going to leave some threads hanging at the end of *Back to the Future II*, let's at least tell the audience that's there's a whole other movie and here's a little taste of it. But they were still upset that the movie ended in a sort of a cliffhanger. I had always argued that part two should have been sold as the second part of the trilogy, so that even before the public went into the theater, they knew that this was part two of three. If we had warned the audience before they saw the movie, they wouldn't have been so upset that the ending left them in the air. Unfortunately, this never happened. *Back to the Future II* had a record opening, but we fell off 50 percent the next week because audiences thought they were being conned. We should have learned from the test preview; the audience needed to be educated.

"*Back to the Future III* has the least amount of profanity of the three pictures. Bob Zemeckis and I got real tired of getting all these letters from fundamentalist groups and people who were offended by the language, although under the PG rating, we were allowed to have a certain amount of profanity. People were writing, "These were such good movies, why did you have to spoil them by putting so much cursing in them?" Bob Zemeckis and I thought about it. If it helps the movie or makes a point, yes, Marty's got to call Biff an SOB, absolutely, but maybe he doesn't need to say 'godammit' quite so often."

Aside from the *Back to the Future* trilogy and Steven Spielberg's *1941*, which will be explored later on in this book, Robert Zemeckis and Bob Gale collaborated on *I Wanna Hold Your Hand* (1978), *Used Cars* (1980), and *Trespass* (1992). These three films went through changes for the most peculiar reasons. I *Wanna Hold Your Hand* was Robert Zemeckis's first film; Bob Gale cowrote the script with him and produced the film as well. The story was about a group of teenagers who try to meet the Beatles on the eve of their first appearance on *The Ed Sullivan Show*. The turning point on that film occurred before it was even shot, when Universal's legal department told the filmmakers they could not use real footage of the Beatles on *The Ed Sullivan Show*. Ned Tanen, who was then the head of the studio, eventually saw the first cut of the film and said, "You have to show the Beatles at the end; that movie does not work without it." According to Gale, Sid Sheinberg agreed and said, "Let the Beatles sue us. I would have the legal rights to the court case. We would have the Beatles reunited in court to sue Universal, and that would be a movie to go see." So Zemeckis and Gale got the right after that screening to go back and shoot one more day of the Sullivan sequence the way they had initially intended to do it, with doubles out of focus in the background and with black-and-white monitors showing real footage of the Beatles on the Sullivan show in the foreground.

Trespass was originally entitled *Looters*. With the Los Angeles riots occuring two months ahead of the release date of the film, Universal decided to change the title. But before the riots broke out, the movie had already been tested to so-so results, and one of the reasons was that Ice Cube died in the film. "Twenty-five percent of the audience walked out," Bob Gale recalled. "It was horrifying, and then, with the riots breaking, we were afraid the movie might not be released at all. The studio told us, 'Either you guys do a new ending, or we're gonna put you on the shelves and forget it.' And so we did, but it took several times to get it right."

But by far, the most intriguing change Zemeckis and Gale had to make was on their film *Used Cars*, a black comedy about the rivalry between used-cars salesmen and their outrageous schemes to get customers.

Bob Gale: "The only thing that got cut out of *Used Cars* never got to preview. It was something that the studio insisted that we change in the scene when the car salesmen do a commercial at a football game wearing Groucho Marx glasses. The propman on the film had found these glasses that instead of having a fake nose had a penis for it. We thought that was one of the funniest things we'd ever seen, and we thought to ourselves, you know, these car salesmen, that's exactly the kind of things they would do. So we shot the scene with these glasses. When we sent the dailies to Columbia Pictures, I got this call from the head of production just ripping me apart for putting these pornographic images in the movie. How could we possibly do this? Had we lost our minds? This has gone beyond the grounds of taste. I got my head handed to me on a platter about this.

"Columbia was outraged about this scene. I kept telling them to wait until they saw the scene cut together. I got on an airplane [the movie was shot in Phoenix] and screened the scene for Columbia. Frank Price [the head of the studio at the time], who by the way I have absolute admiration and respect for, turned around and said, 'It's the most disgusting thing I've ever seen. You have to redo this.' And so we reshot the scene with normal Groucho glasses. However, if you have access to the videotape or the laserdisc and you single-frame through the sequence, you'll see there is still one shot in that sequence where one of the guys is wearing a set of dick-nose glasses. In fact, an actual image of that was in one of the TV spots. It was one of the laughs that we had on the TV censors! It was only a few frames, but it was on national television."

In 1992, Robert Zemeckis directed *Death Becomes Her*, from a script by Martin Donovan and David Koepp. The film you saw, however, was not the one you could have seen; a part played by comedian Tracey Ullman was entirely cut out, and the ending was completely reshot after the film was sneak-previewed.

The film you saw is about Madeline Ashton (Meryl Streep), an affected, narcissistic show-business personality whose beauty is collapsing as rapidly as her career. Her worst enemy is also her former friend Helen Sharp (Goldie Hawn), a shy, repressed, unattractive, and unsuccessful writer. Madeline steals Helen's fiancé, Dr. Ernest Menville (Bruce Willis), a plastic surgeon, and marries him. Years later, Madeline and Ernest have a miserable life together; Madeline's career is dead, and Ernest now specializes in making corpses look good for funeral homes. Helen, however, has transformed herself from an overweight, obsessive mental case into a famous—and sexy—author. Helen wants revenge and convinces Ernest to murder his wife. Meanwhile, out of desperation, Madeline visits Lisle von Rhuman (Isabella Rossellini), a beautiful, underdressed enchantress, who grants her the secret of eternal youth, encased in a little bottle.

Unaware that Madeline has swallowed a potion that not only rejuvenated her but also has made her immortal, Ernest tries to kill his wife, only to realize that he's now stuck with a living corpse! On trying to murder Helen, Madeline discovers that her enemy also took the potion, and after years of hating each other, Madeline and Helen bond, hoping that Ernest will forever take care of their bodies. First, though, they have to make sure he drinks the magic potion as well. They knock him out; when Ernest wakes up, Lisle tries to convince him to drink the potion. She slits one of his fingers with a dagger, dips the blade in the potion, and drips it into the cut. His hand miraculously becomes youthful. Still, Ernest resists temptation and escapes. Many years later, Helen and Madeline, still alive but decaying, lonely, and miserable, attend Ernest's funeral.

Unlike them, Ernest has had a full and happy life. On their way out, they trip down a set of stairs and break to pieces. Still able to move her lips, Helen casually asks Madeline if she remembers where she parked the car.

The film that was sneak-previewed in Phoenix to a test audience was different from what you ultimately saw in your local cinema. In the original version, Ernest, who has a drinking problem, visits a bar called Dominick's and befriends Toni, the bartender, played by Tracey Ullman. Her character was introduced in the first half of the film, right after we saw Ernest on the job and before Madeline went to the beauty parlor. In that bar scene, Ernest gleefully watches Madeline being strangled in a film on TV; after she dies, Ernest tells Toni she can now turn the TV off. Toni was an understanding, likeable character—at one point in the scene, she puts napkins beneath the head of a drunken man who's slouched over the counter at the other end of the bar. Ernest complains he's been wasting his life, has made the wrong choices, and says there's gotta be a bright side, a way to start over again.

The Toni character did not appear again until the end of the film. The release version shows Ernest falling from the roof into a swimming pool and escaping, but initially, he found the potion in the pool, grabbed it, and left with it. Lisle tells Madeline and Helen to get Ernest back. While the two women search for him at home, Ernest finds refuge with Toni at Dominick's. Because he has the potion, for the first time he can do something about his life and get rid of both Madeline and Helen. Ernest urges Toni to take the potion to the *New York Times* and have it analyzed if anything ever happens to him. Toni encourages him to go to the police. As they're trying to find a solution, the drunken man we saw earlier sitting at the end of the bar rises and falls again. This time, he's dead.

By now, Madeline and Helen have figured out Ernest must be at Dominick's. When they show up, the police are questioning Toni; a body is laid out on a stretcher outside the bar, covered with a blanket. Toni explains that the man is Ernest. Madeline and Helen want to search the body to get the potion back. Luckily, Ernest, who's been hiding, manages to throw the potion to Toni before Madeline and Helen have a chance to find out that he's still alive. The two women get into their car and leave, realizing that from now on, it's just going to be the two of them together. . .forever. Ernest knows that eventually they'll realize that the body was not his; Toni reassures him that by the time this happens, he'll be far, far away. Maybe Toni is right, but then what? Twenty-seven years later in Switzerland, Madeline and Helen are traveling; they're still beautiful but they're bored. They see an old couple. . .it's Ernest and Toni, happy, sitting and having a picnic. Ernest takes Toni's hand and covers it with his right hand—the one that Lisle had made look youthful—which, unlike the other one, is that of a twenty-five-year-old. . . .

Director Robert Zemeckis told the magazine *Cinefex*:

"The original ending was soft and didn't keep with the tone of the picture. Even though Bruce did a wonderful job acting the part of this gentle old man, and the makeup was really terrific, the problem was you still knew it was the same Bruce up there that you'd seen for the whole rest of the picture. And we were asking the audience to accept all this right at the end, which is tough; whereas you ask the audience to suspend their disbelief early on—Goldie's getting fat is a good example of that—because you are still in the process of telling them what the rules of the movie are. By ending the movie at his funeral as he is eulogized, the audience could use its own imagination to envision how Bruce had turned out, which seemed to give the sequence more power."

Perry Katz, executive vice president of marketing at Universal Pictures, who organized the test screenings for the film, said:

"The audience did not understand, in the original ending, what the problem was with being young and beautiful forever. Basically, the negative impact of eternal life was not clear. David Koepp rewrote the ending. Now when we see Meryl Streep and Goldie Hawn at the funeral, they've become a twisted mass of flesh. In addition to being bored, they're constantly at each other's throat. With this new ending, the negative impact of eternal life was obvious. This version got great results when we tested it."

Another example of a scene that confused sneak-preview audiences took place when Isabella Rossellini tries to convince Bruce Willis to drink the potion. Originally, Willis just said, "But then what?" and ran away. "People did not understand why he did not want to live forever," Perry Katz observed. New dialogue was added in which Ernest explains the downfalls of living forever and says eternal life would mean seeing everyone else dying and hanging out with Madeline and Helen forever. He concludes: "This is a nightmare!"

With the movie due for release at the end of July, reshooting began toward the middle of June. "It's something that was hard to see until you feel it with the audience," Zemeckis commented on the original ending and on his decision, "but we wouldn't have done it if it jeopardized the release pattern and marketing strategy we had in place." By then, trailers of the film featuring Tracey Ullman had already been shown in theaters around the country.

The Tracey Ullman scenes seemed to slow down the picture and to belong to another movie altogether. On one hand, you had an outrageous black comedy, and suddenly the scenes between Willis and Ullman brought the story down to reality. Also, Ullman, who is known for her outrageousness, was having to play a quiet, rational character, which sent the story in a whole different direction. The old ending was it seems a bit sappy, although visual-effects art director Doug Chiang, on staff at George Lucas's Industrial Light and Magic (ILM), wanted an interesting last look at Madeline and Helen and had planned on superimposing briefly, almost subliminally, skulls over their faces. Chiang wanted to pay tribute to the last shot of Hitchcock's *Psycho* in which, for a few seconds, the skull of Norman Bates's mother is superimposed over Anthony Perkins's face. When Zemeckis realized he had to shoot a new ending without Tracey Ullman, it did not make sense to keep her in the film at all anymore.

Prior to the sequence at Ernest's funeral, a new scene was

added with Madeline and Helen at the house looking for him, realizing that they lost him, and comforting themselves that at least they've got each other; they'll just have to take care of one another. Madeline says, "I'll paint my ass and you'll paint mine." Suddenly, they realize that they're stuck with each other forever, and their cheery mood grows somber.

The new ending, however, maintained the message of the story. The priest's eulogy refers to the fact that Ernest found the secret of eternal life in the hearts of his friends and the secret of youth in the hearts of his children and grandchildren. In that new sequence, there is a picture of Ernest as an old man near his coffin. That still was actually taken as a test for Bruce Willis's makeup as an old man for the original scene in Switzerland. "The photo was scanned into the computer," Zemeckis explained, "and Bruce's face was actually grafted onto a different picture—that of a mountain climber."

The filming of the very last scene was a technical challenge. Madeline and Helen stumble outside the church looking for a can of spray paint. Unlike the initial concept of the story, both women are deteriorating and constantly need touch-up on their bodies. New makeups had to be created fast. Kevin Haney, who had supervised the prosthetic makeups designed by Dick Smith, was on his honeymoon in Belgium, and Michael Mills (who had designed Bruce Willis's makeup during production) was called in for the reshoot. Special-body-effects artists Tom Woodruff, Jr., and Alec Gillis went back to the molds of Meryl Streep's and Goldie Hawn's bodies they had built for other scenes. They made several sets of limbs and torsos that could break apart easily, as well as other dummies that were used for the various angles required for that intricate scene. ILM did the compositing and added Streep and Hawn's faces to the two heads spinning around for the last shot.

Tracey Ullman however was not the only casualty in *Death Becomes Her*. Jonathan Silverman had a small role as Madeline's agent. His three short scenes were reduced to a cameo appearance in the final version of the film, and he can be seen asking Helen if she still has his number at her book-signing reception. Originally and earlier in that scene, Silverman was discussing Madeline's pathetic career with a starlet, revealing only at the end of the conversation that he's her agent. Later, Silverman had a bit with Meryl Streep in which she begged him to get her the center square on *The Hollywood Squares* TV game show.

Adam Storke, who plays Dakota, Madeline's stud boyfriend, also had an additional scene that ended up on the cutting room floor. In it, he is in bed with Madeline; he stands up and stares at his naked body in a mirror. He complains about his love handles, although he doesn't have any. Madeline is carrying on about Helen and thinks that Dakota's comments are directed at her, not at his body. The scene ends with Madeline staring at herself in another mirror, this one placed above the bed, noticing a crease on her face, and blaming the pillows! Later, after drinking the potion and coming home, Madeline had a phone conversation with Dakota, forgiving him for his behavior and promising to meet him later. That bit was eliminated as well for the final cut.

Every movie needs to be tightened up after the initial rough cut. Sometimes even perfectly good scenes have to be sacrificed if, as Bob Gale explained earlier, they don't help the plot or convey important information about the characters. In an earlier version of *Death Becomes Her*, for instance, Madeline and Ernest's wedding was much longer. Also, when Ernest is looking for Madeline at the hospital after he's supposedly murdered her, there was initially an extra bit with an old lady asking a nurse for a doctor for her dog. Shortly thereafter, Ernest finally found Madeline in the hospital's morgue. Initially, he had to convince a mortician working on the dead body of a priest to step out. Once alone, he finds Madeline and tells her that what has happened—she's still alive—which is a sign that they're meant to stay together. While he's carrying on, the slab with the priest slides down and hits Ernest, who then screams, "It's a miracle!" The interaction with the mortician and this gag with the priest were entirely cut out.

More significant was the deletion of several sequences following the scene at the hospital's morgue. The way that scene ends in the release version of the film shows Ernest screaming miracle. We immediately cut to Ernest painting Madeline's body, shortly followed by Helen's arrival at the couple's mansion. In fact, a whole day is missing in the story. Originally, Ernest and Madeline got out of the morgue. Madeline said to the mortician on her way out, "False alarm." There was a scene in which Ernest went to meet Helen and explained that he had had a reconciliation with Madeline. Assuming that Madeline is dead, Helen thinks that Ernest is having a psychotic episode.

The next morning, Rose, the maid, walks in and finds the kitchen a mess. She opens the fridge and sees Madeline in it. Nonchalantly, Madeline says, "Close the door," and Rose replies, "Yes, ma'am." She then awakens Ernest, who immediately asks, as he routinely does every morning, "Is it up yet?" (Ernest always refers to Madeline as "it"), and Rose replies, "It's up, sir, but it's in the fridge." Ernest becomes frantic; other maids have found Madeline and are hysterical. Ernest covers his wife with avocado and tells the maids that Madeline is on a new health thing. Finally, he gives them all a year's salary, explaining that he and Madeline are selling the house and moving to Europe. Wishing the couple a good life, the maids leave. Ernest then struggles to get Madeline up the stairs. She complains she's sweating, to which Ernest replies, "I don't think it's sweat, honey. I think you're defrosting." Madeline starts crying, and Ernest consoles her by promising she's going to be his greatest masterpiece yet. The scene ends with Ernest losing his grip on his wife and Madeline stumbling down the stairs. This was entirely cut out. Part of that scene, though, was used in one of the trailers for the film, and a picture of it is featured on the back of the laserdisc and videotape jackets.

As funny as this scene was, it simply did not advance the story, and it seemed too long a period without the Helen character. Although in the release version we never find out what happened to the maids and why they have suddenly deserted the mansion, it's obvious that logic had to be sacrificed to tighten the plot.

The sneak-preview process marked a positive turning point on the making of *Death Becomes Her*. The fact that the ending, which worked on paper, did not work on film forced the director to reevaluate what led up to it and to focus predominently on the Meryl Streep, Goldie Hawn, and Bruce Willis triangle.

RIDLEY SCOTT'S *BLADE RUNNER* AND *LEGEND*

I t took ten years before director Ridley Scott could see his 1982 science-fiction masterpiece *Blade Runner* the way he had originally intended it to be. The screenplay, loosely based on a novel by Philip K. Dick entitled *Do Androids Dream of Electric Sheep?*, was written by Hampton Francher and David Peoples. The setting of the story is a grim, sleazy, claustrophic Los Angeles, circa 2019. Harrison Ford portrays Deckard, a former police detective à la Philip Marlowe, forced back on the job. He is a blade runner, an expert cop who specializes in killing replicants, genetically engineered human beings (such extermination is called "retirement"). Deckard's mission is to retire four renegade replicants from a top-of-the-line Nexus 6 series. They have escaped from an "off-world" colony and have come to Los Angeles. These replicants were created by Tyrell (Joe Turkel), whose sexy secretary Rachael (Sean Young) is also a replicant but doesn't know it. Rachael is different from the other replicants; she's been implanted with memories. Therefore, she has feelings. Deckard succeeds in eliminating Zhora (Joanna Cassidy), one of the rebel replicants, but receives an order from his boss Bryant (M. Emmet Walsh) to retire Tyrell's secretary as well. Rachael, however, saves Deckard's life when Leon (Brion James), another one of the rebel replicants, assaults him; Deckard decides to protect Rachael.

In the meantime, Batty (Rutger Hauer), the leader replicant, asks Sebastian (William Sanderson), an employee of the Tyrell Corporation, to take him to his boss in hopes he can increase their life spans—replicants can only live four years. When Batty realizes that his quest has failed, he kills both his creator and Sebastian. Deckard tracks down Batty and Pris (Daryl Hannah), the two remaining replicants. After retiring Pris, Deckard has a final and near-fatal confrontation with Batty. But when he has the opportunity to kill Deckard, Batty choses to shut himself down and retires willingly. Deckard goes home and leaves the city with Rachael, grateful that his partner on the force, a man named Gaff (Edward James Olmos), who found out he was hiding Rachael, decided not to retire her and to let them go.

That's the *Blade Runner* you saw in 1982, but that's not the more ambiguous, more sophisticated film Ridley Scott wanted to do. The voiceover narration by Harrison Ford and the happy ending with Deckard and Rachael taking off in a spinner (flying car) to greener pastures—literally—were both added after initial, unsuccessful sneak previews. Essentially, Ridley Scott wanted the audience to think that Deckard himself was a replicant. The director originally wanted to show Deckard sitting "playing the piano rather badly because he was drunk, and there's a moment where he gets absorbed and goes off a little on a tangent, and we went into the shot of the unicorn plunging out of the forest. It's not subliminal, but it's a brief shot. Cut back to Deckard, and there's absolutely no reaction to that, and he just carries on with the scene."

During the film, on two occasions, Gaff makes two figures—one paper origami figure of a chicken and another with matches of a man with an erection. At the end, when Deckard leaves his apartment with Rachael, he finds the origami figure of a unicorn. In the theatrical version, it simply tells the audience that Gaff has been there; if the unicorn dream had been included, it would have meant that Gaff knew that Deckard's memories had been implanted and that therefore he was a replicant. "One of the layers of the film has been talking about private thoughts and memories," Ridley Scott declared, "so how would Gaff have known that a private thought of Deckard was of a unicorn?"

The producers never liked this idea—which, by the way, did not exist in the Philip K. Dick novel. "Is he or isn't he a replicant?" producer Bud Yorkin kept wondering. "You can't cheat an audience that way." Harrison Ford agreed: "I tangled with Ridley. My biggest problem was that at the end, he wanted the audience to find out that Deckard was a replicant. I fought that because I felt the audience needed somebody to root for."

The version of *Blade Runner* that was previewed at the beginning of 1982 in Denver and Dallas did not have any unicorn, but there was still a hint that Deckard might be a replicant. (Before Deckard and Rachael make love for the first time, you can see for a brief moment a glint in Deckard's eyes, the same all the other replicants have. Also, at the end, Gaff tells Deckard, "You've done a man's job.") Unfortunately, the response from the test audience was not overwhelming. Although seeming to like the film—there were no walkouts during the screenings—the audience pointed out that the story was somewhat confusing and that the ending simply did not work. Basically, it had expected something else from the director of *Alien* and from the actor who had saved the galaxy in *Star Wars*. Unfortunately, *Blade Runner* was closer to Stanley Kubrick's *2001: A Space Odyssey*.

The producers of the film—which included the Ladd Company and Michael Deeley, in association with Jerry Perenchio and Bud Yorkin—and Warner Bros., the distributor, were not pleased with the results. Exhibitors who had attended the sneak previews were also nervous. Yorkin confessed at the time, "After much talk, so much anticipation about the film, the cards were very disappointing. We all were in a state of shock." Production on *Blade Runner* had been plagued with numerous difficulties, including delays and problems between the cast, the producers, the crew, and the director. The film seemed cursed and set for failure.

Ridley Scott went to England to oversee the sound dubbing. "It was after he'd gone," production executive Katherine Haber related to *Details* magazine, "that Bud Yorkin wrote Ridley a very curt letter that said I've had enough. Yorkin then investigated the happy ending and the voiceover narration as it appeared in the film." The purpose of the narration by Harrison Ford was to guide the audience through the most obscure parts of the film. A first draft was written by novelist-screenwriter Darryl Ponicsan. His version was tossed away, and Ponicsan was replaced by Roland Kibbee, a television writer. Ridley Scott and his editor, Terry Rawlings, hated the narration. But no one more so than Harrison Ford: "It was in my contract that I had to do voiceovers, but I hated them. Ridley hated them as well, but when the film went over-budget, they made me do it. I went kicking and screaming to the studio to record it." Katherine Haber, who was present during the recording session of the narration, went as far as saying that Ford "purposefully did it [the voiceover narration] badly, hoping it wouldn't be used."

The narration was used in several strategic places:

The first voiceover comes in at the beginning of the film, when Deckard is waiting for a seat at a sushi bar. He is reading his newspaper and looks over at a large blimp/screen advertisment for life in an off-world colony. Deckard defines himself as an ex-cop, ex-blade runner, ex-killer.

Shortly after that, Deckard sits at the bar; the second narration reveals that his ex-wife called him sushi. . .cold fish, in other words. This element does not exist in the story beyond this brief narration.

The third voiceover occurs when Gaff (the character played by Edward James Olmos) asks Deckard to follow him to the police station. The narration brought something new to the plot; there is some animosity between Gaff and Deckard. Gaff speaks a language called "City Speak", a mishmash of Japanese, German, Spanish, and "what have you." Deckard explains in the voiceover that although he knew what Gaff was saying, he pretended he didn't understand: "I didn't want to make it easy for him."

The fourth voiceover is brief and takes place during the meeting between Deckard and his boss Bryant (M. Emmett Walsh). The narration explains that the term "skinjobs" used by Bryant means "replicants." Deckard indicates that Bryant is the kind of man who would have called black men "niggers."

This comment makes Bryant less likeable, and by drawing this parallel, Deckard shows he has sympathy for replicants and sees them as deserving respect.

The fifth narration comes when Deckard takes off in the spinner with Gaff, after the meeting at the police station. Deckard explains that he originally quit his job because it involved too much killing. Deckard says he had to accept his mission—retiring the rebel replicants. Otherwise, he would have been eliminated. If the job turned out to be too much, Deckard reveals he could always leave. Deckard then mentions that Gaff, who is up for a promotion, doesn't want him back on the force.

Voiceover number six was added when Deckard and Gaff visit Leon's hotel room and explains how Deckard got the lead. Leon is the replicant who kills Holden, a blade runner, at the beginning of the film, during a Voigt-Kampff (V-K) session (the V-K machine is used by blade runners to reveal if someone is a replicant or not).

During that same scene, Deckard checks the bathroom and finds a scale in the tub. He then looks through drawers and discovers family pictures. Voiceover number seven explains that the scale is not human, (It is synthetic.) that replicants don't have any and that they don't have families either.

When Deckard gets home, he is confronted with Rachael, who's been waiting for him. She tells him she's not a replicant; she's got memories, even family pictures. Deckard explains that these memories are implants; she is a replicant and doesn't know it. Rachael leaves. In voiceover number eight, we find out that the childhood memories that Tyrell implanted in Rachael's mind are, in fact, his niece's. Deckard comments on the fact that replicants are not supposed to have any feelings. . .and neither are blade runners. Deckard is confused: "What was happening to me?" Deckard also wonders about the pictures he found in Leon's room, and if, like Rachael, these rebel replicants need to create memories for themselves.

Narration number nine follows Deckard's shooting of Zhora; he explains he feels badly about shooting a woman in the back despite the fact she was a replicant. He also mentions his feelings for Rachael.

Narration number ten takes place toward the end of the film; Batty saves Deckard's life and lets himself die. Deckard doesn't understand why Batty did not kill him. He speculates: maybe replicants love life, not just theirs, anyone's. Maybe the rebel replicants just wanted answers and to find out who they were. Deckard concludes: "I could just watch him die." This narration existed already in the preview print. It was slightly different and longer; originally, Deckard said he watched Batty all night.

The last voiceover occurs in the last scene of the film, when Deckard and Rachael fly off to a new life. In this happy ending, which was added after the sneak previews, Deckard states the obvious: Gaff came to his place in search of Rachael and decided not to retire her. Deckard says Rachael is a new prototype of replicant—no termination date. . .termination undetermined. Deckard concludes: "I didn't know how long we have together. Who does?"

If the main intention of the narration was to eliminate any doubt that Deckard was a replicant, it was accomplished. The voiceover narration made the audience lazy; it justified everything and characterized everyone. "You're looking at a red door," editor Terry Rawlings said, "and it's telling you it's a red door." Initially, Ridley Scott had wanted the audience to think; the voiceover did not permit it anymore. "I think voiceover is very difficult to make work," Scott said, "and it rarely does—it did in *Apocalypse Now* and *Out of Africa*, that's it." In that sense, the version that was released in 1982 totally contradicted the director's initial creative ideas and intentions.

After the sneak previews, the ending was yet another problem that had to be addressed. The last shot showed Deckard and Rachael getting into an elevator; the doors close on them—The End. It was the first time in his career that Ridley Scott had experienced the preview process, and he confessed that the audience's negative reaction puzzled him. In any case, the ending had to be changed. "I didn't fight it," Scott recalled.

"I thought, 'My God, maybe I've gone too far. Maybe I ought to clarify it.' I got sucked into the process of thinking 'Let's explain it all.'"

A new scene to follow the shot of Deckard and Rachael getting into the elevator was written. The goal was to create an uplifting feeling, and the shots of mountains, nature, and beautiful landscapes which we see through the windows of the spinner accomplish just that. Originally, the footage was to be shot in Utah, but because of bad weather, the producers turned to Stanley Kubrick and asked to use stock footage he had shot for the opening credits of *The Shining*.

The scene of Harrison Ford and Sean Young inside the spinner was shot in the Hollywood hills, with the vehicle on the ground, although in the film, we get the illusion they're flying.

Blade Runner, complete with the narration and the new ending was sneak-previewed again, this time in San Diego. The print was similar to the version that was released on June 25, 1982, except for a short bit which introduced Batty making a call in a phone booth to Chew (James Hong)—who, we later find out, designs replicant eyes for the Tyrell Corporation—and for a shot at the end, of Deckard reloading his gun during his final confrontation with Batty. The results were encouraging, and the film was finally released to mixed to negative reviews; while most critics agreed that the film looked good, they thought it had no real substance to it. As devastating as it may have been to Ridley Scott, the narration was criticized and declared dull. "Screenwriters Hampton Francher and David Peoples saddle him [Deckard] with a narration full of tough-guy clichés that were hoary in 1949, let alone 2019," Michael Sragow wrote in *Rolling Stone*, mistakenly crediting the two writers for the voiceover [Roland Kibbee, who did the job, did not get screen credit]. Pauline Kael of *The New Yorker* found "Scott's creepy, oppressive vision requires some sort of overriding idea—something besides spoofy gimmicks, such as having Deckard narrate the movie in the loner-in-the-big-city manner of a Hammett or Chandler private eye. This voiceover, which is said to have been a late addition, sounds ludicrous, and it breaks the visual hold of the material."

On the other hand, if the critics did not like the film, there was still hope with the audience. After all, *Blade Runner* had been changed entirely, based on the public's response. Unfortunately, the competition that summer was stiff; *E.T.* was the film everyone wanted to see. . .over and over again. The lavish *Blade Runner* opened strongly, but interest in the picture faded quickly. The film had cost a little over $27 million and barely made its budget back domestically.

The first of several new versions of *Blade Runner* was released on videotape and laserdisc by Embassy Home Entertainment. That version was, in fact, the European version of the film; while it did not feature additional scenes, it included fifteen seconds of extra—gory—footage. Three shots were added when Batty murders Tyrell by forcing his thumbs into his eyesockets. In the theatrical version, we never saw blood; Ridley Scott cut away from the violence by putting in a shot of Tyrell's pet-replicant-owl and by staying longer on Batty's face. For the European release, the close-up of the owl was removed, and the shots of Batty were trimmed. Three added close-ups showed Batty's fingers pushing hard into Tyrell's eyesockets and blood spurting out.

Later, Deckard is attacked by Pris, one of the three rebel replicants. She jumps on top of him, paralyzing him by squeezing her legs around his neck. Two shots of Pris holding Deckard by his nostrils before she drops him on the floor were added. In the U.S. version, Pris just releases her legs from around his neck and drops him. Also new were two other shots, one of Deckard and another one of Pris, at the end of that same scene. In this new version, Deckard shoots Pris one additional time, and her moving frantically on the floor before Deckard gives her the *coup de grâce* is longer.

Finally, when Batty and Deckard are chasing each other at the end of the film, Batty drives a nail through his own hand. Two close-ups of the nail ripping through the flesh that did not exist in the initial version of the movie were added.

In 1989, by coincidence, Michael Arick, director of asset management at Warner Bros., stumbled across a 70mm print

of *Blade Runner* in the vaults of Todd-AO, a sound production
house in Los Angeles. Obviously, nobody knew that print
existed. Several months later, the Cineplex Odeon on Fairfax
in Los Angeles announced a classic film festival featuring
70mm prints. Arick was contacted for the *Blade Runner* 70mm
print he had found in the Todd-AO vaults. But everyone was
in for a big surprise; that print of the film was missing the
voiceover narration—except for the terse comment on Batty's
death at the end, and the last shot showed the elevator doors
closing on Deckard and Rachael. The film did not have the
happy ending! This was obviously a work print that had been
used for one of the sneak previews. The music for the climactic chase sequence between Batty and Deckard even had
temp music, borrowed from *Planet of the Apes* by Jerry Goldsmith and from *Humanoids From the Deep* by James Horner.

In fact, there are many other differences between that version and the one that was released in 1982:

- The opening titles only say: Harrison Ford in *Blade Runner* (this logo and titles were also used in the trailer).

- There's no prologue about the Tyrell Corporation, replicants, and blade runners, as in the release version.
  Instead, there's a fictitious replicant definition from the
  New American Dictionary 2016 edition: "Replicant: See
  also: Robot (antique), Android (absolete), Nexus (generic).
  Synthetic human with paraphysical capabilities, having
  skin/flesh, culture. Also: Rep, Skin Job (slang). Off-world
  uses: combat, high-risk industrial, deep space probe. On-
  world use prohibited. Specifications and quantities: information classified."

- The extreme close-up of an eye intercut with views of Los
  Angeles in 2019 in the opening sequence is missing. So
  are two shots of Holden—the blade runner who is about
  to interview Leon—watching the view from his office
  window. On the other hand, we hear clearly the voices of
  air controllers during the aerial shots over Los Angeles. In
  this work print, the sound effects are usually louder. (Later,
  when Deckard is in his elevator, we distinctively hear

Rachael coughing next to him; Deckard had not seen her, and, surprised, he pulls his gun on her. In the finished film, Rachael's coughing is barely audible, making Deckard's reaction seem rather odd.) Other effects tracks, like the voices on the blimps, are also different from those in the release version.

- Leon shoots Holden; we stay longer on the victim toppling over what looks like a typewriter. The wound in his back is more obvious.

- Deckard at the sushi bar; there's an additional close-up of the food he ordered.

- A shot of Bryant serving Deckard a drink is missing. Bryant's line, "I need the old blade runner. I need your magic," is also missing in the work print.

- There's an additional line of dialogue when Bryant, showing Deckard profiles of the rebel replicants, says, "That's Leon. Amunition loader on intergalactic runs. He can lift four-hundred-pound atomic loads, all day and night. The only way you can hurt him is to kill him." These lines do not exist in the release version.

- Deckard makes the following comments when analyzing the picture he found in Leon's apartment: "Hello Roy," and later, "Zhora or Pris?" These lines were deleted for the theatrical release.

- There's a dissolve between the scenes in which Deckard gets information on a snake scale from a Cambodian woman and his searching for the man who manufactured it. The dissolve indicates that time has gone by. This distinction is missing in the theatrical release; we just cut from one scene to another without any dissolve.

- Right before Deckard enters the club where Zhora is performing, there's a brief scene outside on the street deleted for the theatrical version, with two girls wearing hockey masks, dancing in a large plastic bubble, while Deckard is talking to a policeman.

- After Leon is shot by Rachael, he does not topple over Deckard the way he does in the release version.

- The love scene between Deckard and Rachael is similar in both the work print and the release version, but the score is different; therefore, the tone of the sequence is slightly changed.

- Batty tells Tyrell: "I want more life, father," not "fucker," like he does in the release version. Tyrell's murder in the work print is closer to the European version; there are two gory close-ups of the thumbs going into Tyrell's eyesockets and another one when Batty releases his fingers. Still, the European version is more violent.

- Batty has an additional line in the work print when he comes after Sebastian. He says, "Sorry, Sebastian. Come, come."

- When Pris attacks Deckard, the additional shots of her holding him by the nostrils are present, as in the European version. They were removed for the U.S. theatrical version.

- After Batty dies, there's an additional long shot showing Gaff's spinner rising on the side of the building. In the release version, the spinner is out of focus and can barely be seen rising behind Batty.

The audience present at the Fairfax 70mm-film festival loved this new—old—version of *Blade Runner*, but when it was screened for Ridley Scott, who usually refuses to watch his films after they've been completed, the director declared this was not his cut. He said that the only version he would approve would include the unicorn sequence. Scott also complained that this print of the film was a test work print and a faulty dupe. At the same time, the director was excited at the idea of finally being able to recut his film. "When the studio showed this version to me, I thought, 'We've gotten so close; why not complete this as I'd like to see it today, for audiences who appreciate this material and who are ready to see it in its undiluted form.'" The work print of *Blade Runner* was shown at UCLA as part of the Los Angeles Perspectives multimedia festival, and the evening included the reading of a telegram sent by Scott to the audience, in which he said that this version still didn't include his unicorn shot and that therefore, it wasn't a director's cut. No doubt about it; Ridley Scott refused to be associated with that version of *Blade Runner*.

Barry Reardon, president of domestic distribution at Warner Bros., and Peter Gardiner, the company's vice president of operations and corporate film and video services, decided to release the newly discovered print in two theaters only (the Nuart in Los Angeles and the Castro in San Francisco). In a strange twist of fate, *Blade Runner* was going to be tested again, nine years after the initial release. The studio created a campaign and advertised the film as "The Original Director's Version of the Movie That Was Light Years Ahead of Its Time." In the opening week, *Blade Runner* broke house records at the Nuart, where it grossed $53,560, and at the Castro, where the film made about $94,000.

At last, Barry Reardon told Ridley Scott they would finance the final restoration of *Blade Runner*, with Peter Gardiner in charge of the project at Warners and Michael Arick, who had by then left the studio, handling Scott's end of it. Helping as well on the project was Les Healey, who had been first assistant editor on the film.

Since the unicorn sequence had never been shot, Ridley Scott, back in London, had to choose a proper shot of a unicorn amongst trims from his next film *Legend* and inserted it in *Blade Runner*. Or at least, this seems to be what really happened, since Scott has always been evasive when it comes to the origin of the unicorn shot. Later, Arick and Scott found out that the original negative for the unicorn scene had been lost. Warners was going to clean up the work print and rerelease it although it did not include the unicorn sequence. On hearing the news, Scott announced via his agent that he would run full-page ads in the trades if Warners released the work print as the director's cut. Luckily, the studio decided to give Arick three weeks to recut *Blade Runner*, under the director's supervision, in a version that would finally please Ridley Scott. The positive copy of the unicorn shot was cleaned up and added to the film. The gory shots from the international version that were shown in the U.S. video release could not be located in time to meet with Warners' deadline and could not be included in the director's cut.

Vangelis's music was remixed digitally; it is especially different in the sequence that now features the unicorn shot. A hospital scene with Deckard visiting Holden (the blade runner who is shot by Leon in the opening sequence) which had never been edited into the film, could not be cut in mainly because the sound track had been destroyed. The official director's cut does not contain any narration, happy ending, or gory violent close-ups from the European version, but includes the unicorn sequence. Another change: the voice of the commercial on the blimp at the beginning of the film says something slightly different than it did in the original theatrical version; it now names a sponsor instead of referring to the benefits of owning a replicant. One example of something that was never fixed takes place at the beginning of the film. Bryant says four replicants are running in the streets. Later, he says six escaped and one got fried. . . . What happened to number five? In the script, there was indeed a fifth replicant, a woman named Mary, who was reaching the final stages of her four-year lifespan. She died right before Deckard arrived for his confrontation with Pris and Batty. That part was never shot, but the dialogue was never changed.

Another gaffe occurs when a Cambodian woman reads the serial number off the snake scale in a microscope; the number we see is different from the one she gives Deckard. While efforts were made to correct the dialogue, the results created an awkward transition on the sound track. There was no time to bring back actors for looping, and so these—ultimately insignificant—errors remained. Some other inserts or scene extensions, like the girls wearing hockey masks dancing outside Zhora's club, were simply not added per Ridley Scott's request. In the case of the girls, for instance, the director thought they looked cheesy. As for the one line of narration that was present in the work print, Scott decided to take it out for consistency.

"I have no interest in seeing the director's cut," Harrison Ford said. "Making the movie was an unpleasant experience I do not wish to relive." Well, everyone else felt differently. The new *Blade Runner* received positive reviews and became the hit movie it deserved to be. The box-office and critical success of the director's cut proved how rereleasing older films could be good both from a financial and creative point of view. The results on *Blade Runner* were even more fantastic, considering the fact that the film had initially been poorly received. "In a funny kind of way, it [the film] didn't hit the pulse ten years ago," Ridley Scott said. "But then it became influential in terms of certain kinds of movies, and then you had MTV; I thank them for re-educating the film audience to feel more comfortable in enjoying this kind of movie." Scott has said that the bleak view of the future he created in *Blade Runner* was too shocking at the time the film first came out. "Today, it's much less so. Many changes in American cities and life over the past decade have paralleled what we showed on-screen. It's rather chillingly accurate in some ways."

The *Blade Runner* saga shows that sneak previews can sometimes destroy a picture and confuse a director's vision. Who should be trusted? The public or the filmmaker? In the case of *Blade Runner*, the answer is rather obvious. The success of the new cut proves that ten years after the film's initial release, audiences are more educated and open-minded and have progressed emotionally. The director's cut of *Blade Runner* is obscure and ambiguous, but it has more meaning, more substance. It accomplishes more by saying less.

Ridley Scott's next film after *Blade Runner* was the flawed and ill-fated *Legend*, starring Tom Cruise. The film was a faerie-tale about the struggle of good versus the forces of evil. Although the original version was 125 minutes, it was then reduced to 113 minutes, was tested to poor results and trimmed even more. *Legend* was first released in Europe by Twentieth Century Fox; the running time was roughly 94 minutes. It then sat on the shelves of Universal Pictures, the U.S. distributor of the film, for a while. (*Legend* came out in Europe at the end of 1985 and was released in the U.S. in April 1986.) Sidney Sheinberg, president and chief operating officer of MCA, Inc. felt the film did not appeal to teenagers. To correct this, it was decided to have the film trimmed even further and to replace entirely Jerry Goldsmith's brilliant sound track with a new score by the German rock group Tangerine Dream (who had enhanced *Sorcerer* and *Firestarter*, among others.) Goldsmith's work had already gone through changes when the film had been reduced from its initial running time to 94 minutes for its European release; cues were removed, edited, repeated, or edited together to make new ones, resulting in awkward-sounding orchestrations. Some of the temp music remained (a few cues from Goldsmith's score for *Psycho II* and library music by British composer Tim Souster). Goldsmith had encountered similar frustrations with Ridley Scott on *Alien*; some of his favorite cues were dismissed by the director in favor of some classical music from Howard Hanson's *Symphony No. 2* and even music from Goldsmith's own score for John Huston's film *Freud*! "What could I possibly say about this?" the composer declared. "I think it's [*Legend*] one of the best scores I've ever written—certainly, it's gotten me some of my best reviews. I shouldn't really comment on this, though I don't think Tangerine Dream's music will make this movie any more accessible to twelve-year-olds." Scott sympathized with Goldsmith but decided that, while his music was appropriate for European audiences, America needed a broader, more threatening score. "I just hope Jerry [Goldsmith] will forgive me. We worked together before, and his was a great score for *Legend*."

When *Legend* was finally released in the U.S., it ran 89 minutes; not many scenes had been taken out, but sequences had been rearranged. In addition to Tangerine Dream's new score, a song by Bryan Ferry was tagged on for the end credits. Despite these changes—and Tom Cruise—*Legend* failed to attract teenagers; it was a flop across the board and was hissed by the critics. In light of the success he had with his director's cut of *Blade Runner*, perhaps Ridley Scott will one day consider doing a new cut of *Legend*.

JAMES CAMERON'S *THE ABYSS, ALIENS,* AND *TERMINATOR 2: JUDGMENT DAY*

A nuclear missile submarine sinks under mysterious circumstances. The U.S. Navy asks the crew of civilian divers working on "Deepcore," a prototype underwater oil-drilling habitat, to help in the rescue operations. The mission is authorized, although Bud Brigman (Ed Harris), the rig foreman, does not believe his crew is qualified for the job. Transferring to Deepcore to coordinate the operation is a four-man team of Navy SEALs, led by Lt. Coffey (Michael Biehn). The mission represents a double jeopardy for Bud when his soon-to-be-ex-wife Lindsey (Mary Elizabeth Mastrantonio) joins the party. The seemingly routine mission takes on an unexpected twist when Coffey turns psycho and steals an atomic warhead. After a battle that claims Coffey's life, Bud decides to sacrifice himself to deprogram the weapon. Luckily, he is rescued by the NTIs, an alien race that lives underwater. Deepcore's mission is over. Bud and Lindsey are reunited.

This version of *The Abyss* was released in 1989 by Twentieth Century Fox. The film was written and directed by James Cameron, who had made a name for himself with *The Terminator* (1984) and had followed this mega-hit with *Aliens* (1986), one of the most successful sequels in film history. The initial cut of the film, as it was tested in Dallas, was much longer and included a subplot that was later cut out for the first release of *The Abyss.*

The subplot depicted our world on the edge of a nuclear war. After Bud is rescued by the aliens (NTIs) and is safe in a waterproof chamber, they communicate with him by displaying a newscast on a water wall. First, they show a newscast announcing the world is on the outbreak of war. Bud realizes that the NTIs know what's happening in the world above water. They then show a newscast interview with a seismologist, revealing that a giant wave is moving toward the shoreline of every continent. Bud tells the NTIs he knows they're doing this; they can control water. But why are they doing it? On the screen of water, the NTIs show Bud nuclear explosions, hinting at the fact that the world is going to destroy itself. Bud refuses to believe that human beings are going to go through with a nuclear war until the NTIs show him a montage of all the atrocities humans are responsible for (James Cameron referred to this montage as "Atrocities Greatest Hits"). Bud looks down; he knows the NTIs are right. The aliens then create a giant tidal wave that threatens to wipe out several of our cities as a warning to mankind. The NTIs decide to stop their action; Bud asks why: "You could have done it. Why didn't you?" The NTIs display on the screen of water the message Bud had sent to Lindsey prior to his rescue: KNEW THIS WAS ONE-WAY TICKET, BUT YOU KNOW I HAD TO COME. LOVE YOU, WIFE.

"The original goal of the film," Cameron declared, "was to tell a story of a kind of apocalypse in which we are all judged by a superior race, and found to be worthy of salvation because of a single average man, an Everyman, who somehow represents that which is good in us: the capacity for love measured by the willingness for self-sacrifice." This sequence was the heart of the film. "The divine image of the suspended wave," Cameron said, "is an image straight from my dreams. It is the source of inspiration for the entire film. My single recurring nightmare, throughout my life, was that of a vast wave rolling toward the shore, miles high, turning day into night. That dread, in my subconscious, became inextricably interwoven with the dread of death, and the specific dread of nuclear holocaust."

The tidal-wave sequence was created by George Lucas's Industrial Light and Magic (ILM). Yuri Farrant, a surfing photographer, was sent to Waimea, in Hawaii, to shoot large waves. The footage of waves approaching and receeding were satisfying, but the wave coming to a stop had to be re-created in a studio by Paul Haston, with a motion-control device undulating it. Live footage was shot in Santa Monica with three hundred extras and actor Tom Isbell playing a reporter. The other elements and other locations combined miniatures and matte paintings with, in the case of the Russian naval base, live elements. Still, when *The Abyss* was screened to a test audience the first time, the shots of the wave coming to a stop were unfinished.

The Dallas test screening revealed that the tidal wave was the sequence that was hated the most . . . and loved the most. Half the audience liked it because they thought this was the message of the film, while the other half said the sequence seemed to belong in another movie. The big issue after the test screening was the length of the film. "The enemy," James Cameron said, "was our collective knowledge at the time that a film had to be two hours. . . ." Barry Diller, then the head of the Fox studios, told Cameron that this cut of *The Abyss* was too much movie for today's audiences. "Hey, people wouldn't even line up for a David Lean film now, so don't take it so hard," Diller told him.

James Cameron was under pressure to reduce the running time, and Fox wasn't telling him what to cut out. "They were saying," Cameron told the *Los Angeles Times*, "'we've got to make it shorter because it's not going to be successful. Exhibitors are going to freak.'" Having final cut on his film, he had to decide what to eliminate to make it shorter. Cameron was reluctant in cutting anything out of his movie, but the film had cost a hefty $45 million, and the director felt he had to play the game. He finally elected to cut out the entire wave sequence along with the subplots that built up to it, including the scenes mentioning the possibilities of World War III. Without the tidal wave, this particular issue had no more resolution, and so it made sense to delete it. "I lost the nuclear disarmament theme as a clear agenda of the film," Cameron said, "but felt it was still implicit, though now operating at a symbolic level." The story on the oil rig with the threat of the Coffey character armed with the warhead now served as a metaphor for the way the rest of the world would react in the face of a nuclear war. The scope of the story had diminished, the message was less obvious, less literal. In the release version of the film, Bud is saved by the NTIs and put in the waterproof chamber. Bud stands up and says, "Howdy. . .Uh. . .How you guys doing?" The NTIs simply display Bud's message of love to Lindsey on the water wall.

Fox was shocked by Cameron's choice; obviously, the tidalwave sequence had cost a lot of money, and for it to end on the cutting room floor seemed wrong. The love story between Bud and Lindsey was what Cameron had decided he wouldn't touch. "I knew that with the scene of Mary [Elizabeth Mastrantonio] drowning and Ed [Harris] bringing her back to life, I had sort of captured lightning in a bottle from a performance standpoint. The most logical thing to take out was the drowning scene, because it's the one thing that is really kind of a divergence in the story line." Still, the love story remained intact. For Cameron, the test-screening process on *The Abyss* was a confusing experience. "These test-market screenings are dangerous. In this case, it wasn't the studio messing with me. It was me messing with me. It was *me* losing perspective and becoming reliant on a process. I had never used test-market screenings to influence my own thinking. I didn't understand how to use the tool."

In order to find out if he was right, Cameron decided to do a second test screening of *The Abyss* without the tidal wave sequence and its subplots, in Canoga Park, California. He also accelerated the end credits to save another minute, removed some establishing scenes on the oil rig, and eliminated development of secondary characters. The running time was down to two hours, and twenty minutes; the film was still over two hours, but at least it was shorter. The studio was willing to go with it if the test screening showed improvement. The audience approval rating for the movie went up about twenty-five points. Cameron was happy that, although he had lost the great spectacle of the tidal wave, his characters remained

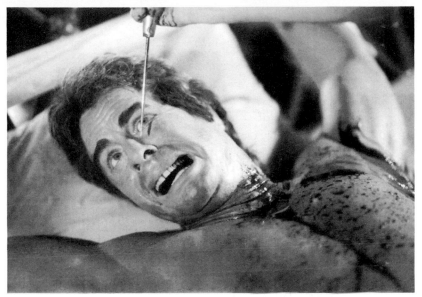

One of the many shots from *Basic Instinct* that caused the film to be slapped with an NC-17 by the MPAA. Director Paul Verhoeven had to delete it in order to receive an R rating. (Special makeup effects designed and created by Rob Bottin.)

Angie Dickinson is killed in *Dressed to Kill*. . .and so was that particular shot. To avoid an X rating, director Brian De Palma had to water down his film dramatically.

Louise Fletcher and Richard Burton in the original ending of John Boorman's *Exorcist II: The Heretic*, before it was cut out only a few days after the disastrous opening of the film.

After showing *Dr. Strangelove* to a test audience, Stanley Kubrick decided to delete a pie-throwing sequence which originally concluded the film.

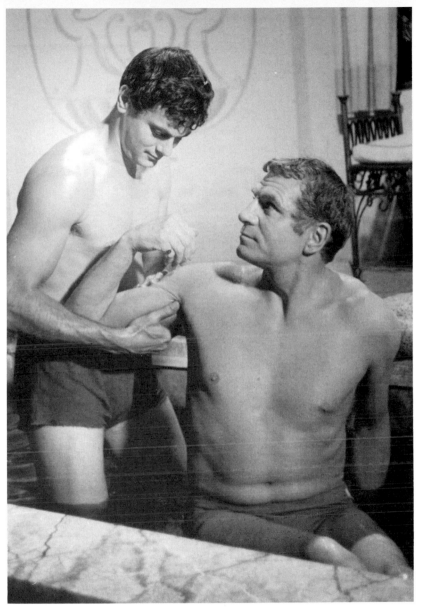

"Any suggestion that Crassus finds a sexual attraction in Antonius will have to be avoided," Geoffrey Shurlock of the Code Administration advised regarding the controversial bath sequence between Laurence Olivier and Tony Curtis in Stanley Kubrick's *Spartacus*. The scene was deleted in 1960 but restored in the film thirty years later.

The eleven-minute "Happy Endings" musical number in Martin Scorsese's *New York, New York* was deleted for the original 1977 release of the film and was eventually restored in 1981.

Test audiences were initially split on the climactic tidal wave sequence from James Cameron's *The Abyss*. It was deleted but found its way back into the film along with other additional footage for *The Abyss Special Edition*.

Michael Biehn and Linda Hamilton in the deleted dream sequence of James Cameron's *Terminator 2: Judgment Day*. That scene can be seen in the laserdisc special edition of the film.

The deleted "colony" sequence from James Cameron's *Aliens* was restored by the director in a laserdisc special edition of the film.

Unicorns did not bring luck to director Ridley Scott. His fairy tale *Legend*, starring Tom Cruise, flopped, even after the film was recut and rescored. It also took ten years from the initial release of *Blade Runner* before the notorious shot of a unicorn meant to explain that Harrison Ford is a "replicant" was added to the film.

A scene of Richard Dreyfuss at a power station that appeared in the original version of *Close Encounters of the Third Kind* was deleted by director Steven Spielberg from the special edition of the film.

Footage showing Richard Dreyfuss inside the mothership, which was not featured in the original version of the film, was added for *Close Encounters of the Third Kind: The Special Edition*.

Penny Marshall's role in Steven Spielberg's *1941* was reduced to an unbilled cameo for the theatrical release but was restored in the television version of the film.

After test screenings, Tracy Ullman, here with Bruce Willis, was entirely cut out from Robert Zemeckis's *Death Becomes Her*.

William Friedkin's *Cruising*, starring Al Pacino, is an example of a film that was threatened by a special interest group before it reached the cutting room. The movie also had problems with the MPAA; that particular scene had to be trimmed and altered before the film could be issued an R rating. Still, several exhibitors either refused to show *Cruising* or warned patrons that it should have been rated X.

intact. So, to the chagrin of many, *The Abyss* came out destituted of the tidal wave. Van Ling, who began his career at Lightstorm Entertainment (Cameron's production company) as research assistant/visual-effects liaison on *The Abyss* and became head of production and director of marketing and promotion, had this to say about the test screenings and the deletion of the tidal-wave sequence:

> It's my opinion and the opinion of some of the folks in post-production that the numbers were false in the second sneak preview. Unlike the preview in Dallas, where nobody in the audience knew what the film was, the second preview was filled with Cameron fans who would automatically have a greater appreciation for the film anyway. You're comparing different test subjects. It was the same demographically, but if you account for taste, it makes a big difference. That's just a theory.

Cameron also had his own thoughts on the results of test screenings of *The Abyss*:

> We were basing a lot of our decision-making on that, which I've learned since then is really a mistake. You have to do very broad demographics if you're going to do test screenings and use them to change the cut of a picture. Because you can't just cut the picture for one part of the country or one group of people.

The Abyss, which came out in the summer of 1989 against the competition of films such as *Batman, Lethal Weapon 2, and Star Trek V*, was different from *Aliens* and *The Terminator*, the two films Cameron was known for. This time, while the spectacle was still there, his new movie had more of a human story, and this time, the monster was not an alien queen or a robot from the future. As Cameron explained it, in *The Abyss*, the monster was the human race itself. The reviews were mixed, and although the film grossed $60 million domestically, it wasn't the mega-hit that Fox, or Cameron, had expected.

While the film was still playing in theaters, James Cameron asked video editor Ed Marsh to put together a longer version of *The Abyss*, featuring scenes that had been deleted in the post-production process even before it had been shown to test audiences, as well as the tidal-wave sequence. Yet that rough cut of what would later become the special edition sat on the shelves of Lightstorm Entertainment for two years. The truth is, Cameron had doubts about doing a special edition of *The Abyss*: "It seemed like a no-win proposition. If we restored the scenes and the result was disappointing, then the special-edition project would be a failure. If we restored the scenes and the result was better, then we'd look like bozos for not doing it right the first time."

A series of events resolved that conflict and motivated the release in 1992 of *The Abyss Special Edition*. In order to understand the process through which this event was made possible, it is important to explain the different steps and reasons that led up to it.

In 1986, James Cameron directed *Aliens*, the sequel to Ridley Scott's *Alien*. Both films set new standards in the science-fiction genre. With the possibilities offered by the laserdisc market, Cameron agreed to release a new version of *Aliens* with additional footage. "The concept of a special cut or edition of a film is a new and exciting development, made possible by the specialized markets created by video," James Cameron wrote in his introduction to the *Aliens* special laserdisc edition. "The economic realities of feature-film exhibition, at least domestically, demand that a commercial film not exceed two hours. Every minute beyond that magic number carries the penalty of lost revenues. *Aliens* pushed the envelope with its release length of two hours and seventeen minutes, and I am grateful to Twentieth Century Fox for supporting the film at that running time." Now, with the special-laserdisc-edition concept, Cameron was able to recut *Aliens*, without any time constraint, and reinstated twenty minutes of footage. Although he declared he was satisfied with the version that had been released initially, he believed that the new edition was "the best possible version of the film in the absence of time constraints."

With the additional footage, the new version of *Aliens* runs 154 minutes. Eight minutes of this additional footage had already been restored for the *Aliens* network premiere on CBS. "It was a real important project for me to get done because I wanted people to see it," Cameron said of the extended version. While many sequences were added, other scenes never made it back into the film, even for this special edition. As Van Ling explained:

> One of James Cameron's main tendencies on special editions is not to just put everything back in. You still have to think about pacing, and so there are scenes that don't go back in. In *Aliens*, for instance, there was a scene in which Ripley [Sigourney Weaver] was looking for Newt [the little girl played by Carrie Henn] and she found Carter Burke cocooned [Burke was played by Paul Reiser and was the evil character willing to sacrifice human lives to bring back specimens of the alien creatures]. That scene was shot. Burke says, "God, I can feel this thing moving inside my chest." Ripley thinks, "Nobody deserves this," and puts a grenade in his hands, pulls the pin, and runs. It goes off. She's in a way sparing him from a horrible death [an alien is incubating in his body]. It shows Ripley has compassion, but it's pretty cold compassion. The scene was cut for pacing. The audience knew that Burke had been killed [although we never see him die], and now it was just about Ripley trying to find Newt. The scene with Burke in the cocoon was a diversion from the real emotional and narrative thrust.

Incidentally, a similar scene in Ridley Scott's *Alien* also remained on the cutting room floor. At the end of the film, when Ripley is escaping, she finds Dallas (Tom Skerritt) still alive, cocooned. Above him, the body of Brett (Harry Dean Stanton) is also encased in a cocoon. Dallas begs Ripley to kill him, and using a flame thrower, she burns down the whole alien nest. That scene, along with other sequences that focused on character development that mainly showed that

Ripley had difficulties imposing herself as a leader of the other crew members, were cut out for pacing.

About seventeen segments were restored in the special laserdisc edition of *Aliens*. Most of them involved character development; in other words, most of the action sequences were already in the release version of the film. In the new cut, however, we find out that Ripley, who was in hypersleep for fifty-seven years, had a daughter who passed away. The scene begins with Ripley sitting on a bench in a park. She grabs a remote control and switches off the image of the park; we realize that she was, in fact, sitting in front of a screen. Burke comes in, and Ripley asks if he was able to track down her daughter. He avoids the issue until he finally reveals that Amanda (Amy) Ripley McLaren died two years before, at age sixty-six, and that she was married with no children. She was cremated, and her ashes are kept in Wisconsin. The scene ends with Ripley saying, "I promised her that I'd be home for her birthday. Her eleventh birthday." She breaks down in tears. Although it was never mentioned in the first *Alien* that Ripley had a child, this element plays a major role in the new cut of *Aliens* because it reinforces the bond between Ripley and Newt, the orphaned girl. A touching scene during which Ripley talks to Newt about her daughter and explains the origin of babies was also restored in the special edition, putting a larger emphasis on the human angle of the story. This element makes tough Ripley appear vulnerable, tender, and ultimately more sympathetic.

By far, the most interesting sequence that was restored takes place on planet LV-426, where we meet Newt, her parents (the Jordens), her brother Timmy, and other members of the colony before they're attacked by aliens. The sequence is introduced by a discussion between two employees of the Weyland-Yutani Corp. The company's motto is "Building Better Worlds," and that's exactly what the colony is trying to do on LV-426. We then follow the Jordens as they discover a giant spaceship—already seen in *Alien*—which turns out to be the home of thousands of alien eggs. Jorden and his wife decide to go inside the spaceship, leaving behind in their truck their daughter Newt and their son Timmy. Later, the mother returns in a panic and calls for help on the radio. Her husband has a facehugger (the beast that lurks inside the alien eggs) clawed to his face; Newt sees her dad lying on the ground with that thing on his face and starts screaming. None of this was shown in the release version. Instead, we cut from Ripley at the inquest explaining what happened to the crew of the Nostromo (the ship in *Alien*) to a scene with Burke telling her that they lost control with planet LV-426. In the theatrical version, we reach the colony with Ripley and her small army after everyone but Newt has been killed or cocooned by the aliens.

The special laserdisc edition of *Aliens* was an enormous success. Several other factors played an important role in the release of *The Abyss Special Edition*. One was the success of Kevin Costner's *Dances With Wolves*; the film was three hours long, and no one seemed to mind. The release of the director's cut of *Blade Runner* also proved that there was a real market for new cuts of films that had been changed for their initial run. ILM had created for *Terminator 2* some groundbreaking computerized visual effects; this time, the tidal-wave sequence coming to a stop could look right. Getting *The Abyss Special Edition* underway suddenly seemed not only tempting but logical. That the tidal-wave sequence had been cut from the film was well-known among film buffs and Cameron fans. Plus, a novelization of Cameron's script by Orson Scott Card had been published at the time the film had first been released and had remained faithful to the initial story. The general public knew what they had missed. It is important, however, to point out that neither the new version of *Aliens* nor *The Abyss Special Edition* should receive the label "director's cut." Cameron was happy with the way both movies were released in their time. Calling these special editions "director's cuts" would imply that Cameron did not have final cut on his movies. James Cameron made all the cuts himself and made all the decisions.

When Cameron got involved with *The Abyss Special Edition*, he was just stepping out of the enormous success of *Ter-*

minator 2, which he directed for Carolco and Tri-Star Pictures. In 1992, Cameron signed a five-year, twelve-picture deal with Twentieth Century Fox valued at $500 million, along with the clout to put movies into production without Fox's approval. The first to come out after the deal was signed was *The Abyss Special Edition*. There was some speculation around the fact that in allowing Cameron to rework *The Abyss* was merely massaging the director's ego. "There is probably an element of that," Cameron told the *Los Angeles Times*. "They want to preserve relationships, and they should, because if I was in their position, I'd do the same thing."

With Fox's approval, work on *The Abyss Special Edition* began, but not before Cameron had set some ground rules: No scenes from the original film could be taken out or even altered—although Cameron admitted there were a few things in the film that made him cringe! Alterations on the sound track could only be made in order to accomodate the new footage. Finally, as with the *Aliens* special edition, not every scene had to find its way back into the film; only the elements that helped the story had to be taken into consideration. "We didn't slavishly put back every single scrap of film that was shot, because issues of pace and style are still important," Cameron declared. "It still has to be a good movie."

Lightstorm production supervisor Steven Quale, who had been a production assistant on the film, edited the added footage under Cameron's supervision. Van Ling produced and supervised the project, while sound editor Dody Dorn and sound designer Blake Leyh returned to complete the audio work. The necessary actors also returned to loop some additional dialogue, except for Kidd Brewer, Jr., who played Finler, an oil digger aboard Deepcore. The actor had died tragically in an accident about a year after the film was released. "Though sloppy vaulting procedures resulted in the loss of all of our original production-sound recordings from the set," Cameron said, "it was possible to reconstruct his dialogue from scrap-dailies transfers." James Cameron dedicated *The Abyss Special Edition* to Kidd Brewer, Jr.

The special edition presented another problem. Alan Silvestri, who had composed the music for the film, was not available to score the additional footage, and composer Robert Garrett was hired in his place. Van Ling said:

> We used new music for the wave sequence and also when the ark rises. For the ark, we, in fact, had to replace Silvestri's music because we had added three shots and couldn't track the music correctly. Bob [Garrett] is a synth composer and a longtime friend of James Cameron's. He had done some music for *Aliens*; he did some computer synth-tone music that was used when you first see the alien queen. For the wave sequence, we had a debate on whether we wanted music at all, or if we just wanted the roar of the wave. James said, "Let's try to come up with some music for that scene." Silvestri, by the way, never did a score for the wave. Bob, on the other hand, had composed some temp music for *The Abyss*. His score for the wave sequence is just a variation on that.

Aside from the tidal-wave sequence, most of the other footage that was added gravitates around the possibility of World War III, concerns character development, creates a deeper human story, and fleshes out the relationship not only between Bud and Lindsey, but also between Bud, his entire crew, and Coffey, the enemy. At the time, everyone involved with the special edition knew that the tidal wave was the sequence that would get the public's attention. Van Ling had this to say about the technical challenges that were faced on this particular scene:

> There are only three shots in the entire wave sequence that were worked on, and they were three composite shots. The two shots in Santa Monica where the wave is hovering over people and birds fly across in the foreground were existing shots that we just scanned into a computer—we cleaned them up and added some matte artifacts. Thanks to the technology that was developed at ILM for *Terminator 2*, we were also able to do the shot of the wave stopping right this time. ILM did this entirely as a computer graphic.

Twenty-eight minutes of additional footage were restored for *The Abyss Special Edition*. Three minutes of expanded credits finally brought the running time to about 171 minutes. A quote by Friedrich Nietzsche ("When you look into an abyss, the abyss also looks into you") was restored as well; it had initially been taken out because the film *Criminal Law*, which was released just prior to *The Abyss*, used the same quotation. *The Abyss Special Edition* ultimately was perceived as an entire new movie and new experience.

As explained in the first chapter, when widescreen movies are released on tape and laserdisc, they have to be cropped on the sides so only the most obvious action elements appear onscreen. That process is known as pan and scan. When *The Abyss Special Edition* was released on laserdisc, Fox and James Cameron offered both a letterbox version and a director's pan-and-scan version—meaning the pan-and-scan transfer was supervised by the director. "I am quite proud of the pan-and-scan transfer of the film," Cameron said, "and believe it to be superior in many ways to the letterbox, due to the poor resolving power of NTSC* video. The film was shot in the Super-35 process to allow for improved video transfer, and the result is that the pan-and-scan transfer does not suffer many of the horrible cropping losses normally associated with a widescreen film." Basically, the director had to redirect his film for the pan-and-scan version. Watching that version versus the letterbox one is a totally different experience. Some of the images in the letterbox edition are too small, whereas in the pan-and-scan edition, you feel closer to the characters. With the latter, you trade scope for intimacy. Van Ling noted:

> James Cameron's point of view is that when you transform a book into a movie, you try to make sure the spirit of the characters and the thread of the story stay intact.

*NTSC: (National Television Standards Committee) NTSC is one of the three TV standards used worldwide, the others being Secam and Pal. NTSC is mainly used in the U.S., Canada, Mexico, Japan, and South Korea. NTSC is 525 lines of horizontal resolution. Pal and Secam have 625 lines and offer a better and more consistent color balance.

James's mandate when he goes from a rectangle to a square is not to preserve the movie aspect ratio as much as it is to preserve the story and the spirit of the picture. "Pan-and-scan" has a pejorative connotation, so I designed a logo for *The Abyss Special Edition* laserdisc box set: a TV frame inside a film frame with a brain in the center; it indicates that the pan-and-scan was done with some intelligence.

There's yet another version of *The Abyss* worth mentionning: the airline version. When a movie is licensed to be shown on an airline, the restrictions are tight. One of the main restrictions is—again—time; the film has to be ninety minutes or under. Strong language or intense scenes are taboo; obviously, people don't have the option of walking out if they can't take the film! Some of the original editors were brought back to cut the airline version of *The Abyss*, which differs from the original theatrical version in many ways:

The Abyss opens with the amazing crash of a submarine. That sequence was one of the last ones to be shot. At the time, Fox was worried about the cost of the film and suggested the scene be deleted. The studio wanted the film to begin with helicopters coming down and for people to say: "A sub crashed and we're off on a rescue mission!" This was a cost-cutting measure since the crash involved major special effects. On the other hand, that spectacular opening sequence was a great hook. Luckily, Leonard Goldberg, the president of Fox at the time, agreed and the scene was shot. It is indeed an incredible moment. Unfortunately, when a film is shown on an airplane, you can't have any large vehicle crashing. So, in a strange twist of fate, the crash of the submarine was entirely deleted for the airline version of *The Abyss*, and the film begins with helicopters coming down on a ship for the rescue mission.

Cut out as well is the scene in which a rat is plunged into breathing fluid for an experiment. The search inside the wreck of the submarine was also trimmed down; in the airline version, only one body is floating inside the control room. Obviously, the close-up of a crab crawling out of the mouth of one of the victims is out. Some scenes were cut strictly for time. For example, the sequence during which Lindsey confronts Coffey, yells, blows her top, and is finally told to calm down is out. This deletion obviously gives the scene an entirely different tone.

After it was generally recognized that *The Abyss Special Edition* was better than the version that had originally been released, Fox Broadcasting announced that it had programmed the film and had already advertised it. "We thought they would save us a four-hour slot or split it over two nights so that they could show the complete version of the film," Van Ling explained.

> They said no; we are giving you two and a half hours for the special edition, including commercials, meaning the film had to be trimmed down to 115 minutes. We had to cut out twenty-five minutes! We thought, "this is going to look strange; we just released 178 minutes of the film, and now you want us to cut it out!" We refused to do it. We felt that if we cut anything out of the special edition and TV viewers hated it, Fox would say Lightstorm did it and Cameron approved it. So we suggested they take the airline version. The running time on it is 118 minutes, so we told them they could time-compress it. Basically, they fast-motion the whole movie through a machine; if you program the machine to play the film at 101-percent speed, you save three minutes over the course of 118 minutes. You don't even see it. They time-compress films on television all the time. But, of course, we made Fox put a title card up front saying that the film had been edited for television.

With the success of the special editions of *Aliens* and *The Abyss*, it seemed inevitable that sooner or later, a new version of *Terminator 2: Judgment Day* would be put together. But here again, Cameron was pleased with the way the film originally came out. "I see it not as a fix, but as an opportunity to do greater justice to the characters who live and breathe within the 136-minute confines of the film. This special edition [of *Terminator 2*] in no way invalidates the theatrical cut. It simply restores some depth and character made omissible by the theatrical running time and now made viable again by the home theatrical/laserdisc format."

Originally, three major elements were removed to keep the film at a reasonable running time, which have now been restored for the laserdisc version.

The first scene was a dream sequence, shot in one day, with Michael Biehn reprising his role as Kyle Reese. In the first *Terminator*, Sarah Connor (Linda Hamilton) got involved with Reese, who died at the end of the picture. In the sequel, Sarah is thought insane for predicting a nuclear war and for revealing the existence of the Terminator, and is locked away at a state hospital. In the dream sequence, Reese visits Sarah in her cell; he begs her to take care of their son John and tells her she must fight, that the future is not set. This scene with Michael Biehn was featured briefly in one of the early trailers for the film. (Incidentally, James Cameron got some of his own medicine when his cameo appearance in *The Last Action Hero* (1993) ended on the cutting room floor. There's no report so far of a special edition of the film restoring that missing part.)

Right after Sarah, her son John (Edward Furlong), and the Terminator (Arnold Schwarzenegger) escape from the hospital, they find refuge in a gas station. The Terminator has been shot, and Sarah removes the bullets from his back. Again, what is known as "the chip-removal scene" had to be deleted for time; in that scene, Sarah basically removes the Terminator's brain and wants to keep it shut off. John fights his mother, and they put the chip back in, after John has switched it into the "write" mode—instead of the "read" mode—meaning the Terminator can now be more human and learn things, whereas before, he was programmed. This scene tells us that the Terminator is programmed by us; we make the machine what it is. This scene also presents for the first time John going against his mother and shows his leadership taking over. Following that sequence was a scene in which the Terminator is trying to learn how to smile. As Van Ling explains it in *Terminator 2: The Book of the Film*, with that particular scene out in the release version, Cameron had to find a way to explain the Terminator's ability to imitate human expressions; so a bridging line of dialogue for the Terminator was added in post-production: "The more contact I have with humans, the more I learn." The interesting ramification of that would be that the longer the Terminator stays on earth, the more human he can become, to the point where he might even stop killing. In the theatrical version, the Terminator starts learning the second he arrives on earth; in the special edition—and in the original concept of the film—he only starts learning specifically when he is switched over to the "read" mode.

A lot of the fleshing out of Miles Dyson (Joe Morton), the black scientist whose research might lead to a nuclear war, was initially cut out but was restored in the special edition. The scenes show how blind Dyson is to the implications of his work and how he even neglects his own family.

Altogether, about sixteen minutes of additional footage found its way back into the *Terminator 2* special edition laserdisc. But not everything was restored; for instance, there was a scene during which the T-1000 (Robert Patrick) is searching John's room. Missing as well, although featured on the laserdisc separately in a supplement section, is the first ending (known as "Future Park" or "Coda Park") that was shot but not used after the film was sneak-previewed. That ending shows Sarah as an old woman with her son and his daughter in Washington, D.C. John has become a senator. . .meaning that, thanks to them, Judgment Day, the nuclear war, never came. Sarah is sitting on a bench in a park and talking into a tape recorder, telling her story. This justified and explained the narration featured at the beginning of the film. Cameron liked the idea of that ending on paper, but on film, it didn't work. A preview confirmed—as Cameron might have suspected it himself—that the ending was too philosophical, not story oriented. It was an interesting idea because it negated an entire time line; it seemed that happy and peaceful final moment belonged in another movie. Instead, the film ends on a road at night with Sarah's narration suggesting that if a Terminator could learn to have feelings, maybe there was still hope for the human race as well. That new ending was tagged on less than a month before the film was released. While the original ending seemed to conclude the story completely, the one Cameron ultimately chose for the film hints at a possible sequel.

There's an interesting story surrounding the release of *Terminator 2* in Great Britain, as related by Van Ling:

> Basically, the British Board of Film Classification has two major ratings: a 15 rating which corresponds to our PG or PG-13 and an 18 rating which is the equivalent of an R. The film was an R here for the language more than anything else. In England, the language was not such a big deal, and the Board told us that if we just made a few cuts, the film could be released with a 15 rating, and we could make a hell of a lot more money. They proposed a list of cuts, mostly predicated on the violence; specifically, they were saying don't show any violence happening to people who aren't deserving of it in some way. In their mind, the idea of the innocent bystanders, which in the case of *T2* is mostly guards, security officers, policemen should not be shown casually being knee-capped. They're very conscious of that because of the Irish Republican Army. The only cut that James Cameron condescended to was when Sarah hits a guard, she hits him about four times, not six. They said okay and released the film with a 15 rating and with literally one second and a half cut out of it. When they came to release it on video with the same rating, they asked us to do more cuts. They said they could control the people going into the theaters but that they couldn't control people at home.
>
> We weren't exactly happy about that because we think that's a double standard. They wanted us to make the cuts because we were the best qualified to do the job. There's two ways you can take that; one is you can take that as they respect us enough to want us to basically amputate our own children. Or you can take it as meaning if we have the production company do the cuts and if there are any complaints, they'll just say Cameron did

it and approved the cuts. We agreed to make the cuts based on a videotape that they sent us showing what they wanted done. It was amazingly horrific, and none of it made too much sense. It ended up looking like a bad cut of the movie.

James Cameron is very adamant; if someone wants him to cut his movies, he wants everybody to know about it. He insists on putting banners ahead of the TV versions of his films saying "Edited for Television." So he tried to make the cuts as obvious as possible for the British Board of Film Classification. All the cuts are as jarring as possible, and we also put a card at the head of the film, saying "This film has been edited in accordance with the guidelines of the British Board of Film Classification," as a disclaimer. They did release later an 18-rated/American cut of *T2* on videotape.

While some may find it odd for a director to keep cutting and recutting his films, James Cameron has on three occasions taken on the task of looking at his work and deciding to take it a step further, knowing he might seriously jeopardize his initial choices. Through the different cuts of his films, Cameron has been able to establish a dialogue with his audience.

STEVEN SPIELBERG'S *CLOSE ENCOUNTERS OF THE THIRD KIND* AND *1941*

Close Encounters of the Third Kind (also known among buffs as *CE3K*) was one of the most successful films of all time, even saving Columbia Pictures from bankruptcy. *CE3K* cost the studio $19 million and returned to the company, within a few months of its November 1977 release, $120 million. During the shooting, the pressure was on, and it looked like director Steven Spielberg was not going to make the November date. "Between my first writing of the screenplay and the making of the motion picture, certain compromises had to be made as a result of budget and schedule," Spielberg declared. At the time, Columbia had been changing administrations, and the stock of the company was low. According to the director himself, it was the first time that a studio was going to fall into the abyss; Columbia needed a hit that not only would fill the coffers again but also would reestablish the dying image of the company. Executives at the studio told Spielberg that he had to make a hit and informed him that they were changing the release date from mid-December to November. But because Spielberg was heavily involved in working with Douglas Trumbull and Richard Yuricich on the special visual effects for the film, he never had the time to add certain scenes or fine-tune others. Basically, as Spielberg put it, the film we saw in 1977 was a work-in-progress that was never finished. Actually, the only thing that the director changed after sneak-previewing *CE3K* to a test audience was the background song "When You Wish Upon a Star" from Disney's *Pinocchio* during the final mothership scene. "I felt the song was going to be perceived as wistful thinking," the director said. *CE3K* did save Columbia Pictures, and for a while there were discussions over the possibilities of doing a sequel *because the film was released*

Instead, a year after the initial release of the picture, Spielberg asked the studio to give him money to recut the film the way he would have done it had he had seven more weeks to finish it back in 1977. In exchange, he promised he would show the inside of the mothership. Columbia Pictures agreed. "When a really successful picture like *The Sting* or *American Graffiti* is released," said Robert Cort, who was then Columbia's marketing vice president, "we're saying, 'If you loved the picture, come see it again. If you never quite got your backside into the theater, come see it for the first time.' Now we've got a third reason. 'Come see what you couldn't see before.' It gives the rerelease a little marketing hook." The irony in all this is that Spielberg admitted later that he never wanted to show the inside of the mothership, but that was the only way he could get Columbia to commit to what he himself referred to as "a rather unorthodox idea." He declared at the time, "I've had the opportunity to see how the film plays for audiences. Film is not necessarily a dry-cement process. I have the luxury of retouching the painting."

It wasn't the first time that Spielberg had the opportunity to add scenes to one of his films; his telefilm *Duel* (1971), based on a short story by Richard Matheson, about a businessman (Dennis Weaver) who realizes that the driver of a truck is out to get him, was extended from seventy-four to ninety minutes for foreign markets. The opening sequence was different; in the theatrical release version, Weaver starts his journey in a series of road shots filmed through the windshield from his point of view; the TV-movie begins with a shot of the open road. Spielberg added a scene for the theatrical release, during which Weaver stops for a train and the truck tries to push his car forward. George Eckstein, the producer of *Duel*, also wrote an additional scene of Weaver calling his wife (Jacqueline

Scott). Spielberg did not like that scene but kept it in to satisfy Cinema International Corporation, the foreign distribution
arm of Universal and Paramount at the time, which first
released this longer version overseas.

Close Encounters of the Third Kind/The Special Edition was
made with a budget of approximately $2 million for about three
months of work. Here in detail are the differences between
CE3K as it was released in 1977 and *The Special Edition*, the
scenes that were cut out, changed, or added.

The first change comes right after Barry (Cary Guffey), the
young boy who is eventually kidnapped by extraterrestrials,
escapes into the night. In the first version, Spielberg cut from
that scene to a close-up of a Pinocchio music box playing
"When You Wish Upon a Star." We meet the Neary family
(Richard Dreyfuss portrays Roy Neary; Teri Garr is his wife
Ronnie; they have three kids, two boys and a girl). Roy Neary
is playing with his son's toy train; two cars run into each other.
Ronnie orders the kids to go to bed; they argue and want to
watch *The Ten Commandments* on television. The phone
rings; Ronnie answers. It's Earl, Roy's boss at the power station. Suddenly, the power goes off. Spielberg decided to extend
this sequence for *The Special Edition*. This time, we cut from
young Barry escaping into the night to a panoramic shot of
the city at night. We find out why Roy is playing with the toy
train; he is, in fact, explaining to his older son what a fraction
is, using the example of a train in the middle of a bridge and
asking the teenager how far the train has to move in order to
avoid a collision with an oncoming one. The son can't figure it
out. This leads into an argument involving Roy, his wife, and
his three kids. He wants to take them to see *Pinocchio,* but
the kids want to go play Goofy Golf, instead. Ronnie complains
that Roy has put some of his equipment on her breakfast table.
In the background, Toby, the Nearys' daughter, is hitting her
doll against the metal bar of her playpen. Roy yells at her,
"Toby, you are close to death!" He tries to convince his kids
that *Pinocchio* is better than Goofie Golf, but they vote against
his choice. We then pick up the scene as it was originally cut,
with Roy's boss calling. (As we will see later, Spielberg took

out a number of scenes showing Roy fighting with his family for *The Special Edition*.) This more than compensates for the other missing sequences and definitely sets the Neary family as dysfunctional.

In *The Special Edition*, Spielberg cuts directly from that introductory scene of the Neary family to Jillian Guiler (Melinda Dillon) looking for her son Barry in the woods. The director deleted a lengthy scene that appeared right after the Neary family sequence in the first version of the film and which had Roy on the job at the power plant. That one showed workers arguing with one another. The power went out in the entire town; one worker figures that riots have errupted, while another one says there's nothing they can do because the failure is not due to human error. (In fact, UFOs are flying over town and sucking out the electrical power.) The scene ends with a supervisor telling Roy to check a plant in another area that he's familiar with. The sequence at the power station created more jeopardy for the Dreyfuss character and also told us that the whole town, plunged into darkness, was going crazy. At the same time, since we never see how the situation affects other individuals, it justifies why the scene was ultimately taken out.

Spielberg included a new—and humorous—shot for *The Special Edition* that didn't exist in the first version: a UFO stopping in front of a large McDonald's billboard and flashing lights on it before taking off again, during the scene in which Roy Neary is in his van, trying to catch up with the flying saucers. At the same time, Spielberg deleted in that sequence a line from an old man saying, "They can fly rings around the moon, but we're years ahead of them on the highway," after seeing the UFOs fly by.

In the initial version of the film, Spielberg cut directly from a scene between Roy and his wife watching the sky at the spot where he had had a close encounter to the next morning at the Nearys' home. He added a new sequence in between these two scenes, which he shot specially for *The Special Edition*. The director of photography on the additional scenes was Allen Daviau. (Vilmos Zsigmond, William A. Fraker, Douglas

Slocombe, John Alonzo, Laszlo Kovacs, and Steve Poster all worked on the original production of *CE3K*). In that new sequence, the U.S. Army and scientists discover a ship in the middle of the Gobi desert. The ship is called Cotopaxi, and although it's never mentioned in the film, it is the name of a real American cargo ship that disappeared in the Bermuda Triangle. The model for the ship, built by Greg Jein and his staff, is an exact replica of the real Cotopaxi. That scene was actually in the original *CE3K* script, and Spielberg had always wanted to shoot it. At last, he was able to fulfill his dream, and the scene was shot in White Sands, New Mexico. The only problem with the scene is that it starred Bob Balaban and J. Patrick McNamara, who were both part of François Truffaut's entourage in the film (French director Truffaut played a scientist named Lacombe), but not Truffaut himself, who was unavailable. His absence seems awkward and is strongly felt.

Gone from *The Special Edition* is an argument between Roy and his wife right after he got fired from his job. In the first version, Ronnie asks her husband what's happening to him and tells him she's not getting a job. Roy is lying on his bed staring at a crumpled pillow. Ronnie's voice fades out as Roy becomes aware that the shape of the pillow means something (it resembles the shape of a mountain—Devil's Tower—where the close encounter of the third kind takes place at the end of the film).

In some cases, Spielberg changed the order of several sequences for *The Special Edition*. This is how the continuity worked originally:

- Roy is fired and has an argument with his wife.
- Roy goes back to the highway junction where he first met Barry and Jillian. Many other people have come and are waiting for the UFOs. Instead, they are chased by air force helicopters.
- Lacombe goes to India and discovers that the local population of a village was also visited by extraterrestrials.
- Lacombe gives a conference.
- Lacombe and his staff do research at a telescope station.

This particular group of scenes was rearranged for *The Special Edition* as follows:

- Roy is fired (the argument is cut).
- Lacombe goes to India.
- Lacombe gives a conference (that scene was lengthened; after sharing his discoveries with his colleagues, Lacombe gets a standing ovation).
- Roy, Jillian, and other people wait for UFOs at the highway junction.
- Lacombe and his staff do research at a telescope station.

The kidnapping of Barry, the little boy, follows the scene at the telescope station in both versions. In *The Special Edition*, we immediately cut from the kidnapping to Lacombe and the army trying to figure out ways to scare the population away in order to prepare secretly for the close encounter at Devil's Tower. Spielberg took out from the original cut a scene at the air force base. At the beginning of the sequence, Jillian is being harassed by reporters asking about the kidnapping of her son by extraterrestrials. Roy and Ronnie have come to the base with other people for a press conference. While the army insists that they do not believe in UFOs, people argue that they know what they saw. The scene turns to ridicule when a man says he saw Big Foot once. Others say that the army is conducting secret tests. The scene ends with Roy drawing compulsively on a newspaper (the headlines read COSMIC KID-NAPPING and shows a picture of Jillian) the shape of the Devil's Tower and breaking his pencil. With that scene out for *The Special Edition*, we're led to believe that Jillian never reported the kidnapping of her son.

In another scene at the Nearys' dinner table, Roy helps himself to mashed potatoes and starts building a mountain out of his serving. He realizes that his wife and kids are staring at him and apologizes for his behavior. His family doesn't seem to understand. Spielberg trimmed down that scene for *The Special Edition*. Originally, the scene began without Roy at the table. In *The Special Edition*, Roy is already sitting at the table when the scene begins.

Curiously, Spielberg added in *The Special Edition* a long sequence that he had not used in his initial cut, during which Roy freaks out and goes in the shower with his clothes on. He's locked himself in the bathroom, and his wife breaks the door open. Roy explains that he doesn't understand what's happening to him. Ronnie yells at her husband, saying she hates him and that because of him they've lost their friends and that their family is falling apart. She even suggests they go into therapy. Roy's older son comes in and starts yelling at his dad, calling him a crybaby; he slams the bathroom door over and over and then runs out. Roy begs his wife to hold him and tells her he's scared. Ronnie gets away from him and locks herself in the bathroom. The kids are crying and close their bedroom doors. Spielberg had decided not to put that scene in the first version because, at the time, he felt it was too strong. He decided to put it in *The Special Edition* after realizing that all the characters in the film had a turning point except for Ronnie. Originally, you never really understood why she left her husband the next morning; that scene showed her breaking down and justified her reaction.

However, Spielberg took out for *The Special Edition* most of the sequence during which Roy decides to build a replica of the mountain in his living room the morning after his breakdown. The scene showed him throwing bricks and plants through the kitchen window, grabbing the fence around a duck pond, arguing over garbage in front of his neighbors and his family. The only segment of the scene that remains in *The Special Edition* is when Ronnie takes off in her car with the kids. Roy unsuccessfully tries to stop her and rolls over the car. Originally, that scene continued; Roy stands up, ignoring his neighbors, climbs through the kitchen window using a small ladder, which he pulls in after him. The scene ended with offscreen sounds of Roy stumbling over broken dishes. Although Spielberg liked that whole sequence, the critics didn't; whether the reviews had any influence on the director or not, he decided to trim the sequence for *The Special Edition*, feeling that the scene was a bit redundant anyway because Roy's madness had already been established. The tone of the scene in the first version is both tragic and comedic; in *The Special Edition*, the tone is just tragic.

Roy has the television on while building the mountain inside his living room. He looks outside at his neighbors; offscreen we hear the soap opera *Days of Our Lives*. In the first version, we heard: "This is Macdonald Carey, and these are the days of our lives." Curiously, in *The Special Edition,* Macdonald Carey does not say his name.

Finally, Roy arrives in Wyoming where he believes a close encounter is going to happen. He parks by the train station while the population, who thinks the whole area has been contaminated by toxic gas, is evacuating. This sequence was rearranged for *The Special Edition*. This is how it originally was edited:

- Long shot of the train station; Roy arrives in his car and stops.
- An elderly man is selling gas masks.
- Roy gets out of his car.
- Panicked people are trying to get aboard the train.
- Farmers on horses are bringing cows to the station.
- Roy walks in front of the gas-mask salesman and goes to a barricade.
- Roy tells a guard (played by Carl Weathers of *Rocky* fame!) that he has to go make sure his sister is safe. He says her name is Smith. The guard tells Roy that he's got orders to shoot anyone who tries to break through the roadblock, and advises Roy to pass on the word. Roy gets the hint.
- Roy gets to his car; he's bought a gas mask and a dove in a cage (when the bird dies, he'll know he's reached the infected area). Suddenly, he hears a woman calling his name; it's Jillian.
- Roy looks for Jillian. They find each other and hug.

And now *The Special Edition*:

- Long shot of the train station; Roy arrives and stops his car.
- The gas-mask salesman bit. (Spielberg chose a different

angle on him, and this time, we hear him say, "Even my dog wears one.")

- Roy gets out of his car and hears a woman calling his name; it's Jillian.
- Panicked people are trying to get aboard the train.
- Roy looks for Jillian. They find each other and hug.

Steven Spielberg did not make any other changes until Roy actually walks inside the mothership. In the first version, after he disappeared inside the spaceship, we cut to Lacombe and then to an extraterrestrial coming out, doing the hand signs with the scientist, leaving no doubt that they can communicate with each other. The main reason why most people went to see *The Special Edition* was to see the inside of the spaceship. "We imagined a lot of things about the inside and outside of the mothership that never got photographed," special-effects wizard Douglas Trumbull declared at the time he was hired to design that particular sequence—and before he got to work on it. "We want the inside of the mothership to give a more heightened sense of the spectacular nature and unlimited power and resources of these extraterrestrial beings." Trumbull added that in the first version of the film, the mothership was more abstract. "We want to show that it's a giant intergalactic aircraft carrier, the docking place for the smaller saucers, a combination of church, planetarium, immense ship, and the vertical assembly center at NASA. We want to try to give a suggestion of the limitless grandeur of the universe."

Although Spielberg maintains he still likes the ending of the first version better and admits in retrospect that he sold out to Columbia Pictures and, as mentioned earlier, showed the inside of the ship only to be able to recut the film, this moment is truly magical. The original mothership sequence (the exterior of it that is) was shot in a hangar in Mobile, Alabama. The new sets for the interior of the spaceship were built at TBS Studios, and Spielberg, who was directing *1941* during the week, lensed this additional scene on weekends. The sequence ends with a shower of glitter and light. We then cut back to Lacombe and the extraterrestrial coming out to do his

hand signs. Could it be that the shower of light has transformed Roy into an extraterrestrial?

Right before *The Special Edition* came out, Spielberg found
himself in the center of a storm. Norman Levy, then Columbi-
a's president of distribution, said that according to standard
practice, the eight hundred or so prints of the first version of
CE3K would be junked, but that a few pristine prints would be
stored in the company's vaults. "There will never be any reason to re-release the first version," Levy said. Spielberg was
furious and had the last word in the matter: "There will be two
versions of *Close Encounters* showing for the next one hundred years, as far as I'm concerned." Michael Phillips, who
produced the film with his former wife Julia, declared on the
matter at the time: "This, *The Special Edition*, is now the
definitive version. I would think that the first version may continue to exist in the studio's vault as an historical piece, but
as far as I'm concerned, it's this version that counts." The version that's shown on television and that aired for the first time
on ABC on November 15, 1981, combined both versions of the
film and ran 143 minutes.

Columbia decided to push the initial Easter release of *The
Special Edition* to the summer of 1979. "We're not going to
take any chances," Norman Levy said. "We want to make the
picture available during the peak of the summer." In order to
make any profit, the studio had to gross at least $6 million. A
new campaign was launched, with a new poster, curiously
showing a shot of Dreyfuss among extraterrestials outside the
spaceship, which exists in both versions of the film. The television spots and trailers announced: "When you saw *Close
Encounters*, you wanted more. Now, you have more!" Even
Dell Books went in for the ride and released a new and revised
novelization of the film written by Spielberg. The original running time of the film was 135 minutes and had been reduced
to 132 minutes. Sixteen minutes of footage had been deleted;
seven minutes of previously discarded footage had been reinstated, along with about six minutes of newly photographed
scenes, making for a net reduction of three minutes. With that

in mind, *Variety* speculated that audiences would be disappointed and that *The Special Edition* and its new ending was above all a great teaser for a sequel.

The reviews for *The Special Edition* were spectacular; critics agreed that with this new cut, the film had become a classic. "What has happened is a phenomenon in the annals of film," Arthur Knight wrote in *The Hollywood Reporter.* "Director Steven Spielberg has taken his 1977 flawed masterpiece and, by judicious editing and addition of several scenes, has turned his work into an authentic masterpiece." Critics were glad that Spielberg had trimmed the scene in which Roy goes crazy and decides to build a mountain in his living room. "What flawed the earlier *Close Encounters* is what proved fatal in *1941*," Arthur Knight wrote. "His sense of humor can turn a character into a grotesque." While most critics loved this new version of the film, Pauline Kael of *The New Yorker* tore apart each of the changes:

- Regarding the desert sequence: "Not a bad idea, but it's not a good shot, and it duplicates other material."
- About Roy no longer causing a commotion in his neighborhood: ". . .when his wife drives off with the children, the neighbors are still gathered around watching."
- Regarding the fact that Barry's mother doesn't report the kidnapping of her son and the news conference with the air force is cut: ". . .the ruthlessness of the air force and army men who keep the cranks and dreamers from their objective is puzzling." Kael also wrote that a shot of other astronauts going inside the spaceship had been lost, making it look like only Roy goes inside. This is a falsity. This shot, I believe, never existed.

Scott Fivelson of the *Los Angeles Times* wrote an article entitled "Another 'Close' Call" in which he ridiculed Spielberg's intentions and wrote that the director was at work on yet another version of his film: *Rough Draft of Close Encounters of the Third Kind.*

Producer Michael Phillips had this to say at the time about the whole concept of recutting the film: "I just hope it doesn't lead to a trend in which filmmakers 'redo' their movies. That would simply be dreadful. Some filmmakers might start withholding a few minutes from the first release so they could add this material in the reissue and get people to spend their $5 again." Phillips, who said that *The Special Edition* was more of an action picture than the original version, did add however that Spielberg's attempt was honest and that his new cut gave the movie an entirely new dimension. At the same time, his fear about a trend in rereleasing movies with new added footage has certainly come true.

Before he did *CE3K*, Spielberg was known as the man who did *Jaws* (1975). The response from test audiences on *Jaws*, which like *Close Encounters* was shown in Dallas, had been incredible. "Which scenes did you dislike? None," coproducer David Brown recalled in his book *Let Me Entertain You*. "Which scene did you like? All. On one card someone wrote, "This is a great film. Now don't fuck it up by trying to make it better." We did try, and we did make it better. Following that preview, a shock cut of a fisherman's decapitated head floating into frame was filmed at night by Spielberg in editor Verna Fields's San Fernando Valley swimming pool and produced a scream of such magnitude that I could hear it outside a theater every time the scene was playing." By the way, that scene was in the original screenplay; part of it had been shot during principal photography in the daytime. The scene featured Roy Scheider, Richard Dreyfuss, and Carl Gottlieb (who played a local reporter and cowrote the script as well). When Spielberg decided to reshoot it after the sneak preview, he only used Scheider and Dreyfuss and while part of the scene was shot in Verna Field's swimming pool, long shots were filmed on the Universal backlot, using a tank rented from MGM studios that had been built for the Esther Williams spectaculars.

Unfortunately, with *1941*, the film Spielberg chose to direct after *CE3K*, the experience the director had enjoyed with test audiences on *Jaws* and *Close Encounters* did not repeat itself.

1941 was written by Robert Zemeckis and Bob Gale, based on a story by Zemeckis, Gale and John Milius. *1941* was a large-scale production set in Los Angeles during the panic-stricken days following the attack on Pearl Harbor, when most of the population of Southern California believed that a Japanese invasion could come at any time. Like *Jaws* and *CE3K*, *1941* was screened in Dallas—in October 1979. The film was set to be released on November 14. The test audience was selected to represent a twelve-to-forty-nine age span in what Spielberg himself described as "an IBM-type programmed preview audience. They had no idea what they were seeing, since telephone calls were made that said only 'Come to a Hollywood sneak preview.' " A similar tactic had been used on both *Jaws* and *Close Encounters*.

1941 was a coproduction between Columbia Pictures and Universal Pictures; Columbia handled overseas distribution, and Universal distributed the film domestically. The sales and production executives from both companies were invited to the test screening. Eight hundred patrons showed up; later on, Spielberg and Universal said that the preview sampling did not accurately represent the probable audience for the film. *1941* was targeted for the same audience that had liked *National Lampoon's Animal House* (1978) and watched *Saturday Night Live* on television, since the film starred John Belushi and Dan Aykroyd. In any case, conflicting reports came out of that screening; executives from Columbia and Universal were supposedly nervous and panicked about the mixed reaction the film received from the test audience. Spielberg described the audience's reaction as positive, citing spontaneous laughter and applause. The director said that the preview cards were generally excellent. "I use a preview as much as I use a movie camera," Spielberg told *Daily Variety*. "It's a process of trial and error, to make the film work in the best way possible." The director concluded that it was essential for a comedy to be tested. He had learned nonetheless an important lesson: "I learned not to invite Universal and Columbia executives and sales people to previews anymore. Let them stay home and watch *Laverne & Shirley* on television. I'll preview my pictures and make the changes."

Nevertheless, *1941* had to be changed; generally, the audience—and the executives—felt the first forty-five minutes of the film were too long. "It's very expository, and there was some restlessness and lack of laughs," Spielberg said. "My job right now is to fix those forty-five minutes. Other than that, the film is what it is." But Spielberg needed more time to apply his changes; the midNovember release and a charity premiere had to be cancelled, and the film was reset to come out in December. Another preview took place in Denver, and finally, *1941* came out. According to *Variety*, seventeen minutes had been cut, reducing the running time to approximately 118 minutes (including six minutes of end credits alone!). "The movie at this point is exactly what it's going to be," Spielberg said. Unfortunately, the film was bashed by the critics and ignored by the public.

1941 is one of these rare cases where the television version includes great scenes that didn't exist in the theatrical release. Incidentally, the *Jaws* television version includes, for instance, a funny bit that did not exist in the theatrical release, showing Robert Shaw buying piano wire for shark hunting at a music store and singing "Ode to Joy" with a kid playing the instrumental on a clarinet. Watching *1941* on television is like discovering a new, richer, more outrageous, and much longer film (thirty minutes of footage were added, bringing the running time to two and a half hours). Of course, profanity had to be overdubbed for television. The first sequence of *1941*, in which Spielberg duplicated the opening from *Jaws*, starred the same actress, Susan Backlinie, swimming naked and having an encounter, not with a shark, but with a Japanese sub. Obviously, the nudity was substituted with less explicit shots for television. Also out is a short bit of John Belushi in his aircraft scratching himself. But at the same time, while many sequences were extended and short bits added here and there, some entirely new scenes were included and can only be seen in the television version of *1941*. Inevitably, because most of the added scenes did not star John Belushi and took place essentially in the first half of the film, Belushi's role in the TV version seems less important.

In the theatrical version, the scene at the diner at the beginning of the film, which introduces several of the main characters, was followed by Capt. Wild Bill Kelso (Belushi) landing in his airplane at a gas station/general store in Death Valley. The television version breaks that continuity with two added sequences.

In the first one, we meet Betty Douglas (Dianne Kay) and her friend Maxine (Wendy Jo Sperber) with other USO girls listening to Miss Fitzroy (Penny Marshall), the hostess at the Hollywood USO. That scene is hilarious as Miss Fitzroy explains that the girls will not be able to dance with civilians. "You're going to have to smile at men who you would never give a second glance to in peacetime. . ." and then, "You're going to have to dance and dance close with men you might find repulsive." At the other end of the ballroom, soldiers are on their knees. Penny Marshall's role was reduced to a bit part for the theatrical version of *1941*, as she only appears during the jitterbug contest and says a couple of lines. Her name does not appear in the end credits of either version.

The second sequence, added in the TV version, takes place at a department store. Wally (Bobby DiCicco), a dishwasher who will stop at nothing to go dancing with Betty at a jitterbug contest, wants to buy a zoot suit. Customers are listening to the radio; a woman is frantic: "They bombed Pearl Harbor, now they're gonna come here!" Wally manages to steal the suit by having his pal Dennis (Perry Lang) crank an air raid siren, resulting in a sudden panic in the department store. A man dressed as Santa shows up with a gun and wearing a Civilian Defense armband. Sydney Lassick, who starred as one of Jack Nicholson's fellow inmates in *One Flew Over the Cuckoo's Nest* and played the schoolteacher in Brian De Palma's *Carrie*, and whose part as a salesman had been entirely cut from the release version of 1941, saw his role restored for the TV version. Other important added sequences include a new scene introducing Claude (Murray Hamilton), a civilian aircraft-spotter whose post-Pearl Harbor defense duty finds him later on in the story, perched atop a ferris wheel in Pacific Ocean Park, and his friend Scioli (Lionel Stander), who has transformed his car into a homemade tank! The scene establishes that Claude is afraid of heights and shows Scioli's wife beating up and kicking the car/tank. Later, a few minutes were added when Claude and Herb (Eddie Deezen) arrive at the amusement park.

In the theatrical version of *1941*, Slim Pickens, who plays Hollis Wood, a rustic American, is seen in his truck—that bares the inscription HOLLIS "HOLLY" WOOD: XMAS TREES—while Japanese, arriving on shore, spot him. In the theatrical version, that sequence is immediately followed by Hollis on the Japanese sub. In the TV version, however, that segment is entirely different. Japanese disguised as Christmas trees reach Hollis's lot and take pictures of each other in their costumes. Hollis Wood shows up and is kidnapped after an hilarious altercation in which Hollis tries to cut down the Japanese Christmas trees!

An entire sequence was added at Betty Douglas's house, which faces the shore. The family is having dinner; Betty's parents, Ward and Joan Douglas (played by Ned Beatty and Lorraine Gary) talk about getting black curtains and redoing their home, while one of their sons is eating his pea soup through a gas mask. Ward takes Betty aside and has a discussion about her duties at the USO: "I don't know what they've told you down at the USO, but you're going to meet a lot of strange men. . .men in uniform. . .boys a long way from home. . .lonely, desperate. . .they only have one thing on their minds. Show'em a good time." That scene, however, is sort of a replay of the speech Miss Fitzroy gave the USO girls at the beginning of the film. Other added bits with the Douglas family show Joan Douglas arguing with her husband when the army decides to put a tank in their backyard, and a sequence showing Joan taking a bath and the Japanese peeping on her from the surfaced sub offshore.

Following the scene between Ward and Betty Douglas is yet another added sequence, this one with the tank crew in their barrack. Sgt. Tree (Dan Aykroyd), an hyper-patriotic soldier, tells his crew that there'll be no dancing for them; "We've just been posted on combat readiness." Tree exits, furious, when he realizes that Sitarski (Treat Williams) is missing, gone to the USO dance. That scene also introduces Ogden Johnson

Jones (portrayed by black actor Frank McRae), who is unable to impose authority on redneck racist Foley (John Candy), a member of the renegade tank crew. Another funny line from Aykroyd was added in the sequence following riots on Hollywood Boulevard and has him asking the crowd: "Do you think Santa Claus is cute? Do you think the Japs believe in Santa Claus?"

Many scenes with Wally are longer in the TV version (the scene in the diner, for instance, at the beginning of the film, his confrontation with Sitarski in the garage at the Douglas's home, and when Wally is aboard the tank all have added bits. In another extra scene, Wally shoots down a police car). A funny additional scene takes place outside the USO: Wally is arguing with Sitarski over Betty; Sitarski walks away after setting Wally's zoot suit on fire. Shortly thereafter, Dennis shows up with identical twin girls, the same ones who were spotted in the department-store sequence. That segment did not exist in the theatrical version.

Tim Matheson portrays Capt. Birkhead, an army stud whose ambition is to "do it" with Donna Stratton (Nancy Allen), Gen. Stilwell's (Robert Stack) secretary. The problem is Donna can only "do it" in an airplane. The Birkhead character lost a great deal of humor as most of Matheson's lines were either deleted or changed for the TV version. The line "She'll bat your balls out of the ballpark," referring to Donna, was deleted. Birkhead's description of the B-17 aircraft to Donna, loaded with sexual innuendos, was altered: the words "forward thrust" were replaced by "flying capacity" and the line "when this baby delivers its payload" became "when this baby delivers its bombs." Also, when Birkhead and Donna are finally having sex while flying in the airplane, Tim Matheson had a line: ". . . just as soon as I make it over these hills," as he stared down at his costar's provocative cleavage. The line was kept, but the visual was substituted by a long shot of the plane literally flying through the Hollywood hills! Nancy Allen's double entendre: "Do you think it will stay up for a long time?" was also changed and became for television: "Do you think it'll fly for a long time?" Matheson, however, has a couple of additional bits which did not exist in the theatrical release. His first scene in the TV version shows him making out with a reporter inside a car. Later, he unsuccessfully tries to convince Donna that the car he's driving feels like an airplane, hoping to seduce her.

Another short addition shows the Interceptor Commander (played by director Samuel Fuller) giving the order to go to "condition blue." In the theatrical version, we see him ordering "condition yellow" and later on "condition red" only. These different steps were explained by Gen. Stilwell in an earlier scene, during a press conference; this dialogue only exists in the television version. Stilwell also has several additional moments in the TV version; the scene in the movie theater where he is watching *Dumbo* was extended, as was Stilwell's altercation with John Landis, the director of *The Blues Brothers* (1980) who turned actor for *1941* and who plays a messenger.

Other minor changes include John Belushi riding a motorbike through a paint factory and additional lines by Michael McKean and David Lander (Lennie and Squiggy from TV's *Laverne and Shirley*) who portray Willy and Joe, two soldiers named after the cartoon characters of Bill Mauldin.

Altogether about twenty-eight changes were made for television (they include shot deletions or substitutions and dialogue replacements), while about thirty-three elements (which include new scenes and bits extending sequences) were added to the initial theatrical release of *1941*. The extended television version, which also plays on cable, gave a second chance to *1941*; the film has by now developed an amazing cult following. If there was any doubt when the film was released, *1941* is today one of Steven Spielberg's greatest achievements.

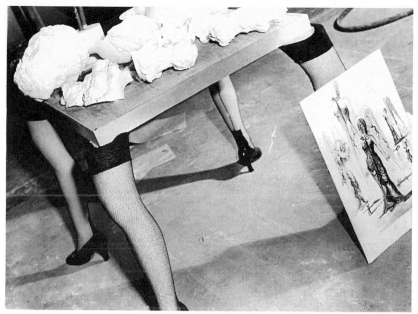

Salvador Dali designed the dream sequence for Alfred Hitchcock's
Spellbound, starring Ingrid Bergman and Gregory Peck. Producer
David O. Selznick hated the results and reduced the sequence dra-
matically.

A brief glimpse of that table, designed by Dali, survived the cutting.
On it are portions of heads for a statue of Ingrid Bergman and at the
bottom is a sketch for the Grecian costume she wore; these elements
were designed for a segment that ended on the cutting room floor.

Alfred Hitchcock and Ingrid Bergman get ready to shoot the dream
sequence. . .from which the actress was entirely cut out.

Test audiences rejected the original ending of Hitchcock's *Topaz*; they could not accept the idea of a duel between Frederick Stafford and French actor Michel Piccoli.

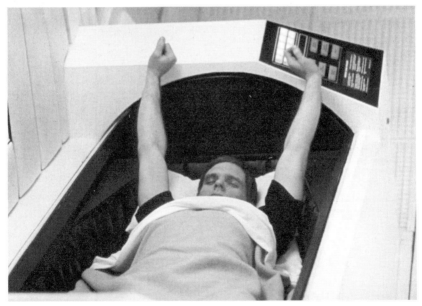

After sneak previewing *2001: A Space Odyssey*, Stanley Kubrick decided to cut out about twenty minutes from the film, including this sequence with actor Keir Dullea that detailed the routine life aboard the spaceship Discovery 1.

The original ending from William Friedkin's *The Exorcist* showed Rev. William O'Malley, S.J., and Lee J. Cobb discussing movies and quoting the famous closing line from *Casablanca*: "Louis, I think this is the beginning of a beautiful friendship."

Before/After. Eric Stoltz was replaced by Michael J. Fox in *Back to the Future* after a few weeks of shooting. As a result, Christopher Lloyd, who played inventor Doc Brown, had to reshoot some of his scenes.

Linda Blair possessed in a deleted sequence from William Friedkin's *The Exorcist*.

Harrison Ford visiting a colleague who's been shot by a replicant at a hospital of the future was filmed but never used for Ridley Scott's *Blade Runner*.

This gruesome scene from Paul Verhoeven's *Robocop* starring Peter Weller, caused the film to receive an X rating and had to be toned down. (Special makeup effects designed and created by Rob Bottin.)

This scene from Steven Spielberg's *Jaws*, in which Roy Scheider's son (Chris Rebello) tries to save an "estuary shark victim" (Ted Grossman), never made it into the film.

Although this shot was not in the final cut of William Peter Blatty's *The Exorcist III*, it was used to promote the film in Europe.

Although Brian De Palma removed most of the gore from the notorious chainsaw scene in *Scarface* starring Al Pacino (left), there was still a battle between the filmmaker and the members of the MPAA who wanted to rate the film X for violence and strong language.

JOHN BOORMAN'S *EXORCIST II: THE HERETIC*

The story of *Exorcist II: The Heretic*, as it was released on June 17 1977, takes place four years after *The Exorcist.* Regan MacNeil (Linda Blair), who was possessed by a demon as a child, has forgotten what happened to her in Georgetown. She is under the care of Gene Tuskin (Louise Fletcher), a child psychologist. Father Lamont (Richard Burton) is instructed by Cardinal Jaros (Paul Henreid) to investigate the strange circumstances surrounding the death of Father Merrin (Max von Sydow) during Regan's exorcism. Despite Dr. Tuskin's reluctance, Father Lamont, using synchronized hypnosis, penetrates Regan's subconscious. He learns that Pazuzu (represented by plagues of locusts), the demon that possessed Regan, is still alive within her. Regan discovers that she has special healing powers and eventually guides Lamont to Africa to search for Kokumo (James Earl Jones), who, as a child, was possessed by Pazuzu and was exorcised by Father Merrin. Lamont finds Kokumo and understands through the example of the locust that although Regan has been brushed by the wings of evil, there's hope she'll turn and guide the world to goodness. Finally, Lamont's journey takes him back to Regan's house in Georgetown where he is confronted with Pazuzu-possessed Regan. He tears out her evil heart, and the house collapses. Evil has been defeated. Sharon (Kitty Winn), Regan's confused secretary/companion who also appeared in *The Exorcist* and who believes she's been touched by evil, kills herself. Dr. Tuskin tells Regan that the world will never understand what happened. Hand in hand, Regan and Lamont leave together.

When *Exorcist II: The Heretic* was released, it seemed for director John Boorman that the nightmare was finally over; the production of the sequel to *The Exorcist*, one of the most successful movies of its time, had been "hell." To begin with, actor Lee J. Cobb who played Lt. Kinderman in the first film, and whose role was pivotal for the sequel, died of a heart attack the day he received the new script. Then, producer Richard Lederer had to be hospitalized for open-heart surgery two weeks after getting involved with *The Heretic*. Director Boorman contracted a mysterious and severe virus during the filming, and the production had to be suspended for five consecutive weeks. It turned out he was suffering from San Joaquin Valley Fever, named after a fungus found in the earth of the Southwest, which was the origin of the dust used in the African sets for the film. It affected Boorman's lungs, acting like a case of pneumonia. At the same time, his wife developed an ulcer, and one of his daughters discovered she had a tumor. In the middle of production, Louise Fletcher's husband had to be rushed to the hospital for heart surgery, and actress Kitty Winn became ill and learned that she was suffering from a rare kidney disease. When she was hospitalized, Louise Fletcher sent her a note saying: "There's no Pazuzu," referring to the demon that possesses the character played by Linda Blair in both *The Exorcist* and *The Heretic*. When the pain got worse and before she went on the operating table, Kitty sent a note back to her costar: "Who says there's no Pazuzu?"

Whether or not the Devil itself was trying to stop the production of the film, *Exorcist II: The Heretic* was, at the time, the largest launching in Warner Bros. history. The film came out on Friday, June 17, in 735 theatres and grossed $5.8 million in its opening weekend despite mixed-to-negative reviews; back then, this made the film Warners' biggest two-day opening. But just when John Boorman and Warners thought they had a major hit on their hands, the film dropped 60 percent the second weekend. The most eagerly awaited sequel had become the most hated film. "An extremely nervous and tension-filled audience came and wasn't rewarded," producer Richard Lederer declared. "So they responded with derision and couldn't wait to tell other people not to come." Director Stanley Kubrick had warned Lederer and had told him that, in order to work, the sequel would have to outvomit the first film, perhaps by having the characters vomit in rainbow colors. Kubrick could not have been more right.

Exorcist II: The Heretic was being ridiculed by audiences across the country. In Los Angeles, for example, a private screening, held at the Academy of Motion Picture Arts and Sciences on the Thursday prior to the Friday opening, generated a lot of laughs. The following day, patrons at the Hollywood Pacific Theatre threw things at the screen and booed the film. One of the biggest laughs came at the end during Louise Fletcher's final speech about the world not being ready to understand what happened after the Georgetown house has been destroyed. Although I will do an in-depth comparision of the two different versions of *Exorcist II: The Heretic* later on in this chapter, it is interesting to note here that Louise Fletcher hated the original ending of the film and had predicted during the filming that audiences would laugh at it.

Only a few days after the opening, Warner Bros. notified the nation's exhibitors that the studio was changing the ending of the film and that new final reels would soon be shipped out to them. At this point, the press couldn't find out who was responsible for the new ending. Who had ordered it? Was it the studio, the producer, or the director himself? Finally, John Boorman came forward and explained that he had recut the ending of the film the day after the Friday opening. "I cut it by telephone from six-thousand miles' distance," Boorman said. "I had a print at home [the director lived in Ireland]. I worked on it, and I called them [Warner Bros.] with the frame numbers for the cut." He flew back to L.A. to see the audience reaction to the new cut at the Pacific Theatre. "I was quite pleasantly surprised; the picture got applause at the end." At the same time, an anonymous source at Warners revealed that the new cut had not had any ameliorating influence on audience reaction. "We're victims of audience expectation, based on the first picture, " Boorman speculated. "The sin I committed was not giving them what they wanted. There's this wild beast out there, which is the audience. I created this arena, and I just didn't throw enough Christians to it." He also confessed that the whole experience had terribly shocked and hurt him. He claimed that the hostility toward the film was mainly centered in L.A. and New York, where so-called sophisticates came to the movie to laugh at it and to make others laugh.

Boorman, who had been offered the first *Exorcist* and had passed on it because he felt the story was cruel toward children, wanted to do something different with *The Heretic* (the script was written by William Goodhart). He claimed he wanted his film to have a "visionary quality" and to be about "spiritual evolution." "The problem for people going to this is that they expect the other reality. And in the present climate—you see it in *Star Wars*, which is a brilliant but mindless film—people resent being asked to contribute anything. I thought I had produced a film which was thoughtful and beautiful and involving." Boorman finally declared that he was doing further recutting of his film. In fact, he insisted that he was not just recutting the film, he was refashioning it. He said at the time that this was just an experiment, that he wasn't sure of the results, and that he planned on screening the new version—which he called "Mark IV" to a test audience. "To some extent, I'm allowing the audience to recut it. People think of cutting and recutting as a defeat, but it's not. As Irving Thalberg said, 'films are not made, they're remade.'"

The extensive recut version of *Exorcist II: The Heretic*—the "Mark IV" version—was tested at the Village Theatre in Westwood on a Sunday night to favorable audience response. The film ran 110 minutes, about seven minutes shorter than the original. The audience had no way of knowing that it was being used as guinea pigs for the new cut and reacted more positively than the one that had watched the original version of the film. There was little laughter, and the film even received applause. Boorman said he would offer to show this new cut to critics with his humble apologies. He even admitted that, in his original cut, he had created difficulties for his audience but had not guided them properly; he hoped that this new version would now reveal the film that had always been there.

Warners had to decide whether it should go to the expense of a new print order in an attempt to boost the weak box-office results of the $11 million movie. The cost could amount to more than $1 million, and finally, Warners decided to release Boorman's new cut only in foreign markets.

Today, *Exorcist II: The Heretic* can be seen on home video only as it was originally intended. But here is, in detail, the different changes that John Boorman felt he had to bring to his film in order to satisfy his audience:

The first thing you notice when watching the "Mark IV" version of the film is that the score for the opening credits is different. In the original version, Boorman used a dark, slow music cue, mixed with chanting (the score was composed by Ennio Morricone). At the end of the credits, we go to a black screen and hear the screams of a woman. This sound bite makes the transition to the first scene of the film, during which Father Lamont is about to exorcise a young girl. The scene takes place in a hut in South America. In the "Mark IV" version, Boorman used a more upbeat music cue for the opening credits; it moves much faster and is more ethnic/African sounding. In this revised version, Boorman added a prologue, narrated by Father Lamont, using a montage of stills: "Father Lancaster Merrin died in Georgetown, near Washington, D.C., while attempting to exorcise a twelve-year-old child, Regan MacNeil. The name of the spirit that possessed her was Pazuzu, an Asyrian demon traditionally known as the "king of the evil spirits of the air." Father Merrin had first encountered this demon in Ethiopia forty years earlier when it possessed a young African boy. Father Merrin believed the human spirit was on the threshold of a great leap forward either into goodness or evil. His teaching inspired many disciples of whom I was one, and his death dispirited us deeply."

The narration is accompanied by stills borrowed from both *The Exorcist* and from *Exorcist II: The Heretic*: Father Merrin standing in front of the house in Georgetown [this still was actually used for the poster of *The Exorcist*]; a close-up of Father Merrin during the exorcism; a close-up of Regan possessed; a shot of Regan on her bed and, at her side, the statue of Pazuzu; a close-up of Father Merrin as a young priest; a close-up of Kokumo as a teenager, posessed by Pazuzu; a still of Father Merrin praying by Regan's bed; a close-up of Father Lamont at the Vatican. We then meet Lamont on the streets of a South American shanty town, climbing up stairs. Lamont's narration continues: "So it was that four years later I climbed a hill in South America with a heavy heart, for it had fallen to me to carry on Father Merrin's struggle." We then cut to Lamont inside the hut, trying to exorcise the girl who ultimately puts herself on fire. Boorman deleted one close-up from the original cut of Lamont looking in his Bible at a picture of Father Merrin and saying, "Father Merrin, in the valley of the shadow of death, be at my side."

The new prologue improves the beginning of the film; audiences were able to relate to the story, but at the same time, it is an illogical device since Lamont dies at the end of this version of the film. How could he be narrating the prologue if he is destroyed in the end? French critic Michel Ciment argues this point by using the example of *Sunset Boulevard*, in which William Holden, who's been killed by Gloria Swanson and is floating dead in her swimming pool as the film opens, narrates the story. (Originally, Billy Wilder had William Holden, dead, miraculously waking up at the morgue and telling his story to other cadavers.) Unfortunately, in the case of *Exorcist II: The*

Heretic, it seems this device was used as a handy solution to clear the path for the audience, not in an attempt to break conventional movie-story rules like in *Sunset Boulevard*.

The original cut went from the hut to Regan rehearsing a tap-dancing routine ("The Lullaby of Broadway"), immediately followed by Regan in session with Dr. Tuskin. We then met Lamont in Rome, at the Vatican, in conference with Cardinal Jaros. The "Mark IV" version is paced totally differently. We go directly from the scene inside the hut to a much shorter version of Lamont's visit to the Vatican. Compare the dialogue in both versions:

The beginning of the scene is similar in both versions:

PRIEST: Cardinal Jaros, may I present Father Philip Lamont, Society of Jesus.

JAROS: Would you care to explain your refusal to accept this task?

LAMONT: Your Eminence, I believe I should be relieved from all possible responsibilities of which I'm not worthy.

JAROS: Father Lamont, I have not asked you to perform another exorcism. I simply requested that you investigate the circumstances surrounding the death of Father Merrin. You have performed exorcisms. You knew Father Merrin. Furthermore, you were exposed to his teachings. I cannot think of anyone more qualified for. . .for this assignment.

The dialogue that follows was entirely deleted in the "Mark IV" version:

JAROS: Philip, it's so good to see you. Merrin's reputation is in jeopardy. His writings have been impounded.

LAMONT: I'm not surprised. No one in the Church wants to hear about the devil. Satan has become an embarrassment to our progressive views.

JAROS: Merrin was rather more extreme, I'm afraid. He argued that the power of evil threatens to overthrow the power of God himself.

LAMONT: So, they found a heresy to nail him to. . . .

JAROS: Well, many of the theological college believe that he died in the hands of the devil during that American exorcism. Some, and they're close to the Pontiff, go so far as to suggest that he was a satanist. At the end, I mean.

LAMONT: Perhaps Father Merrin led us astray. Perhaps he took a path that no one could follow.

JAROS: But how he inspired us, Philip. [Jarros shows Lamont a picture of them together as young priests.] Here, remember? Christ is hard to follow too.

LAMONT: We were young. Today, wherever I look I see only evil. God has fallen silent.

JAROS: I cannot move to safeguard Merrin's testament until all the facts about this last exorcism are clearly known. You will conduct the investigation. You will act discreetly in all confidence, reporting to me alone.

LAMONT: I'm not worthy.

JAROS: You are a soldier of Christ. You must make yourself worthy.

In the "Mark IV" version, Boorman immediately cut from Jaros saying: "I cannot think of anyone more qualified for. . . for this assignment" to:

LAMONT: I'm not worthy.

JAROS: You are a soldier of Christ. You must make yourself worthy!

Obviously, some of the elements in the lengthy speech that appeared in the initial cut are now evoked in the opening voiceover narration. In the original scene, however, we understood Lamont's doubts about the Catholic Church better and his argument with Jaros gave his journey an even greater danger. In the "Mark IV" version, this first encounter with Jaros is so short, it seems out of place and awkward.

In the first scene between Dr. Tuskin and Father Lamont, Boorman felt he needed to establish that the priest was also a psychologist: "This is an attempt to establish the situation more clearly for the audience," Boorman explained, "and give more authority to the characters." The following dialogue was added for the "Mark IV" version.

LAMONT: Strangely enough, in your paper on, what did you call it, "Psychotic Eruptions of the Unconscious", you describe cases that are very much like demonic phenomena.

TUSKIN: Are you a psychologist?

LAMONT: Yes.

One of the most laughable segments in the original cut of the film occured when Regan, Dr. Tuskin, and Father Lamont successively go under hypnosis with the help of a machine called a synchroniser, and roll their eyes. Boorman trimmed these shots and made them seem more real, less forced, and less ridiculous.

Right after this sequence, Boorman took out several lines of dialogue and rearranged shots:

In the uncut version, Lamont says, referring to his experience under hypnosis: "It was horrible, utterly horrible and fascinating." We then hear the sound of the synchroniser. This subliminal message and Burton's delivery seems heavy-handed. Boorman reduced the line to "It was horrible" and took out the sound effect. Also in this sequence, Lamont and Tuskin originally had a longer argument. The following lines were deleted for the "Mark IV" version:

TUSKIN: Look, we don't know all that much about synchronised hypnosis yet. It could have just as well been a dream, a fantasy, an hallucination, not a memory at all.

LAMONT: Names, just names. Better to see the face than hear the names.

John Boorman also cut a couple of lines during a scene between Sharon (Kitty Winn) and Father Lamont:

Uncut version: "Mark IV" Version:

SHARON: When I'm with her is the only time I'm at peace. Why would that be? I can't understand it. It frightens me.

LAMONT: Have you tried a psychiatrist or a priest?	LAMONT: I'm not here for you.
SHARON: I'm talking to one now, aren't I?	
LAMONT: I'm not here for you.	

In the early part of the original version, Tuskin asks Lamont: "Don't you ever need a woman, Father?" He replies, "Yes." This hint at Lamont's confused sexuality was cut out. Following that scene, Lamont and Regan experiment a second time with the synchroniser. While under hypnosis, their minds travel to Africa, and we see a succession of quick shots of landscapes from the point of view of a locust. For the "Mark IV" version, the director trimmed that sequence and took out a shot of zebras running. Also out is a quick exchange between Dr. Tuskin and Father Lamont after the hypnosis session; in the "Mark IV" version, the scene ends with Tuskin saying: "But Regan told us it was something she remembered from the museum." In the uncut version, the scene went on a little longer:

LAMONT: I want to ask her.

TUSKIN: Just a minute. Take it easy. I want to look at you. [She takes his pulse.]

Boorman also decided to make the scene during which Regan gets an autistic girl talking shorter. After the girl starts to talk, her mother arrives and is naturally in shock by her daughter's miraculous recovery. The original scene was much longer; the mother's reaction was simplified. (In the uncut version, the mother goes: "You're talking! Talking! She's talking! Oh, God!" In the "Mark IV" version, the mother just says, "Oh, God!") Also out is the following exchange between the mother and Dr. Tuskin:

MOTHER: You keep talking. You keep talking.

TUSKIN: Come on in my office.

MOTHER: No. Her father would never forgive me if he didn't hear her. I've got to take her home.

Father Lamont and Dr. Tuskin have discovered that Regan has special healing powers. This triggers an argument between them. Originally, that particular scene was longer:

LAMONT: We got to fight that demon that's inside her. It's preventing her from reaching full spiritual power.

TUSKIN: Demons? We make our own demons up here! You're obsessed with the idea.

LAMONT: I'm not obsessed. I'm not. I admit I'm fascinated, but I know the dangers. Father Merrin himself was afraid that he'd fall into admiration.

TUSKIN: How about adulation?

This is how John Boorman changed this scene:

LAMONT: We got to fight that demon that's inside her.

It's preventing her from reaching full spiritual power.

TUSKIN: You're obsessed with the idea.

It is interesting to notice that Boorman kept the same shot of Dr. Tuskin saying "How about adulation?" and just replaced her dialogue. If one looks closely, the new line ("You're obsessed with the idea") is slightly out of sync.

John Boorman decided to delete a whole discussion between Father Lamont and Regan about French theologian Teilhard de Chardin, even though the inspiration for *Exorcist II: The Heretic* came from his writings. At the same time, Boorman felt the speech was too difficult for the general audience and decided to cut it out. This is how the scene was originally intended:

LAMONT: In fact, a French priest, Teilhard de Chardin thought that we'd all come together eventually in some sort of mental telepathy. A kind of world mind in which everybody would share.

REGAN: When is that supposed to happen?

LAMONT: I don't know. Father Merrin himself believed that with modern scientific research it could happen quite soon. I mean the kind of research that Dr. Tuskin is doing. But if it happens before we're ready, we may find ourselves pointing toward the wrong direction, toward Satan.

This scene takes place at the American Museum of Natural History in Manhattan. Originally, the ending of that particular scene was awkward and concluded with Father Lamont saying, "Kokumo [referring to the African boy exorcised by Father Merrin], if he can tell me how he has survived Pazuzu, I'll come back and let you know." The same scene in the "Mark IV" version simply ends with Regan saying, "His name was Kokumo."

Boorman then decided to refashion the following confrontation scene at the Vatican between Cardinal Jaros and Father Lamont entirely. While he took out some dialogue in the earliest part of the scene, he added a very interesting speech for the "Mark IV" version that did not exist initially:

Original version:

LAMONT: I must go to Africa right away, because if I can find this man Kokumo, it will prove beyond doubt that the exorcisms were valid. But more than that, you remember how Father Merrin prophecied that the new man would rise to purge evil from the earth? They may already be among us. Kokumo could be one of them. I saw him in a vision. I saw his power over evil.

JAROS: I've asked you to investigate the exorcisms of Father Merrin, not to step into his shoes. You're in dying need of prayer. I suggest you make a retreat.

LAMONT: A retreat? Why not an advance?

JAROS: Lamont, you're openly in defiance of the Church, I beg you to reconsider. I have no choice but to relieve you of your assignment. You're to refrain from any further action. We'll speak again after your retreat.

The "Mark IV" version:

LAMONT: I must go to Africa right away because if I can find this man Kokumo—I saw him in a vision. I saw his power over evil.

JAROS: Lamont, you're openly in defiance of the church, I beg you to reconsider. I have no choice but to relieve you of your assignment. You're to refrain from any further action. We'll speak again after your retreat.

LAMONT: Merrin looked evil in the face and recognized it everywhere and named it and fought against it, desperately alone until the end, and we, we deny him, why? Because he was trying to show us the way to the kingdom of Christ upon earth? That's something that deep in our hearts we've given up hope on. What you really believe is that the world is incurably sick, lost.

JAROS: Heretic!

LAMONT: That's a denial of our sacred mission!

In the uncut version, before we made the transition to Father Lamont in Africa, there was a shot of Regan outside on the balcony of her Manhattan apartment. In the "Mark IV" version, this shot comes in later, after we've seen Father Lamont praying in a church on the top of a mountain in Africa. Incidentally, the scene inside the church was originally longer; it had more chanting and showed Lamont taking Communion and saying, "I'm mortal sin, disobedient pride. But evil overwhelms us. I had to disobey. I had to disobey."

Later, when Father Lamont tells a monk he flew on the wings of Pazuzu and that the demon showed him where a man died years ago, John Boorman deleted the following line for the "Mark IV" version: "I flew with Pazuzu in a trance. It's difficult to explain. I was under hypnosis." Was this yet another line at which audiences laughed?

The director refashioned the brief sequence during which Ned Beatty takes Richard Burton in his plane to the city of Jepti; the shots are in a different order and the dialogue slightly changed.

The uncut version:

LAMONT: I've flown this route before.

PILOT: When was that?

LAMONT: It was. . .it was on the wings of a demon.

Compare to the "Mark IV" version:

LAMONT: I've flown this route before on the wings of a
          demon.

In the "Mark IV" version, the pilot laughs at Lamont while
we're seeing an exterior shot of the plane; in the uncut version, we actually see him laughing inside the plane. Shortly
thereafter, during the sequence in the African city of Jepti,
Boorman shortened the French dialogue between Lamont and
a local policeman.

The last act of the film is the portion that was changed the
most. The "Mark IV" version is much tighter; Boorman took
out a scene between Dr. Tuskin giving a bath to her two children and being unable to answer the phone. Also gone are a
couple of lines when Tuskin realizes that Regan has taken the
synchroniser.

Uncut version:

TUSKIN: The synchroniser, it's gone. She's way ahead
           of us.

SHARON: I know she is.

SECRETARY: Any news?

SHARON: Regan's taken the synchroniser.

Now, compare to the "Mark IV" version:

TUSKIN: The synchroniser, it's gone. She's way ahead
           of us.

The other following scenes or lines were deleted for the
"Mark IV" version:

- A brief moment during which Dr. Tuskin is watching her
  young patients singing while waiting for a phone call from
  Regan.

- Sharon calling Regan "a stupid bitch" when she finds out that she's going back to the Georgetown house with Father Lamont.

- Dr. Tuskin telling her secretary to call her kids before she leaves for Washington.

- Father Lamont telling a train controller: "She [Regan] belongs to me."

- The scene during which Dr. Tuskin and Sharon are on their way to the airport and are stopped on the freeway by the victim of a car accident was entirely recut. In the uncut version, Tuskin first drives off and then stops her car; when she runs out to help the man, Sharon says, "Well, Regan can wait, I guess." Tuskin calls to the man, "Wait, I'm a doctor. I'll help you." The scene ends with the camera panning from Tuskin helping the wounded man to a plane flying overhead. In the "Mark IV" version, Tuskin just drives off, without stopping for the man.

- The scene with Dr. Tuskin and Sharon aboard a plane was initially slightly longer. In the uncut version, Tuskin turns to a nervous man sitting next to her, right after the plane fell into an air pocket, and says, "Why don't you loosen your tie?" This line was deleted in the "Mark IV" version.

- An incident, in which Father Lamont commands a recalcitrant bus driver who is eating a sandwich to drive him and Regan to Georgetown, is cut.

- A scene in a cab involving Sharon and Dr. Tuskin was completely cut. The police are blocking the road and Tuskin gets out of the cab:

TUSKIN:	What now? I'm going to see into this.
CABDRIVER:	Won't do any good.
SHARON:	She's a doctor.
CABDRIVER:	Doesn't make any difference. This is Washington.
SHARON:	Someone is dying.

- A quick shot of Sharon and Dr. Tuskin inside the cab as they reach Prospect Street in Georgetown was deleted in the "Mark IV" version.
- The sequence during which the cab crashes through the gates of Regan's house in Georgetown was completely refashioned.

In the uncut version, a car drives by the cab. A rock hits the windshield; it shatters to pieces. Father Lamont opens the door to Regan's bedroom, and a swarm of locusts flies in his face. In the "Mark IV" version, Father Lamont opens the door to Regan's bedroom. A swarm of locusts flies in his face. The windshield of the cab shatters.

- After the cab crashed through the gates of the Georgetown house, Boorman added one gruesome close-up of the cab driver dead (his neck impaled on the steering wheel) for the "Mark IV" version that didn't exist originally, but he took out Dr. Tuskin saying, "Sharon, help me. We've got to help Regan."
- The director also removed Regan saying, "Father, let me reach you." Since we don't see Regan saying this line (she is standing in front of Lamont on the staircase), it was simply erased, but the scene itself remained intact— no shots were deleted. In that same sequence, Regan goes to her room and opens her door; she sees herself possessed by Pazuzu on her bed. In the "Mark IV" version, two close-ups of Regan possessed from *The Exorcist* were added.
- In the original uncut version, Father Lamont was seduced by the possessed Regan:

POSSESSED REGAN: Be joined with us, Father.

Lamont jumps with the possessed Regan on the bed and starts kissing her.

POSSESSED REGAN: Kill her.

In the "Mark IV" version, the seduction of Father Lamont was entirely deleted. Boorman used the shot of the possessed Regan saying, "Be joined with us, Father," but dubbed her saying instead, "Kill her." If you look closely, the actress's lips are out of sync.

- In both versions, Sharon sets herself on fire. However, in the uncut version of the film, Dr. Tuskin goes into the street, screaming for help after trying to reach out for Sharon, after she sets herself on fire. All of this is gone in the "Mark IV" version.

- The "Mark IV" ends with the house collapsing Father Lamont screaming Regan's name. Regan appears out of the chaos, completely exorcised; Dr. Tuskin watches her, crying. The police have arrived. Freeze-frame on Regan. The End. Initially, the ending was entirely different: There were additional shots of Dr. Tuskin picking up Sharon's body and Father Lamont surviving the collapse of the house. He meets Regan, Tuskin, and the dying Sharon on the street:

SHARON: I chose evil.

LAMONT: No, Sharon. Your hunger for belief was your truth. *Te absolvo. . .In nominé Patris. . .Et Filii. . .et Spiritus Sancti. . . ."*

REGAN: Sharon. . . .

SHARON: Regan. . . . [She dies.]

LAMONT: The time has come. Now we are saved and made strong. An enemy of the human race is subdued.

TUSKIN: Regan, I'm sorry. I understand now. The world won't. Not yet. [She hugs Lamont.] You have to go. Take care of her.

Lamont and Regan walk off together. The police and people arrive. Dr. Tuskin cries and, as we hear the sound of the synchroniser, we fade to white.

John Boorman conceded at the time he recut the film that his new ending was less hopeful, less triumphant than his initial intent of showing good conquering evil. "It may be presumptuous in this day and age to show good totally winning out." According to the director, the character played by Richard Burton had to be sacrificed for the good of the picture. The revised ending also got around the problem of what audiences felt was the "unreality" of the film. Showing Burton and Blair walking off into a studio-backdrop sunrise and the police and a crowd of people suddenly appearing in the street behind Louise Fletcher simply felt bogus. "This new ending," Boorman declared, "is an attempt to eliminate the second reality that people were concerned about. I should have made it clear that these things were happening in another reality, in a frozen moment of time. The problem was I just didn't do it well enough."

- The director chose a different score for the end credits of the "Mark IV" version. While keeping part of the romantic cue he had used for the uncut version, it suddenly jumps to a Tangerine Dream–like score, also reminiscent of the music used by William Friedkin for the end credits of *The Exorcist.*

Despite Boorman's effort to change his film, *Exorcist II: The Heretic* was badly received. While the "Mark IV" version of the film works on some levels (the best cuts are those that took care of some of the awkward dialogue), it seems more disjointed than the initial cut. At the same time, John Boorman must be commended for delivering a second version drastically different from the first one without having to reshoot any additional footage. Was Boorman's film bad, or was the director the victim of the audience's expectations that *Exorcist II* was going to be a remake—not a sequel—of *The Exorcist*? When he got involved with the project, Boorman refused to take the audience into consideration and went for his vision. Unfortunately, when he decided to recut his film to make it more accessible to his audience, it was too late. *The Exorcist* set the horror in reality; therefore, the audience could identify with the situation and be scared. In *The Heretic*, Boorman set the terror in another reality. Boorman's instinct to create a different tone to his film was right (this intuition worked in the case of *Aliens*, for instance), but unfortunately, he took it too far into a surreal, nonlinear style.

BRIAN DE PALMA'S *DRESSED TO KILL* AND *SCARFACE*

Dressed to Kill

Dressed to Kill (1980) is about Kate Miller (Angie Dickinson), a middle-aged, sexually repressed housewife. She complains to her psychiatrist, Dr. Elliott (Michael Caine), about her husband's pathetic performances in bed and tests her sexual worth by trying to unsuccessfully seduce him. Kate then picks up a handsome stranger in a museum and lives her wildest fantasies with him, but before she leaves her one-afternoon stand, she discovers that he has a venereal disease. She rushes out of his apartment but has to return after she realizes she's forgotten her wedding ring. When the elevator doors open, she is slashed to death by a blond woman with dark glasses. Liz Blake (Nancy Allen), a "Park Avenue whore," is the only witness to the murder and becomes at once the star suspect as well as the killer's next prey. Liz is saved by Peter (Keith Gordon), Kate's son, who is determined to unmask the murderer, since Detective Marino (Dennis Franz), who is in charge of the case, is being totally uncooperative. Peter discovers that the killer is one of Elliott's patients. Liz decides to seduce Elliot in order to check out his appointment book and finds out that Elliott himself was Bobbi, the murderess. Liz is saved by a female undercover cop. It turns out Elliott was a transsexual with a split-personality syndrome; each time he was aroused by a woman, Bobbi—his female alter ego—took over and killed.

When *Dressed to Kill* was submitted to the MPAA, Brian De

Palma, who wrote and directed the film, was informed that it was likely to receive an X; no patron under the age of 17 would be admitted to see the picture. This decision taking him totally by surprise, De Palma argued that there were many other films that received Rs and were as explicit as his.

In 1968, De Palma's second feature film *Greetings*, starring Robert De Niro, had been one of the first movies to receive an X under the new classification code. But because *Greetings* was sort of an underground picture done for a little over $400,000, the film's rating didn't hurt the box office; if nothing else, it got the movie more publicity, and *Greetings* became a commercial success. With *Dressed to Kill*, the situation was different; the film had cost a lot of money, it had major stars in it, and basically, De Palma knew that the difference between an R and an X rating could mean the difference between riches and ruin. Richard Heffner of the Classification and Rating Administration (CARA) referred to *Dressed to Kill* as a "masterwork" but nevertheless declared that he had to give it an X because it was just too strong. At the time, Brian De Palma referred to the MPAA as a board of censors; "I sense a repressive era beginning in the country again. I always gauge these things by who's headed for the White House."

The controversy around *Dressed to Kill* came at the time director William Friedkin, United Artists, and producer Jerry Weintraub were caught in a battle with the MPAA over their film *Cruising*, which dealt with the S&M homosexual world. The irony is that De Palma had at one point written an adaptation of *Cruising* (based on a novel by Gerald Walker) and had created for the story the character of a sexually repressed housewife. When De Palma abandoned *Cruising*, that character became the departure for *Dressed to Kill*. De Palma felt that his film was a direct victim of the controversy that surrounded *Cruising*. In any case, he had to make some strategic cuts in the opening shower sequence, in the murder scene in the elevator, and in the nightmare sequence at the end of the film. He also had to replace some of the dialogue in the scene during which Liz (Nancy Allen) tries to seduce Dr. Elliott (Michael Caine).

The following line was deleted altogether for the R-rated version:

LIZ: [referring to a nightmare she had about a man raping her] All the time he's talking I can see the bulge in his pants.

Also, in the X-rated version, Liz said, "He drops his pants, spreads my legs, kneels down behind me." In the R version, this line became "He drops his pants, he forces me down on my stomach, kneels down behind me."

When Liz strips to her sexy lingerie in front of Elliott, he says to her: "Now, why would you want to do a thing like that?" In the X-rated version, Liz replies, "Well, because of the size of that cock in your pants." In the R-rated version, the word "cock" was replaced by the word "bulge."

De Palma got an R rating after submitting *Dressed to Kill* three times to the MPAA, and here are, in detail, the differences between the U.S. version and the uncut versions of the film that was shown in Europe:

The opening sequence: Kate Miller (Angie Dickinson) is giving herself pleasure in the shower while her husband Mike (Fred Weber) is shaving. A man appears behind her, puts his hand on her mouth, and rapes her from behind. The scene ends with Kate pushing the man's hand away and screaming. (In the close-ups, on the actress's intimate body parts actually did not belong to Angie Dickinson but to Victoria Lynn Johnson, her stand-in and the *Penthouse* centerfold for July 1980.) The following shots were removed from the original cut of the film: two close-ups of Kate's fingers caressing her pubic hair. (These two shots are extremely explicit and leave no doubt in the viewer's mind that Kate is masturbating.) The first close-up was replaced by a shot of Kate caressing her belly, and the second one was substituted by a shot of her caressing her breast. Two shots were entirely removed—and not replaced—when the man rapes Kate. In the uncut version, we see the two bodies around the waist moving, leaving no question that the man is actually having intercourse with Kate. There is also an additional shot in the X-rated version of the man's hand covering Kate's own hand over her pubic area, which was removed for the R version.

Kate is brutally slashed to death with a straight razor by Bobbi (who is, in fact, Elliott in drag) in an elevator. The scene was also "slashed" in order to meet with the MPAA's requirements. In both the uncut and the U.S. versions, a major portion of that scene is missing; the jump on the music track makes the cuts even more jarring and obvious. When you saw the film in the theater, you missed the extreme close-ups showing the razor slashing Kate on her right cheek and then gashing her neck. These were substituted by long shots of the killer assaulting Kate and by one quick—almost subliminal—close-up of her neck, immediately followed by another long shot; but you basically never see the razor slashing up the victim, as in the X-rated version. The whole murder sequence is shorter in the U.S. version and was practically recut entirely. In other words, most of the shots used in the U.S. version do not appear in the uncut version and vice versa. The uncut version is violent, gory, and graphic; the U.S. version is violent but not explicit.

In the last scene of the film, Liz (Nancy Allen) is in the shower and realizes that Bobbi, the killer, is waiting for her by the bathroom door. She gets out of the shower and goes to the cabinet to get a straight razor. She opens the cabinet and sees the killer right behind her. Bobbi slashes Liz's throat with a razor and. . .Liz awakes; it was only a nightmare. The uncut version has an additional extreme close-up on Liz's throat that shows the bleeding, gaping wound.

How did these cuts affect the film? While the changes didn't alter the plot, they definitely affected the director's initial intentions. The U.S. version of *Dressed to Kill* has less impact than the uncut one, but in the end, the changes did not stop the public from enjoying the film. "Actually," De Palma said, "they [the audience] probably wouldn't notice much difference between the two versions. But I do."

In 1981, a year after its initial theatrical release, NBC purchased the TV rights to *Dressed to Kill* for $6.5 million, allowing the network to show the film a total of three runs. It was speculated at the time that in order to fend off the expected attacks from the Moral Majority and other religious groups, the NBC censorship department (also known as "standards and practices") decided to hack about twenty minutes from the film. In fact, the network version of *Dressed to Kill* that's shown to this day is one that boggles the mind. Remember that changes may differ depending on the time the film is shown and also if it's aired by a network or on syndicated television. The following version of *Dressed to Kill* aired on TBS in July 1993:

The opening sequence: Kate is in the shower. All the nudity was, of course, cut out; what remains are close-ups of Angie Dickinson's face and several shots of her husband shaving. When the man appears behind her, all we see is his hand on her mouth and a quick shot of her feet as she is being lifted. The scene ends with Kate screaming. For someone who's never seen the film before, there's practically no way of knowing what just happened. No shots were substituted for the ones removed. The scene is obviously shorter and incomprehensible.

In the theatrical version of the film, De Palma cuts from this scene to Kate having sex with her husband. The camera is above them and slowly pans down toward the couple. Kate fakes an orgasm; her husband taps her gently on the cheek and exits to take a shower. In the TV version, none of this exists; we simply see Kate in bed, all alone, and we hear the shower being turned on in the background.

Several lines were deleted or changed in the scene between Kate and Elliott, her psychiatrist.

In the theatrical version, Kate says, referring to her husband's performance in bed, "He gave me one of his wham-bam specials this morning, and I'm mad at him. Isn't that right, shouldn't I be mad?"

On television, she says, "He made love to me in his usual selfish way this morning, and I'm mad at him." Originally, she added, "I moaned with pleasure at his touch," which was changed to: "I pretended to be thrilled by his touch." Because the dialogue is so different, we do not see Kate say these lines. Instead, the camera is on Michael Caine practically the whole time. But more disturbing is the way this sequence ends. Kate asks Elliott: "Do you find me attractive?" Elliott looks at himself in the mirror, and that's it. The following dialogue was entirely deleted:

KATE: Do you find me attractive?

ELLIOTT: Of course.

KATE: Would you want to sleep with me?

ELLIOTT: Yes.

KATE: Then why don't you?

ELLIOTT: Because I love my wife and sleeping with you isn't worth jeopardizing my marriage. Is it worth it to you to jeopardize yours?

KATE: I don't know.

When Kate is in the museum, she looks at a young couple; the man keeps kissing the girl, who asks him to stop and to look at the paintings. He then caresses her suggestively, and she gets embarrassed. They walk away. In the TV cut, we barely even get a glimpse of the couple.

Kate has seduced a man in the museum. He's waiting for her outside in a cab. She gets in. He grabs her and kisses her. The cab takes off, and the couple make love in the backseat. The man kisses Kate's exposed breasts and removes her underwear. He puts his hands between her legs, and Kate has an orgasm. Her scream dissolves to the horn of a truck parked on the street. In the TV cut, the music had to be cued up and starts as soon as the man kisses Kate (in the film, the music doesn't start until the cab drives off). That's all we see. Next thing we know, the couple is already stepping out of the cab.

Kate wakes up in the man's apartment. In the TV version, we do not see her naked, getting out of bed and getting dressed. We just have a close-up of her looking at her watch, and we then see her by the bed with her clothes on. Gone as well is Kate having a flashback of her making love with the man in the cab and realizing she left her underwear in the cab. The re-editing of that particular sequence creates major gaps and continuity errors.

As to Kate's murder in the elevator: through a curious photographic process, this sequence was tinted in red. When she is first assaulted by the killer, she retreats into the elevator, and the door closes. We get a glimpse of the killer striking at her with the razor in the rearview mirror of the elevator. This shot still exists, but the sounds of the razor slashing and Kate screaming were removed for television. We never see the victim being slashed to death in the elevator. We just have a long shot of Kate falling to the floor and the killer exiting the frame to hide on the side as the door opens. In the release version of the film, when the elevator door opens, we see from Liz's point of view Kate all cut-up and bleeding. In the TV version, we only get the reactions on Liz's face, but we never see Kate, except for a brief moment at the end of the scene. The elevator door closes, and Liz rushes downstairs to ask for help. (The color is now back to normal; no more red-tinted images!) Once on the ground floor, Liz exits, the camera pans to the elevator door, and we see Kate's bloody hand sticking out. That shot was cut for the TV version.

In the rest of the film, mostly only dialogue was changed. . . or in some cases, chunks of it were entirely removed:

Theatrical version:	*Television version:*
DR. ELLIOTT: When was the last time you had intercourse with your wife?	DR. ELLIOTT: When the last time you made love to your wife?
DET. MARINO: Now what the fuck is it to you?	DET. MARINO: Now what the heck is it to you?
MARINO: We got some hot-pants broad cruising for some action. That guy she picked up went down on her, for Christ's sake.	MARINO: We got some lonely woman looking for some action. That guy she picked up made out with her, for Pete's sake.
MARINO: What kind of building is this? Every-	MARINO: What kind of building is this? Every-

body's getting laid after lunch.

body's fooling around after lunch.

MARINO: Let's stop this shit!

MARINO: Let's just talk straight!

MARINO: Let's face it, you're a whore, a Park Avenue whore, but you're still a whore. Now who were you fuckin'?

MARINO: Let's face it, you're a hooker, a Park Avenue hooker, but you're still a hooker. Now, who was your client? Hey, you're no witness, you're a suspect.

LIZ: Fuck you.

MARINO: No, fuck you. Hey, you're no witness, you're a suspect.

MARINO: We got a murder weapon with a nice set of your prints on it.

MARINO: We got a murder weapon with a nice set of your prints on it.

LIZ: That's bullshit. Why would I want to kill her?

LIZ: That's baloney. Why would I want to kill her?

LIZ: How the hell am I supposed to know where he is?

LIZ: How the heck am I supposed to know where he is?

MARINO: You got a lot better motivation than I do, you ass.

MARINO: You got a lot better motivation than I do, You heinie.

BOBBI: Nosy bitch.

BOBBI: Nosy witch.

BOBBI: Hell of a way to lose a patient, but you shouldn't try to fuck 'em, Doc.

BOBBI: Heck of a way to lose a patient, but you shouldn't try to use them, Doc.

BOBBI: I'm glad I took care of that cockteaser.

BOBBI: I'm glad I took care of that teaser.

LIZ: Thank God, straight fucks are still in style.

LIZ: At least escorts are still in style.

LIZ: Are you gonna pump me dry here or invite me in?"

LIZ: Are you gonna pull my hand off or invite me in?"

LIZ: Look, Marino, I'm not interested in your wiseass remarks.

LIZ: Look, Marino, I'm not interested in your wisecrack remarks.

At one point, Liz escapes from Bobbi and finds refuge in the subway, where she's harassed by three hoods.

Theatrical version:

Television version:

HOOD #1: She's bothering you, Sonny?

HOOD #1: She's bothering you, Sonny?

HOOD #2: That's right, that bitch is bothering me.

HOOD #2: That's right.

HOOD #1: What are you going to do about it?

HOOD #1: Hey, lady, where're you going?

HOOD #2: I'm gonna break her fuckin' ass.

HOOD #1: Why break it when you can fuck it first. [Liz tries to run.] Hey, lady, where're you going?

The scene during which Liz tries to seduce Dr. Elliott was already changed for the R version of the film. It underwent further surgery for the TV version:

In the theatrical version, Liz says, "Then he tells me what he's gonna to me and how much I'm gonna like it. He orders me to strip. I do it, keeping one eye on the razor. He drops his pants. He forces me down on my stomach, kneels down behind me, and raises the cold blade. . . ." In the TV version, Liz just says, "Then he tells me what he's gonna do to me."

In the rest of the scene, most of the dialogue was entirely removed:

Theatrical version:

LIZ: I've done most of the bad things you just read about.

ELLIOTT: Do you like doing these things?

LIZ: Sometimes.

ELLIOTT: What do you like about them?

LIZ: I like to turn men on, and I must be doing a pretty good job because they pay me a lot.

ELLIOTT: Did you ever have any sex that's not paid for?

LIZ: Is that a proposal?

ELLIOTT: No. It's what we psychiatrists call a question.

Television version:

LIZ: I've done most of the bad things you just read about.

ELLIOTT: Do you like doing these things?

LIZ: Is that a proposal?

ELLIOTT: No. It's what we psychiatrists call a question.

Theatrical version:

ELLIOTT: My job is to offer you emotional assistance.

LIZ: How about some sexual assistance? Do you want to fuck me?

ELLIOTT: Oh, yes.

LIZ: Then why don't you.

ELLIOTT: Because I'm a doctor and—

LIZ: Fucked a lot of doctors.

ELLIOTT: . . .and I'm married.

LIZ: Fucked a lot of them too.

ELLIOTT: Don't you think we're getting off the point?

LIZ: Do you mind if I take off my coat?

ELLIOTT: No.

LIZ: And the rest too?

ELLIOTT: Now why would you want to do a thing like that?

LIZ: Well, because of the size of that bulge in your pants. I don't think you're so married.

Television version:

ELLIOTT: My job is to offer you emotional assistance.

LIZ: Do you mind if I take off my coat?

ELLIOTT: No.

Theatrical version:

LIZ: Well, what do you think?

ELLIOTT: I think you're a very attractive woman.

LIZ: Would you like to touch me?

ELLIOTT: Yes and no. . .yes because I'm a—

LIZ: Why don't you?

ELLIOTT: I told you why.

LIZ: That's right. You're a married doctor. I remember now. I think you're full of shit.

ELLIOTT: You do. Just because I happen to have personal and professional ethics.

LIZ: Look, doc, I think you're kind of shy, so I'm gonna go powder my nose, and when I come back, I hope to find your clothes right next to mine. If not, we can just get back to the mind fuck.

Television version:

LIZ: Well, what do you think?

ELLIOTT: I think you're a very attractive woman.

LIZ: Would you like to touch me?

ELLIOTT: Yes and no.

LIZ: Look, doc, I think you're kind of shy, so I'm
gonna powder my nose, and when I come back,
I hope to find your clothes right next to mine.

In the theatrical version, when Dr. Elliott gets shot, we see blood spurting on Liz's hands. We then have a long tracking shot from Liz's face to Elliott lying on the carpet. In the television version, we just have the end of the tracking shot with Elliott on the carpet.

The next scene, featuring Liz, a psychiatrist, and two detectives, was not dramatically changed for television; one line is out: "Elliott's penis became erect," and the word "hell" was changed to "heck". However, the scene between Liz and Peter at the restaurant, during which she explains what a transsexual is, was trimmed to excess:

Theatrical version:

LIZ: If you're a man who wants to become a woman,
you take female hormones.

PETER: What do they do?

LIZ: Well, your skin softens, you grow breasts, and
you don't get hard anymore.

PETER: Great.

LIZ: Are you sure you want to know about this?

PETER: Yeah. It's giving me some wonderful new ideas
for a science project. I mean, instead of building
a computer, I could build a woman out of me.

LIZ: Great idea. In that case, I'll give you all the
details. The next step is surgery. Ah. . .let me
remember the exact word Levy told me. Oh
yeah, penectomy.

PETER: What's that?

LIZ: Oh, you know. They take your penis and slice it
down the middle.

PETER: Yeah, yeah, that's what I thought it was.

LIZ: Then castration, plastic reconstruction, and the

formation of an artificial vagina. A vaginoplasty to those in the know.

PETER: And I thought Elliott just put on a wig.

LIZ: Oh, he did. And a dress too, but you see that's no good in bed when you have to take everything off.

Television version:

LIZ: If you're a man who wants to become a woman, you take female hormones.

PETER: And I thought Elliott just put on a wig.

LIZ: Oh, he did. And a dress too.

In the scene in the asylum, after Elliott has strangled a nurse, we had seen him strip her clothes off; that's missing in the television version, and so is most of the last scene of the film during which Liz is in the shower and gets her throat slashed with a straight razor. All that remain are the head and shoulder shots of Liz in the shower. When the killer strikes, only two shots out of the ten original close-ups remain: the hand of the killer holding the razor before the weapon slashes Liz's throat and an extreme close-up of Liz's eyes.

Dressed to Kill, whether it be the X or R version or the television cut, still earned De Palma criticism, especially from women who felt the film was misogynist. A group called Women Against Violence Against Women (WAVAW) organized boycotts and demonstrations opposing the movie and brought pressure on critics who gave *Dressed to Kill* good reviews. "WAVAW does not advocate censorship," Stephanie Rones, a representative of the organization, declared at the time. "We're only asking for responsibility from film critics. What people see on the movie screen is more than art. Its messages influence society." However, does this justify the alteration of a director's vision? Should De Palma censor himself, go against his creative impulse? De Palma has his own answers to these questions: "The problem isn't the Hollywood system but the people who force a moral justification on you. . .An artist basically creates something out of what's in his brain. I'm no documentarian trying to reflect what's going on in society. There is absolutely no correlation between movie violence and actual violence as far as I can see." Obviously, the MPAA and the networks thought back then—and still think the same way today—that they have a responsibility toward parents with children, and that yes, cuts, re-editing, and deletions of certain scenes are necessary. De Palma disagreed—and so did the film's star Angie Dickinson, who declared at the time that she felt the film was not overdone at all and added, "The arts have a responsibility to show us life as it exists. These people [WAVAW] want all movies to be Walt Disney. We should want movies to show the complexities of our consciousness. *Dressed to Kill* is down-to-earth honest."

SCARFACE

When Brian De Palma's film *Scarface* (1983), which had been submitted four times to the MPAA, still got an X rating, the director told Universal Pictures: "Look, you guys are going to have to fire me, and you can finish the process yourselves. I think we are affecting the effectiveness of the film, and I won't work, and I don't care anymore,"

Scarface, a gangster epic written by Oliver Stone, was loosely based on the classic 1932 film. This updated version starred Al Pacino as Tony Montana, a Cuban immigrant who becomes part of the cocaine underworld in Florida. "For those who remember the original Howard Hawks–Howard Hughes *Scarface* with Paul Muni," reporter Todd McCarthy pointed out in an article for *Variety*, "a small irony stems from the fact that each murder in that film was signified with an X fashioned out of lightings and sets." McCarthy also mentioned that the original was the subject of intense pressure for deletions, and was banned or cut in many cities and states. Fifty years later, history was repeating itself, and the X marking that was imposed on the film by the MPAA also meant murder for the filmmakers.

It had taken producer Martin Bregman three years to bring *Scarface* to the screen. His credits include *Carlito's Way* (1993), also directed by De Palma; *Sea of Love* (1989); *Serpico* (1973); and *Dog Day Afternoon* (1975). All starred Al Pacino. The production was dogged by protests from the Cuban community in Miami, claiming that it portrayed Hispanics in an unfavorable way. "Making a movie is like mounting a military campaign. You want nothing coming suddenly from left field," Bregman declared retrospectively. "Demonstrations, that's what worried me. How do you shoot a movie in a street with a demonstration in progress? It's hard enough to do it with everybody's cooperation. It angered me, that nobody asked to see the script before they made judgments. When they did ask, I told them to go to hell." The production was under siege by Commissioner Guillermo Perez, who had already attacked Bregman for making *Serpico*, which he said was an offensive film. Finally, when the media got involved, Bregman decided to shoot *Scarface* in Los Angeles.

Next, Brian De Palma reportedly received death threats from real-life mobsters, and when the film was finally finished, the MPAA refused to give the $23.5-million gangster movie an R rating, claiming the film to be excessively violent not only visually but in the language as well. "It is not excessive," De Palma insisted, referring to the violence in his film. "We previewed it, and no one walked out because of any violence—in fact, nobody walked out!" He told the *New York Times* that *Scarface* was, at best, a middle range R picture. Bregman said that the film's content wasn't even a hard R. What was the problem then? De Palma had been more cautious this time, especially after his problems with the MPAA on *Dressed to Kill*. Even before submitting his film to the rating board, he had trimmed a scene in which a man was tortured and then murdered with a chainsaw. (Though we never see the chainsaw touching the flesh, there was originally a shot, which lasted about twelve frames, of a severed arm.) De Palma also cut down the number of victims in the climactic ending sequence during which Al Pacino machine-guns a large number of people.

The rating board felt that the shoot-out was too violent. De Palma was shocked by the verdict of the MPAA. He thought he had been extremely careful to avoid the use of explicit violence, but he had to keep cutting to satisfy the board. "We would fix one part, and then they would suddenly raise questions about another part that they'd never mentioned before. After the fourth submission, I said to Universal, this is crazy. It's hurting the movie aesthetically and commercially. I'm not doing any more cutting."

De Palma also accused CARA chairman Richard Heffner of having a vendetta against him. "When *Dressed to Kill* came out, I gave an interview calling Heffner a censor, which he is. Since then he has had a personal vendetta against me." Heffner denied such an accusation, saying that he didn't know De Palma well enough to be angry at him or to have a vendetta against his work. "Nothing could be further from the truth," Heffner said in regards to De Palma's accusation. "I appreciate the publicity value of attacks on the mean old censor. But we rate films, not filmmakers. On the invisible scale that we carry in our heads, we felt *Scarface* deserved something stronger than an R. The accumulation of violence and language was just too much. We consider ourselves responsible to parents, and we didn't think many parents would cheer us for giving this film an R rating." De Palma thought Heffner just wanted him to stand down. The director even received the support from movie critic Roger Ebert, who said that Heffner had a personal ax to grind against the filmmaker.

Martin Bregman, who agreed with his director that the film was not full of blood oozing from the screen and that there was no explicit violence, pointed out that the MPAA was also objecting strongly against the word "fuck" and other harsh, sexually derived words (over 180, stated the MPAA). "You go to a playground in New York City and listen to the nine-year-olds," Bregman told Julie Salamon of the *Wall Street Journal.* "You'll hear some words. A kid going to this movie isn't going to go out and contact his local cocaine dealer. We painted that world as bad as it is." Curiously, Jack Valenti, president of the MPAA and chairman of the appeals board, declared in

Newsweek at the time that he'd want his fifteen-year-old daughter to see *Scarface* because it was an antidrug film.

Robert Rehme, then the president of Universal's theatrical motion picture division, declared that under no circumstances would the studio release *Scarface* with an X. Alan Friedberg, president of the Sack Theaters chain in the Boston area, said that the situation with *Scarface* proved the need for an "M for Mature" or "A for Adults" rating. Friedberg agreed that the film was violent and strong but argued that there was no reason to put it in the same category as a porn movie.

The situation had to be sorted out quickly; the film had been scheduled to open on December 9, 1983, in approximately one thousand theaters. An appeal was scheduled for November 8 after both De Palma and Bregman said that there would be no further cutting. Actually, Bregman had been so certain that *Scarface* would receive an X despite the changes De Palma had already applied to the picture that he had arranged for the appeal before the final verdict reached him. If they won the appeal, the world would see what the MPAA considered an X, and De Palma was convinced that everyone would agree that the film didn't deserve one. On the other hand, if they lost the appeal, Universal would either have to accept the X or recut the film against De Palma's wish.

The appeal was heard by a board consisting of about twenty theater owners, studio executives, and independent distributors. The version screened was the second of the different ones edited by the filmmakers, which, De Palma claimed, was hardly different at all from the initial first cut. *Time* magazine film critic Jay Cocks read to the board a letter he had written to De Palma which claimed *Scarface* did not deserve an X rating. He was followed by Maj. Nick Novarro of the Broward County, Florida, police force, who stated that the situations depicted in *Scarface* were true to life. Incidentally, Martin Bregman declared later in regard to the film's verisimilitude that there was not one scene in *Scarface* that hadn't been pulled out of police files. The chainsaw scene, for instance, really happened, only in reality, there were more victims involved. Novarro said that there was a need for movies like

Scarface and insisted that young people should see it. "It shows the ugliness behind the drug trade," he declared.

Also speaking on behalf of the filmmakers at the appeal were Dr. H. Feinberg, a child and adolescent psychiatrist, and Dr. Richard Atkins, a child and adult psychiatrist. Both testified that *Scarface* could not harm anyone over thirteen, because at that age teenagers could differentiate a film from real life. De Palma and Robert Rehme spoke during the hearing, as did Richard Heffner, who was especially upset about the presence of the two psychiatrists. "If you lie down with psychiatrists," Heffner told the board, "you wake up with the fleas of their discontents. I could bring the surgeon general of the United States to say how bad film and TV violence is for children. But we don't do that."

This time, however, the appeals board decided against Heffner and CARA; seventeen ballots (the majority) were in favor of overturning the X rating. De Palma claimed that if he had lost the appeal on *Scarface*, he would have taken his case all the way to the Supreme Court. He argued that an X rating prohibited a parent from taking his or her own child to see a movie. "That seems to me illegal," De Palma said. "I spoke to a lawyer who suggested that if I were to bring a lawsuit against the rating system, I might win. It's restraint of trade." Despite the victory, Bregman was still angry, saying that the ordeal had cost the studio a lot of money and that prints hadn't gone out because of the delays in getting the proper rating for the film. At the same time, some outsiders said that the decision to give *Scarface* an R rating was purely for economic reasons; the verdict had been given by the appeals board, which, unlike CARA, was composed of industry people. "I'm not naïve about the composition of the appeals board," Richard Heffner told the *New York Daily News*. "But since I took over the rating board in 1974, we've rated 3,500 films. The studios have had an economic interest in all of those films, and yet our ratings have only been overturned a few times."

In any case, what audiences saw was the same print that had been initially submitted to the MPAA. "You delete six [fornicates] and one [anatomical] reference and you change a rating," Martin Bregman said. "What the MPAA's saying is all bull——. The worst violence in the film is all suggestive. It's like the shower scene in *Psycho*. It's all in the mind." Did the controversy over cutting or not cutting *Scarface* help the film? Did it give the filmmakers more publicity? According to Martin Bregman, there were still people who wouldn't go see the film because the MPAA had initially classified it an X, and they feared it would be too violent. For the most part, critics mentioned the battle over the rating of *Scarface* in reviewing the film and tried to decide whether or not it had been worthy of the dispute.

Richard Heffner, who believed that the filmmakers promoted their film by attacking the rating system, clarified a few points in an article for the *Wall Street Journal* by arguing that he and his "civilian" colleagues, as he himself called them, did not classify movies in terms of what they found distasteful. "We are not moralist critics or cops," Heffner wrote. He also insisted on the idea that just because a film was true to life, parents should want to expose their children to those realities. "And thanks to the industry's self-imposed rating system," Heffner concluded, "they don't have to. Which is, I firmly believe, just why we don't have censorship in this country!"

Although *Scarface* did not become a blockbuster, it did reach a cult status. Martin Bregman said that the film made so much brouhaha because it was ahead of its time. The battle made De Palma very bitter. "As soon as I get this dignity [back] from *Scarface*," he told *Esquire*, "I'm going to go out and make an X-rated suspense porn picture. I'm sick of being censored. *Dressed to Kill* was going to get an X rating, and I had to cut a lot. So, if they want an X, they'll get a real X. They wanna see suspense, they wanna see terror, they wanna see SEX—I'm the person for the job."

De Palma did indeed try to cross the line between art and pornography with his 1984 thriller *Body Double*, following *Scarface*. Many were outraged that the film received an R rather than an X, despite the sex (the film takes place in the porn underworld) and the violence (a woman is murdered with a giant drill). *Body Double* hardly got the controversial attention De Palma expected—and wanted—to receive. The film was actually playing against Ken Russell's *Crimes of Passion*, starring Kathleen Turner. This time around, it was the Ken Russell film that was threatened with an X rating by the MPAA and that had to be cut down before it received the acceptable R label.

Body Double was motivated by De Palma's anger toward the MPAA; the film seemed to be a defiant act against his detractors. It was almost as if De Palma was begging for an X. He wanted to fight for his images, for his vision, for his creative freedom. "There is no question that my images are strong and effective," he said. "Do I feel responsible for them? Only that they're good."

THE FRIEDKIN CONNECTION

WILLIAM FRIEDKIN'S *THE EXORCIST,* *CRUISING,* AND *TO LIVE AND DIE IN L.A.*

William Friedkin and Bud Smith are two names that go together. Friedkin is the accomplished film director who had a meteoric rise to the top with *The French Connection* in 1971, for which he received an Academy Award. His collaboration with editor Bud Smith goes back to the time when they were both involved with doing documentaries. Their first venture on a feature film was *The Exorcist* (1973). The movie was based on the best-selling novel by William Peter Blatty and grossed $165 million in the U.S. alone, making it one of the all-time successful films. The story dealt with the demonic possession of a young girl, Regan MacNeil (Linda Blair). Her mother (Ellen Burstyn), out of despair, contacts a priest, Damien Karras (Jason Miller), who is himself tormented by the death of his own mother and questioning his faith in God. Damien joins forces with Father Merrin (Max von Sydow) and perform an exorcism on Regan, which ultimately claims the lives of both priests. Regan, however, is freed of the demon that possessed her.

The Exorcist became the target of censorship attempts in the township of Chester, Delaware, even before the camera began rolling. Angry parents demanded that the novel be exorcised from their schools' recommended reading for English classes and banned forever. The parents of one sixteen-year-old girl complained that a novel about the demonic possession of an eleven-year-old was not fit reading for young adults. A steamed group of more than one hundred parents mobbed a meeting of the West Morris Regional Board of Education in January 1972 and engaged in a heated debate over censorship and obscenity. Board member Thorwald Torgersen admitted that he had not read the book because of a long waiting list at the library but refused to have excerpts from it read aloud at the meeting. Fellow member George Polk declared, "If we do not assume the responsibility for some form of restraint, control, censorship, whatever the choice of words, then we are derelicts. The school should provide liberal education with some restraints." This comment, of course, seems illogical and totally contradictory.

While this controversy over the book was going on, William Friedkin was preparing the film in New York with William Peter Blatty (who wrote the screenplay and produced the film) and with Father William O'Malley, a teacher of a senior advanced-placement English class at a Jesuit school in Rochester; O'Malley had been hired as technical adviser and also played the part of Father Dyer, Damien Karras's friend, in the movie. "Anybody who has his wits about him," he said at the time, "would have to realize that everything in the book is written in an absolutely moral context." He suggested as well that the novel shouldn't be required reading if some students didn't want to read it. He pointed out, however, that the novel had not been "required" but "recommended." Despite the controversy, Blatty said that he didn't expect the film to receive an X rating. When asked if he feared a similar banning effort on his novel might occur in other communities, the author replied, "It could. You find insanity everywhere. The spectacle of parents who become hysterical when their children react calmly and maturely to a work of fiction is in itself a suitable subject for psychiatric study."

Bud Smith (one of several editors of *The Exorcist*; the film received an Academy Award nomination for Best Editing) said:

While editing the film, I never worried that it might receive an X. Absolutely not. From the day we started on the film to the final cut, there was never any consideration for the rating or MPAA concern. We just put the film together the way the script was and the way that Billy Friedkin wanted it to be. As far as the language goes with the little girl and the roughest scenes, such as the one with Regan MacNeil in bed saying "Fuck me, Jesus, fuck me," we felt that that might be a problem because it looked like she was really masturbating with the crucifix. But we just sent the film to the MPAA, and the print they saw is the one that was released in the theaters with an R rating. We had nothing but a great phone call from the MPAA saying what a powerful movie it was. The only problem that we had was when I cut a trailer for the film, with music by Bernard Herrmann. I just used icons, demons, faces, crosses coming at you, and the studio [Warner Bros.] thought it was so violent that they were afraid to put it in the theaters. So they didn't.

While there might have been few concerns regarding the MPAA rating on *The Exorcist*, Friedkin was worried about a new ruling given by the United States Supreme Court on obscenity, providing local communities with the right to set up their own criteria and to cut films if they wanted to. But William Friedkin refused to let this decision affect his creative vision while editing *The Exorcist*. He declared at the time that he was concerned, not afraid, and that the law not only threatened the entire film community but also blurred the distinction between garbage and legitimate expression and gave the right especially for small towns to become censors of movies. "*The Exorcist* is not an obscene film or a dirty film. I'm not going to pretend it is. But it deals in highly controversial areas, and as such, I realize I could run into trouble!" At the time, *Paper Moon* (1973), a film by Peter Bogdanovich starring Ryan O'Neal and his daughter Tatum, had been banned in Dallas because the word "shit" was uttered by the nine-year-old actress. Friedkin said he would not start cutting scenes out of his films because, he claimed, all the language and the actions depicted in *The Exorcist* had foundation in the Catholic religion and were actual symptoms of possession. With Warner Bros. (the distributor of the film) behind him, Friedkin was confident that he would not have to compromise his vision for the benefit of local communities.

Trouble actually began after Friedkin believed it was over. *The Exorcist* had received an R rating, and the film was a hit. The United States Catholic Conference berated the MPAA for giving the movie an R, while they felt it deserved an X. The Conference rated the film A-IV, which meant the film could be perceived as objectionable to certain audiences. While having to deal with Catholic censorship, the filmmakers were confronted as well with a far more dangerous reaction from several communities across the country. In Washington, critic Roy Meacham wrote a heated article entitled "How Did *The Exorcist* Escape an X Rating?" in which he reported the negative effects the film might have on young audiences. "Early in the morning on New Year's Day," Meacham said in the piece, "Washington became the first city ever to bar children from a film the review board said they could see. After conferring with the U.S. Attorney's Office, officers from the police department's morals division warned the management of the Cinema Theater that arrests would be made if any more tickets were sold for use by minors." And, indeed, a sign was placed at the box office of the theater that read: "As a result of a ruling by the U.S. District Attorney's Office, no one under the age of 17 will be admitted to *The Exorcist*. Identification may be required." The police were able to interfere in this case because of a provision in the District of Columbia's code which forbid minors from viewing scenes depicting sexual conduct, even if the actors were fully clothed. "Since *The Exorcist* is not a film in which snipping a scene here or there would make any real difference in its suitability for children," Meacham continued, "the review board's choice was to buck the largest production company in Hollywood or pass the film with an R." If the movie industry could not provide safeguards for minors, local authorities obviously had to do it.

In Massachusetts, Mrs. Rita Warren demanded *The Exorcist*

be banned in Boston, and the case was taken to court. Warners issued the following account of the trial in a press release:

> An effort to have *The Exorcist*, the Warner Bros. motion picture hit, banned in Boston has been thrown out of court there. Justice Theodore A. Glynn, Jr., of Boston Municipal Court, after viewing *The Exorcist*, ruled that "it does not meet the guidelines of obscenity as laid down by the United States Supreme Court." The judge's ruling resulted in the dismissal of a complaint by Ms. Rita Warren against Sack Cinema 57 Theatre Corporation, operators of the Cinema 57 Theatre, where *The Exorcist* has been playing record-breaking business since December 26.

MPAA president Jack Valenti responded to the attacks against the board's decision to rate *The Exorcist* R in a statement published in the *New York Times* on February 25, 1974. He objected to the fact that the MPAA's integrity had been challenged and declared that an R was a very severe rating that did not suggest a family picture. It was the parents' decision to decide whether or not they should take their children to *The Exorcist*. "My children are ten, seven, and five. As a parent, I make the decision that they are too young to see many R films, including *The Exorcist*. But there may be parents who would choose to have their fourteen- or fifteen-year-olds see the film. That is their decision, not mine or the rating system's. That is what the rating system is all about: free choice by parents." Valenti explained clearly that *The Exorcist* was essentially a horror film with no excessive violence, with some strong language, but he insisted that it was used only in relation to the film's theme and was kept to a minimum. "Much of what might concern some people is not on the screen. It is in the mind and imagination of the viewer. A film cannot be punished for what people think because all people do not think alike."

As a sidebar, I'd like to mention another cutting measure that came up during post-production on the film, concerning the music score. Bernard Herrmann, who had composed the music for some of Hitchcock's best films, was chosen by Fried-kin to score *The Exorcist* and flew from London to New York to screen the picture. Friedkin told Herrmann he wanted him to write for *The Exorcist* a better score than the one he had composed for *Citizen Kane.* Herrmann simply answered, "Then you should have made a better movie than *Citizen Kane,*" and returned to London. So, finally, Friedkin hired Lalo Schifrin. . . and more problems ensued; ultimately, the Schifrin score was entirely cut out and literally replaced by already existing music. The same thing had actually happened to Herrmann himself, among others, who was fired by Hitchcock on *Torn Curtain* and replaced by John Addison; to Alex North on Kubrick's *2001;* and, as we've seen before, to Jerry Goldsmith, whose score for Ridley Scott's *Legend* was replaced in the U.S. by music by Tangerine Dream. There are of course many other cases.

Bud Smith noted:

Lalo was Billy's second choice after Bernard Herrmann. We spent a lot of time together. We had up to that point classical music by Polish composers as our temp score. It wasn't actually music, it was more like weird sounds. Lalo came in and played a few cues for Billy on a piano. Billy said, "I can't tell what this is; go record it and then I'll know." So Lalo went ahead and recorded some kind of Brazilian type of music. Billy just freaked out and can-celled the scoring on the first half-day. He said, "I will not accept that as my score." Lalo was just let go. We went back to our temp music, and we had the head of the music department at Warner Bros. take the score to Lon-don. He had the London Symphonic Orchestra just dupli-cate everything that we had temped. However, I tried to put in one cue of Lalo's music during the party scene at the MacNeils', and Billy said, "This is shit. It was shit then and it's shit now and it will always be shit." He took the roll of sound film and threw it through the window across the street into the parking lot. He said, "That's where that belongs!"

Many directors recut their films after they've been released: take scenes out, replace shots, add new scenes. It happens more frequently in today's marketplace whether a film is successful or a total flop. Although this practice was rather unorthodox in the seventies, Friedkin flirted with the idea of reshooting a new ending for *The Exorcist*. Curiously, years later, Friedkin made the following contradictory statement: "With everything I've made, I cut it as I thought was right. I may often have been wrong, but I don't think there are any outtakes that would affect the movies that I've made in any ways other than to make them longer and therefore harder to sit through." This comment is even more surprising in light of the fact that, in 1992, Friedkin recut, by his own will, his movie *Rampage*, which was shot in 1986 and released only in Europe. At the time, DeLaurentiis Entertainment Group (DEG), the distributor of the film, had filed for bankruptcy, and *Rampage* was shelved until Miramax picked it up in 1992 for release in the U.S. Based on a William P. Wood novel, the film dealt with the trial of a serial killer. Michael Biehn portrayed an assistant district attorney tormented by the death of his young daughter. He is ordered to seek the death penalty for the killer even though he's against it. Friedkin deleted some scenes, reinstated old ones, and tried to take a stronger stand in favor of the death penalty. But despite some good reviews and the fact that the new version was far less ambiguous, the film failed to generate any business. In any case, Warner Bros. estimated that a new ending for *The Exorcist* would cost them $400,000 and refused to go through with it. Instead, under Friedkin's pressure, the studio made additional prints and gave the film a wider release.

Bud Smith observed:

At first, the film was only released in twenty-six theaters. After the film came out, Billy said it would be good to reshoot the ending. He wanted to add a scene after the family has gone and the priest walks back to the steps. Billy suggested that he should look down the steps and wanted to shoot Jason Miller walking back up and then fade to black. I think it was just a filmmaker's desire to never let go. You work on a film and, at the very end, you don't finish it, you just abandon it. We never shot this new ending for financial reasons but also because Warners had a blockbuster and felt "Why fix it if it ain't broken?"

William Peter Blatty had ideas of his own for a new ending. In it, Father Dyer went into a retreat after the death of his friend Father Karras. One day, while Dyer was taking a walk, a jogger stopped to talk to him about evil. During their conversation, Dyer realized that the jogger had the same voice as Damien Karras. The film would have ended with Dyer looking up and seeing millions of white lights in the daylight sky, while Karras said to him, "We are the light, Joe." In both Friedkin's and Blatty's new endings, there was a desire to show that Karras's faith in God had been restored and that he had been reborn. This concept was, in fact, exploited in William Peter Blatty's novel *Legion*, the official sequel to *The Exorcist*, which Blatty wrote and directed for the screen as *The Exorcist III* in 1991. For a while, Blatty also hoped that twenty minutes Billy Friedkin had edited out of the film would eventually be restored in the home video version, but it never happened. Blatty thought Friedkin had taken out these scenes to hit a two-hour running time; because of these cuts, Blatty felt the preservation of the religious content of the film had been lost. Friedkin argued that Blatty was wrong—it was maybe five, not twenty minutes that had been cut out—and claimed that he had taken out the scenes because he felt that they were out of rhythm and badly done.

Among the scenes that was cut was, according to Blatty, one that many readers of the novel considered their favorite. It featured Father Merrin telling Father Karras in the hallway of the MacNeils' house in Georgetown that the demon's target is not the possessed but those around him or her, the observers. In an early cut of the film, there was a short scene during which Sharon (Kitty Winn) tells Chris MacNeil (Ellen Burstyn) that Regan is having problems with her schoolwork. Regan's medical examination was also longer, but Friedkin trimmed it down, saying audiences would already attribute—and accept—the girl's condition to the supernatural and that attempting to explain her illness would be bogus. Among the most famous missing scenes from *The Exorcist* supposedly occurred after Chris found out that her director—Chris is an actress—Burke Dennings (Jack MacGowran) was found dead. Chris and Sharon are talking, and suddenly, Regan appears coming down the stairs, gliding spiderlike, flicking her tongue like a snake, licking at Sharon's heels, and following her around the house. That scene was present in the novel as well.

Another deleted scene took place toward the end of the film and showed Chris MacNeil and Father Dyer discussing good and evil. From the moment she got the role, Burstyn had refused to say the line "I believe in the devil!" The dialogue was changed, but the scene never worked and was cut out. Also, originally, the ending featured Lt. Kinderman (Lee J. Cobb) having a discussion with Father Dyer (Father William O'Malley) about movies. Kinderman said, "I'm reminded of a line in the film *Casablanca*. At the end, Humphrey Bogart says to Claude Rains, 'Louis, I think this is the beginning of a beautiful friendship.'" Dyer: "You know, you look a little bit like Bogart." Kinderman: "You noticed." That scene was a bit of a replay of the encounter between Karras and Kinderman in the first half of the film, in which we found out that the detective was a film buff and in which he tells Karras successively that he looks like John Garfield in *Body and Soul*, and Paul Newman and Sal Mineo. Both Warners and Friedkin agreed that the film should end prior to that scene, with Father Dyer simply looking down at the steps (known as the Hitchcock steps, since the director had a cameo appearance walking across the top of a staircase in the film *I Confess*—1953). Blatty only was disappointed.

Maybe one day these scenes will be restored in a new cut of *The Exorcist*. So far, the only changes applied to the film occurred in 1979 when it was reissued in 70mm with a remixed sound track. Friedkin added sound effects prepared for the 1973 version that had never been utilized. "We were unable to use a lot of what we had recorded because you couldn't get it on a 35mm monaural track, which is very limited," the director said. Soundmen Robert Knudson and Chris Newman won Oscars in 1973 for their work on *The Exorcist,* and this new version of the film gave Friedkin the opportunity to take their contribution even further.

Curiously, when *The Exorcist* was shown on network television, it wasn't entirely slaughtered. Obviously, the most difficult scene to re-edit was the masturbation sequence, with Regan holding the crucifix to her genitalia and forcing her mother's face down on her. It's basically impossible to see what's really happening in that sequence in the network version; on television, Regan is just throwing a fit, not masturbating as in the theatrical version.

According to Bud Smith:

I remember that we had to reshoot one insert when the priest goes into the chapel and sees the statue of the Virgin Mary. We couldn't show this on television. [In the film, the Virgin had been transformed into a harlot. Glued to the appropriate spot was a sculpted clay phallus in erection. Sculpted naked breasts were also attached.] The insert we reshot just showed specks of blood on the statue. Altogether, I think we only took out a minute and twenty seconds. In some scenes, the dialogue was either deleted or dubbed. Friedkin himself looped Linda Blair when she says to Karras, "Your mother sucks cocks in hell." It became "Your mother rots in hell." In any case, we went according to the network's guidelines on what they wanted us to change. They accepted our version, but the frustrating part was to watch the film interrupted with commercials.

In 1980, William Friedkin directed *Cruising*, which made the controversy surrounding *The Exorcist* seem like a picnic. *Cruising* is about a cop (Al Pacino) who goes undercover in the New York gay/S&M world to catch a serial killer and who discovers he might himself be homosexual. In the end, a suspect is arrested, but another murder occurs, leading the audience to believe that Pacino himself may be the killer.

Bud Smith said:

> The film was based on a Gerald Walker novel. Jerry Weintraub owned the rights, and Billy wanted to make the film, so they formed a partnership. Jerry would produce, and Billy would write and direct the film. We went to New York; our production office was in Manhattan on Pier 40, down in the West Village, near all the gay bars. Friedkin wanted to shoot in practical locations with practical people instead of using extras. So, naturally, it got through the whole community that a film based on gays, murder, and heavy leather was being made. The casting took place on Pier 40. Billy wanted to make sure that everyone who was going to be in the movie was real. As I said, they weren't extras; they were the real thing. We were shooting on the streets or in the bars, and protests against the film began. They would stand behind barricades, blow police whistles, and disrupt the shooting. Anyway, Friedkin proceeded with his vision. The movie wasn't antigay at all. It could have been about guys who worked on the docks as longshoremen, it could have been anything or any particular group of people who got together and there was one murderer among them.

Cruising was possibly the first time that a movie was being threatened with censorship by a special interest group before it even got shot. Gay activists claimed the film presented a horrifyingly inaccurate and one-dimensional portrayal of the way most gay people lived and could endanger the lives of homosexuals. Producer Jerry Weintraub insisted at the time that *Cruising* was not antigay. "Even if it were," he told *Rolling Stone* in 1979, "the gay-rights forces have no right to try and stop us. We have First Amendment rights. We are portraying a segment of the homosexual community, not the mainstream. These are murders that have actually occurred. I promise this will be a well-made, true, factual account of these killings and what's going in this city." It was a column in *The Village Voice* by Arthur Bell that triggered the first wave of protests against *Cruising*.

> I feel like the Godfather of the gay movement. I put out a contract on Friedkin's movie, and I feel confident that it can be stopped. If it gets released, we'll hit the distributors. If the First Amendment applied to me, I'd be willing to give it to others, but we don't have any civil rights in this country, and Friedkin is using our people to exploit us.

Incidentally, Bell had covered in great detail the Addison Verrill–Paul Bateson gay murder case, which ironically inspired *Cruising*. "I realized from Bell's article that these things really do happen," Friedkin declared. "*Cruising* is no exaggeration."

Ethan Geto, a gay activist in New York, told the press that stopping the film was a matter of life and death. "It portrays gay people as psychopathic killers or as victims who invite victimization. Hollywood has carried the message that homosexuals are suicidal, brutal, and violent. Movies and mass communications have a direct impact on people's consciousness and behavior. The joy, affection, love, and fulfillment that exists among gays is suppressed. It's self-defense for gay people to protest this movie and to try to stop it." Gerald Walker, who wrote the novel, was also being attacked by the gay community; "I'm sympathetic to gays who desire not to have life made harder for them," Walker told *New York* magazine, "but what makes them think a movie about a crazy bastard who goes around killing people will touch off a bloodbath? I wish they weren't so hysterical." Meanwhile, demonstrations against the film troubled the shooting daily. One night, a protest led to the arrest of a demonstrator for allegedly kicking a cop in the balls. The next day, an estimated thousand demonstrators showed up at the location, resulting in two more arrests for disorderly conduct, dozens of injuries, and property damage.

The gay community was also angry at New York Mayor Edward I. Koch and at Nancy Littlefield, the mayor's movie aide at the city's office of motion pictures and television, for allowing *Cruising* to be shot in Manhattan. "The function of the office," Koch said, "is to facilitate movie production in New York regardless of script content. To do otherwise would involve censorship." While giving his support to human rights, Koch stressed that his administration could not afford to give support to any group or to violate principles of free expression. When asked if the disruption of the filming was in effect an act of suppression and censorship, David Rothenberg of the Human Rights Commission said that in light of the fact that the different other lifestyles in the gay community had not been previously portrayed on film, it was justifiable to stop the world from seeing only the S&M sector of the gay world. Actually, this comment is not completely accurate. William Friedkin himself had directed in 1970 the screen adaptation of the Mart Crowley play *The Boys in the Band,* about a group of homosexual friends who gather for a birthday party and exchange stories on their empty lives. Yet Friedkin had been assailed by the gay community for using clichés to portray homosexual men. "We're not asking to be censors," Rothenberg said. "We're just asking Hollywood to exercise the same kind of self-censorship they use before dealing with, say, a sensitive black, Jewish, or other minority subject." The battle against the film did not stop. . . .Some extras quit, and some who remained leaked confidential information about locations. On the other hand, John Devere, editor-in-chief of the gay magazine *Mandate*, went undercover on the set, posing as an extra for the film, and believed that *Cruising* could, in fact, send the same message as Richard Brooks's *Looking for Mr. Goodbar* (1977), about the dangers of promiscuity. Devere referred to one particular personal experience in which he had a casual encounter with a young man who was found murdered several months later.

An anti-*Cruising* committee, however, distributed twenty thousand pamphlets calling the film "a rip-off that uses gay male stereotypes as the backdrop for a horrific story of murders of homosexuals. Gay men are presented as one-dimensional sex-crazed lunatics, vulnerable victims of violence and death. This is not a film about how we live; it is a film about why we should be killed." Jerry Weintraub, who met with gay activists and tried to explain that the film was not antigay, declared the script was substantially altered during production (the killer was not depicted as being himself gay, and it became less apparent that the Al Pacino character might be gay by the end of the film). He denied, though, that the demonstrations had anything to do with the changes. Friedkin's approach to the story became extremely ambiguous; *Cruising* is not a "whodunit," and, in fact, Friedkin had a different actor play the killer for each of the murders. There is an interesting sequence in the film during which the suspect meets his father in Central Park; in reality, the father is dead— the discussion only happened in the mind of the young man. This sequence shows that the suspect is deranged and lives in guilt ever since his father died. Friedkin used Leland Starnes, the actor who played the father, to dub the killer's voice throughout the film!

What did Friedkin think of the gay community's reactions to the film? At the time he was shooting the film, the director told Vito Russo, author of *The Celluloid Closet:* "*Cruising* is no more about gay life than Woody Allen's *Manhattan* is about New Yorkers." In regard to one of the most turbulent nights on the set of *Cruising*, Friedkin told Janet Maslin of the *New York Times*: "When I looked into that mob that night, I saw a gang of unruly fanatics blowing whistles, throwing bottles and cans at the trucks, at the actors, and at me. So how could I believe that this group of people was representing the legitimate interests of a very significant minority in this country? A legitimate group, with legitimate interests, does not threaten to kill you." Al Pacino, as always, confined himself to his work and proclaimed, "My responsibility to this film is as an actor—to the part, not the issue."

Despite the protests, the shooting wrapped up on schedule. The gay community would come back full force to protest the film when it was released several months later, despite the disclaimer at the beginning of the film that said: "This film is not intended as an indictment of the homosexual world. It is set in one small segment of that world, which is not meant to be representative of the whole." This insertion, by the way, had been suggested by members of the gay community who had viewed the film. But the battle over *Cruising* was not finished.

Bud Smith recalled:

Each time we sent the film to the MPAA, they kept saying it was too violent, but they were never specific. It finally got down to a situation where basically all the killings with the knife were too violent. It was okay to put the knife in, but you couldn't pull it out, because when you pulled it out, the blood would spurt out. The way we cut the first killing in the hotel room with the victim tied up on the bed, the murderer kept stabbing him in the back. We had the knife in and out, in and out. Everytime, there would be blood spurting in the air and in the victim's face. That one particular killing we had to cut way back down. What we did is that we'd have the knife going in and then cut to a close-up on the victim's face or see a reflection in the glasses of the murderer, etc.

That was probably the toughest scene to try to get past the MPAA. I would hand carry the print from the dubbing stage to the MPAA office, back and forth, and then cut and recut. We finally called in Dr. Aaron Stern [a New York psychiatrist and Richard Hoffner's predecessor as ratings-board chairman] as a technical adviser [Stern received a total payment of $32,000 for the task plus $13,000 in expenses]; he's a psychiatrist, and he would sit with us in the screening room and analyze what he considered should be taken out for rating purposes. Finally, Jack Valenti got involved and called us. We kept working on it until it received an R rating.

There was a scene in the peep show where there was another killing. There was blood spurting on the screen, and that was too much for the MPAA; they just don't like blood spurting! I don't blame them actually. We had to cut out a lot from the scene that takes place in a gay bar.

There was a guy lying in a bathtub, and another one was pissing on him. There was a scene of copulation as you're panning from Al Pacino's point of view; you basically saw guys giving each other blow jobs. Way in the back, there was a guy up in a strap, a leather sling, and someone else reaches out and puts some gel on his forearm and sticks it up his rectum. All of this was in the original dailies.

During the casting of the film, the guys had been put in categories: you either give a blow job or get a blow job, or you do whatever else. Most of the extras who were from the Screen Actors Guild would leave, but there were a couple of them who were gay anyway and agreed to go for it. Going back to before we went to New York to make the film, Billy brought in a stack of magazines, the *Blueboy* magazines, all the gay male magazines, for research. I looked through them, and I said, "Billy, you're not going to show all this are you?" He said, "This is a great story; this is a great detective story that needs to be told." Anyway, he proceeded with his vision. While seeing the dailies, I didn't think about the MPAA, and the first cut they saw of the film had everything in it that Billy wanted in the film. The golden shower scene was in, the blow jobs, the fist-fucking were in. All of that was actually taking place. All of this had to be trimmed down or taken out. In the pan across the bar, I had to put in a matte so you couldn't see the guys giving each other blow jobs. We didn't replace that particular shot, we just blocked part of it with a soft black matte and the viewer thinks it's just a post in the middle of the room.

"No picture has given us so much anguish as *Cruising*," Richard Heffner of CARA told the *New York Times* on the release of the film.

Because the theme is so incredibly unpleasant, we knew that people would want us to punish the film. People are angry. They want to be saved from this film. But it's not the job of the ratings system to punish movies for moral or aesthetic reasons. There was only one thing we could have done that was worse than giving the film an R rating. That was to give it an X to save our necks. We'd have been heroes. Homosexuals would have loved us. But we wouldn't have been correct.

After seeing the final cut, the MPAA and CARA members thought that parents should not be prohibited from taking their children to the film if they wanted to, and rated it R. Well, not everyone agreed, and General Cinema Theatres, who had committed to show *Cruising* even before seeing the film—this practice is called "blind bidding"—refused to show the picture. After *Cruising*, blind bidding was outlawed in some twenty-three states. The chain cancelled the bookings and issued a statement: "General Cinema Corporation policy is to refuse to play X-rated pictures or pictures which in our judgment should be rated X." General Cinema was shown the film a second time, but the management stood by its decision even though United Artists, the distributor of the film, threatened to sue. All across the U.S., other theater chains "regretted" they had to show the film; some issued ads in their local newspapers, apologizing to their patrons for *Cruising*. A source at the Pacific Theatres chain said, "We're not thrilled with the picture, but we're not in a position to be censors for the public." On the other hand, the filmmakers received the support from Alan Friedberg, president of Boston's Sack Theatres and head of the National Association of Theatre Owners (NATO), who took a full page ad in the *New York Times*, reproducing a telegram addressed to producer Jerry Weintraub. In his statement, Friedberg said that although the film was extremely violent and graphic, it was also powerful, compelling, and well-directed, that it should not be banned for its R rating or by the gay community. Although Friedberg later admitted that Lorimar, the producing company of *Cruising*, had paid for the ad, he stated that he had written the actual copy.

In Bud Smith's words:

One day, I was in the San Fernando Valley and walked by a theater that was playing *Cruising*; they had a big sign

saying "This film should be rated X" and that that particular theater was treating it as an X. At the time, there
wasn't that much publicity about any gay rights or any
gay activists or even the heavy leather, the S&M stuff. So
I would imagine that theater owners across the country
would see the film and say, "I don't want to show it to
my audience." That's censorship. That's definitely censorship. That's like taking books out of a library because
you don't like what they say. I think Billy is an artist. No
one is forcing you to see the film. For Friedkin, *Cruising*
was in the same category as *The French Connection*.

Cruising received an R rating from CARA on January 4,
1980, and the movie was released on February 15. Two weeks
later, on March 3, Richard Heffner of CARA and Albert Van
Schmus, administrative director of the ratings administration,
demanded further cutting. Friedkin and Weintraub agreed.
Until then, the two had been reluctant to comment on the
film's rating controversy "because we both feel that as imper-
fect as the rating system may be, it is more desirable than
local or federal censorship. Because we have been supporters
of the MPAA Code, we attempted to defuse the controversy
and ease the pressure on the MPAA."
However, the MPAA, by a series of innuendos, was basically saying that Friedkin and Weintraub had agreed to make
certain changes in order to get their initial R rating but then
did not make these changes. The filmmakers denied such
accusations, although, as it turned out, *Cruising* had to be
rated twice. Friedkin maintained he never received a reversal
certificate of the original rating. "As far as I know, it's [the
new rating] a reaffirmation of the original R." After reading all
the press that was written on the subject at the time, one
wonders if the fuss and confusion that went on was justified
and necessary. Journalist Dale Pollock wrote at length in the
Los Angeles Times about the battle over the rating of *Cruising*
and even went to see the film with a stopwatch to find out if
the controversial shots had indeed been shortened. His conclusion was that they were not. The filmmakers said that they
were. "The changes we agreed to, we made," Friedkin finally

declared. "Had they requested the additional cuts before the certificate of rating was issued, I would have made them too." What ultimately matters in the end is that the *Cruising* we can still see on video is the film that Friedkin wanted.

This from Bud Smith:

There was a line from Roy Scheider in *Sorcerer* saying "I'm going to take you and this fucking truck right into the ditch." [*Sorcerer*, the 1977 remake of the French 1953 classic *Le Salaire de la Peur*, starred Scheider as the leader of an international group of outlaws whose mission is to bring explosives from deep in the South American jungle to neutralize the fire at an oil derrick.] The MPAA objected to the word "fucking," and I know damn well that we put a sound effect over the word. You never hear the word; it's not audible. Yet, years later, the MPAA claimed that line was never changed. Incidentally, we also had problems with CIC, the European distributor of *Sorcerer*. They decided they wanted to recut the film. So they took out the three prologues that took place in Israel, France, and the United States and started the film in the jungle. It was just a hodgepodge of a film, and then, just before one of the trucks explodes, the characters started having flashbacks of the prologues, which was just absurd. I was sent to London to see the film in the theaters. I took a tape recorder and taped the screening. I brought it back so that Billy could hear how the progression went. He sued CIC for infringing his vision. Once the film was cut for U.S. distribution, no one could change the picture.

The last film Friedkin and Bud Smith did together to date was *To Live and Die in L.A.* in 1985. The story is about a Secret Service agent (William Petersen) who goes after a ruthless counterfeiter (Willem Dafoe). It was based on a novel by Gerald Petievich, a former Secret Service agent, who also cowrote the screenplay with Friedkin. Once again, Friedkin had done a film that was not acceptable for an R rating in the eyes of the MPAA. He also had problems with real-life Secret Service agents. *To Live and Die in L.A.* was the second time in his career that William Friedkin was sneak-previewing one of his films to a test audience.

Bud Smith remembered:

We had only previewed *The Brink's Job* in 1978 [the film was about the infamous 1950 Boston armored-car heist] and had made the mistake of taking out fifteen minutes of the film. There was never any time for sneak previews on *The Exorcist* and *Cruising*. We previewed *To Live and Die in L.A.* twice. We recut a scene with Willem Dafoe and Debra Feuer, who played his girlfriend. It was a driving scene and on their way to their house, there was some dialogue which ended with Willem saying, "When we get home, I want you to give me a blow job," something like that. It was real funny, I thought, the way it was presented. Well, the test audience was shocked and wanted that out. I was actually going from Denver to Chicago, where we were conducting two different previews. Billy didn't go; he doesn't believe in previews. So, Alan Ladd, Jr., [who was then the head of MGM, the film's distributor] wanted that scene to be cut out before I got to Chicago. I told him I wasn't going to cut out anything unless Billy told me so. Billy finally agreed and said, "Take it out, put it in your suitcase, bring it back, and we'll put it back in!" [Laughs] But we never did because it worked fine without it, and it wasn't what the film was about. In terms of the MPAA, we had to trim down the lingering time we were on Willem Dafoe's body burning up at the end of the film. There was also a problem with a scene between William Petersen and his girlfriend where he actually takes off his clothes and turns to the camera. That one, we just put in a tighter shot, as opposed to a long shot. There was another scene that we took out between Willem Dafoe and his girlfriend. Billy hooked up a video camera in the bedroom and then went away, leaving them on the bed. He just told them, "You guys do whatever you want. We'll just play back whatever we want." So, they really went at it. I mean, they had a full-on sex scene, which was never put into the movie. However, at the very end, Dean Stockwell is watching some tapes on a monitor; we don't see the whole thing, but that's what he was watching. In any case, I don't remember the MPAA being too tough on *To Live and Die in L.A.*

I met William Friedkin when *To Live and Die in L.A.* was released. He had this to say about the MPAA:

The good side of the MPAA is that without it, you would have to face local censorship, meaning that any state could cut your movie to their taste. The audience feels secure with this rating system because it sounds official. In fact, it's totally unconstitutional. The board was invented by a very smart psychiatrist named Dr. Aaron Stern. His interpretation of the code was fair, but his successor is a very narrow and uptight man. For example, he'll give a PG rating to Steven Spielberg's *Indiana Jones and the Temple of Doom* because he is such a powerful director and producer, and despite the fact that you see in the film a heart being pulled out of a man's chest!

Bud Smith recalled:

I shot the inserts on the money being counterfeited. Billy shot the other angles on Willem Dafoe printing the money. I spent two or three days shooting the different steps on how you print dollar bills, and we did it on both sides, which you're not supposed to do. You're supposed to only print on one side and leave the other one blank. We had a huge box of these twenty-dollar bills, and they were used when Willem Dafoe is throwing the money in the fire at the end of the film. That money was in the props department, and some people took some of it as souvenirs. One guy took it home, and his kid took a bill to a store and tried to buy some stuff. It got back to the

Secret Service. They tracked down the guy, who said he worked on *To Live and Die in L.A.* I was questioned as well, and I told them I didn't take any of the money. As far as I knew, I gave it to the props department, and then it went into the flames. If they had seen the film before it came out, they might have tried to stop the release of it. Who knows?

And William Friedkin said:

I had an ex-counterfeiter on the film. He didn't finance the film [laughs]. One day, the Secret Service told me they wanted to screen the movie. Three of them came and questioned twelve members of the crew. Some of them were interviewed six times! Of course, I refused to screen the film for them. The first reason they gave me was that I had pictures in the film of people who had threatened the life of the President. They said, "How would you feel if those people who threatened the life of President Reagan saw the film and their picture, put it together, and therefore found out that we had them under surveillance?" I answered, "I would feel terrible. So show me the pictures of these people, and if they are in my film, I'll just cut the shots." They refused and still wanted to screen the film. So I suggested they get a court order from the U.S. Attorney. He declined on it because we live in a First Amendment country. They still came back but this time with another reason: They said that the film was a training for counterfeiting. Even if I show the process of counterfeiting in detail, it would be impossible for anybody to learn from the film because you need special kind of paper, colors. Then I understood that those Secret Service agents had come to destroy my movie. The film is based on a book written by Gerald Petievich. He wrote the script with me, and he was a Secret Service agent, one of the most decorated ones. Those agents were obviously jealous. So I finally told them, "If you're really concerned about it and you're not trying to ruin Gerry out of jealousy and envy, then I'll screen the film for the secretary of the treasury, and if there is anything that is a danger to national security, I'll remove it." They never got back to me. But let me tell you this: If they had succeeded in getting the right to cut my film, I would have fought against them even if it had meant going to jail!

Friedkin's background is in documentaries. He is someone who likes to film things the way they would occur in reality. Unlike Brian De Palma or Paul Verhoeven, Friedkin has a very raw visual style. "When I read *The Exorcist,* I was wiped out by it, but I was afraid I could never get it on film. What turned me around was when Bill Blatty let me in on the fact that this story was based on an actual case. I realized then that the film had to be a totally realistic view of inexplicable events. It had to be absolutely flawless in its presentation of real people against real backgrounds." And Friedkin achieved that much and more in *The Exorcist, Cruising,* and *To Live and Die in L.A.*; it all seems real. Maybe that's why so much controversy surrounded these movies. Maybe the real question in the case of Friedkin's films is not "should they be cut down or not, rated R or X?" but "Are we ready for the truth?" Should movies reflect reality or show a distorted, almost glorified vision of it? Until William Friedkin does another *Exorcist,* another *Cruising,* the question will remain unanswered.

PAUL VERHOEVEN'S *BASIC INSTINCT*

asic Instinct was the most awaited and controversial film of 1992. The script was written by one of America's best screenwriters, Joe Eszterhas, a former *Rolling Stone* journalist whose credits include *Flashdance* (1983), *Jagged Edge* (1985), *Betrayed* (1988), *Music Box* (1989), and *Sliver* (1993). MGM, with whom he had a deal, got a first crack at the script; the studio, however, had to turn it down because of uncertainties surrounding the possibilities of the company's buyout. Although the script was sold in less than twenty-four hours, it became the center of a bidding war between Mario Kassar of Carolco and Andy Vajna of Cinergi. Kassar and Vajna were partners until late 1989, when Vajna sold his stake in Carolco to his partner for $106 million to launch his own company. Finally, *Basic Instinct* went to Carolco in June 1990 for $3 million, the highest price paid to that time for a screenplay. Carolco then hired *Betrayed* and *Music Box* producer Irwin Winkler and put him in charge of *Basic Instinct*. On July 19, 1990, Paul Verhoeven was hired to direct. The Dutch director, whose best known films in his homeland were *Turkish Delight* (1973), *Soldier of Orange* (1977), *Spetters* (1980), and *The Fourth Man* (1983), moved to America for *Flesh + Blood* (1985). In 1987, he directed the acclaimed sci-fi action picture *Robocop* and, in

1990, Schwarzenegger's *Total Recall*, for Carolco and Tri-Star Pictures. Verhoeven received an estimated $5 million to direct *Basic Instinct*.

Although the script was submitted to Mel Gibson, Kevin Costner, and Richard Gere, to name a few, the leading role in *Basic Instinct* went to Michael Douglas, who received about $10 million to star with guarantees that brought his fee to $15 million. At that point, Paul Verhoeven, Michael Douglas, Irwin Winkler, and Joe Eszterhas got together to discuss the script; that first meeting was a total disaster. Verhoeven wanted a lesbian sex scene to be added to the story. His argument centered around the fact that the script, which featured bisexual women and lesbians, only had heterosexual sex scenes. Both Winkler and Eszterhas decided to walk off the project, and Paul Verhoeven hired screenwriter Gary Goldman, who had cowritten *Total Recall*, to rework *Basic Instinct*. Winkler was replaced as producer by Alan Marshall. After doing five new drafts, Verhoeven realized that he was back to the original script. Basically, only about a dozen lines had been changed, and a few visual elements had been altered. Eszterhas was satisfied and returned to the project. Goldman never received credit for his—ultimately very small—contribution.

Michele Pfeiffer, Melanie Griffith, Julia Roberts, and Mariel Hemingway were some of the actresses considered for the part of the cold, calculating, beautiful, and insatiable Catherine Tramell. Sharon Stone, who had costarred in Verhoeven's *Total Recall*, got the role, and with a cast in place, the production moved on location to San Francisco.

The story of *Basic Instinct* begins with the brutal murder of Johnny Boz, a retired rock star, by a blond woman. Two clues are left on the scene of the crime: a bloody ice pick and a white silk scarf. Det. Nick Curran (Michael Douglas) is on the case, and his investigation leads him to Johnny's girlfriend Catherine Tramell (Sharon Stone), a novelist whose latest mystery book strangely parallels the brutal end of her boyfriend. Catherine, it turns out, is filled with surprises, and Nick finds out that she is involved with Roxy (Leilani Sarelle), a provocative young woman. But Nick is no angel himself; his killing two tourists (before the story started) earned him the nickname "shooter". . . . Was it an accident? Was he on drugs? Beth Garner (Jeanne Tripplehorn), a police psychologist and Nick's former girlfriend, has all the answers. Although he knows Catherine could be dangerous, Nick is fascinated with her. In a sense, he's finally met his match. Jealous, Roxy kills herself in a car crash while attempting to get rid of Nick. Death surrounds Nick; he is even suspected of having murdered Nilsen, one of his colleagues. Nick continues his investigation and discovers that Catherine and Beth had gone to college together and were romantically involved. By then, Gus (George Dzundza), Nick's partner, tells him that he's made contact with one of Catherine's former roommates and that he's on his way to meet her. Nick suddenly realizes that Gus is falling into a trap, but he arrives too late. Gus has been stabbed with an ice pick. Beth shows up. Nick is convinced that she's responsible for all the killings and confronts her. She reaches into her pocket, and Nick shoots her, thinking she was reaching for a weapon—it was, in fact, a set of keys. The case is closed. Beth was obsessed with Catherine and was responsible for the crimes. Nick comes home and finds Catherine. He makes love to her, unaware that an ice pick is hidden underneath the bed and that Catherine manipulated him into believing she was innocent.

The homosexual community was outraged by *Basic Instinct*. According to gay activists, the story portrayed bisexual women and lesbians as psychotic killers. Screenwriter Joe Eszterhas declared at the time, "I'm a bit hurt by all this. The script has gays and straight villains. I've written three movies specifically about intolerance and injustice done to a minority group. I don't want to be part of anything that lends itself to gay-bashing. Minority groups of any kind have to accept the possibility that among them is a sociopath." Paul Verhoeven agreed with Eszterhas, saying, "What you don't want to say is yes or no to homosexuality in the story. It's just a part of life. I think it's wrong that anytime gay or bisexual characters are introduced, their sexuality has to be an issue."

The producing team felt that the film was not about lesbian killers but simply about homicidal impulses. However, the gay community wanted to be heard, and on April 10, 1991, the film crew was met by members of the Queer Nation affinity group, demonstrating outside a popular country-western gay bar called Rawhide II, against the fact that the film was antilesbian and that the owner of the bar was participating. Gay activitist Judy Helfand declared, "It's not like there are a whole lot of films in the world that portray lesbians and bi-women realistically. They have to be pandering to how men already fear lesbians. That's the main issue. But it certainly hurts that it's a gay bar that's allowing to film it." Ray Chalker, the bar's owner, told the *San Francisco Focus* that he had received threatening phone calls. "Some of the calls were absolutely vicious. One said, 'we're going to get you, fat boy!' And I'm not even fat!" The police arrived and put up barriers. While the shooting went on, the controversy against the film continued. Richard Jennings of GLAAD (Gay and Lesbian Alliance Against Defamation) said, after reading the script, that the story was extremely homophobic for portraying two lesbian or bisexual characters, one of whom was a psychopathic serial killer with a penchant for murdering men. Hollie Conley, a spokesperson for GLAAD, also felt that the film sent a dangerous message "The film industry bears a grave responsibility for the perpetuation of stereotypes and the dramatic increase in homophobic violence over the last few years," Conley said. "For most Americans living in places where lesbians and gays are terrorized into secrecy, movies represent their only source of information about our community, and films tell them repeatedly that we are criminals and caricatures, and that bigotry against us is perfectly acceptable."

All of these points were valid, but still, did they really apply to *Basic Instinct*? Paul Verhoeven and Carolco continued to deny that their film was homophobic. "*Basic Instinct* is a psychological thriller about a police detective investigating a series of brutal, baffling murders," Paul Verhoeven and his producer Alan Marshall declared. "It is not a negative depiction of lesbians and bisexuals." Art Agnos, the mayor of San Francisco who was then up for reelection, issued a statement saying that he was in agreement with the protesters. But he also added that his city would not be in the position of censoring a movie script. Jonathan Katz of the Queer Nation group led most of the protests and said, "Not unless the script is completely rewritten and the premise changed, will we stop the demonstrations." Disruptions went on. The sets were splattered with paint; protesters would chant: "Michael Douglas, fuck you, racist, antigay. Alan Marshall, fuck you, racist, sexist, antigay" and "Hey, hey, ho, ho, homophobia has to go," etc. Gay activists waved American flags, signaling motorists to honk their horns if they loved the local 49ers football team or if they supported the U.S. troops in Kuwait. . . . Their trick to create noise worked each time.

Finally, Carolco went to court seeking a restraining order against Queer Nation and other gay activist groups. San Francisco Superior Court Judge John Dearman granted an injunction; Carolco attorneys wanted the protesters to be kept two hundred yards away from the location where the film was being shot. The judge ruled they may be within one hundred yards but could not use flashlights to disturb the set or be loud. On April 24, Joe Eszterhas, Paul Verhoeven, and Alan Marshall agreed to meet with representatives of GLAAD, Queer Nation, ACT UP, Community United Against Violence, and San Francisco Supervisor Harry Britt at the Hyatt Hotel. The meeting went on for two hours. The gay activists made it clear then that unless the filmmakers were willing to make substantial changes, including changes of gender and sexual orientation of characters, the community would not allow the film to be made in San Francisco. More specifically, they wanted Michael Douglas's character to be transformed into a lesbian and even mentioned Kathleen Turner for the part. They suggested that Catherine Tramell and Roxy should both murder women as well as men in order to make sure that these two characters, one bisexual and the other a lesbian, would not be perceived as men-haters. They asked that the scene during which Nick forces himself on Beth be eliminated from the film.

Paul Verhoeven was flabbergasted, while Joe Eszterhas told the activists that he understood their requests. The activists also asked that there be a disclaimer at the beginning of the movie, saying that it did not represent the gay community. Verhoeven said he would make no further comments on the situation until he saw the proposed changes. Five days after the meeting, Joe Eszterhas delivered his changes, which mainly involved the character played by Michael Douglas. Now, when Nick and his partner Gus were discussing Catherine as a potential suspect, Gus asked if she was gay. Nick replied, "A lot of the best people I've met in this town are gay." In the original script, Nick practically rapes Beth, his former girlfriend. Eszterhas suggested that the scene be softened. Another change included the recasting of one character, and the writer added a disclaimer to be featured before the opening credits of the film: "The movie you're about to see is fiction. Its gay and bisexual characters are fictional and not based on reality." Michael Douglas commented: "Sure we'll run that—I mean, why didn't we have a disclaimer before *Wall Street* that said 'This doesn't mean that every Wall Street banker is a crook'? Or before *Fatal Attraction*—'This doesn't mean that every single woman is a psycho'?" Paul Verhoeven, Michael Douglas, and Alan Marshall felt that Eszterhas's changes undermined the strength of the original material, weakened the characters, and lessened the integrity of the picture itself. The screenwriter, on the other hand, thought that his changes would have made *Basic Instinct* a better film from a dramatic point of view and a better movie from a socially responsible point of view. On April 30, 1991, all the proposed changes were rejected. "I consider his changes patronizing drivel," declared Peter Hoffman, president and CEO of Carolco. "Joe Eszterhas is a sniveling hypocrite, and I have no use for him. Besides, we would never change a script in response to political pressure." The proposed changes were not released to the activists and did not reach them until three days later. Finally, the protesters went back to the streets. The production was met by sixty demonstrators and members of Queer Nation and GLAAD in a downtown alley. They made so much noise that the shooting had to stop. They were also violating the court order. Backed by the San Francisco police department, producer Alan Marshall made citizen's arrests of thirty-one   demonstrators. The activists were cited and released.

In response to the demonstrations, Carolco chairman Mario Kassar, chief executive Peter Hoffman and Tri-Star chairman Mike Medavoy issued this statement: "Censorship by street action will not be tolerated. While these groups have a right to express their opinions, they have no right to threaten First Amendment guarantees of freedom of speech and expression. The filmmakers are men and women of integrity and artistic vision, and we support their work unequivocally. They are dedicated to the rights of all people and to a life free of persecution, harassment, and discrimination. We ask we be accorded the same privilege."

Joe Eszterhas declared that he was sorry to hear about the arrests: "I've always believed in trying to communicate with people, not arresting them. I wish there was more of an effort here to communicate." The screenwriter continued to suggest changes, but Paul Verhoeven refused to give in. Eszterhas claimed that the reason he suggested the changes was to help better the lives of gay people, not hurt them. "Paul Verhoeven is an explosive and dazzling director. I bear him no animosity. I just don't think he understands the societal impact of the script. I frankly didn't understand these things either before the meeting last week." One *Basic Instinct* crew member referred to the screenwriter as a PR genius trying to score a coup by coming out the sensitive guy and making the others the heavies. "He knows damn well his changes are impossible," this anonymous source revealed. "It would cost a fortune to reshoot."

At last, on May 9, shooting in San Francisco was resumed. Although the production was now filming indoors at Warner Hollywood Studios, gay activists continued to communicate to the filmmakers, Carolco, and Tri-Star their anger toward the movie until it was finally released. Gay activists claimed they weren't asking people to boycott the film or trying to censor it; all they wanted was to educate people. Before the movie came out, Tri-Star issued a statement: "We feel this is a terrific film, and we expect that most people will agree with us. Freedom of expression covers filmmakers and moviegoers as well as protesters. Certain groups have initiated plans to reveal the ending of the movie in an effort to destroy the first weekend's box office. Who did it? *Basic Instinct* is a terrific thriller and is not so easy to dismiss in a simple sentence." Joe Eszterhas published an article in the *San Francisco Examiner* to support gay rights and reiterated that the film was not homophobic. He cautioned protesters not to violate moviegoers' civil rights or engage in artistic terrorism by disrupting the showing of the film. After he saw the film, the screenwriter declared, "The picture I saw was 99 percent mine. I'm happy he [Paul Verhoeven] had the wisdom to turn down my changes." Protests against the film after it came out were modest, and *Basic Instinct* became an instant box-office hit. The last word on the issue of *Basic Instinct* and the gay community could go to Judy Sisneros of Queer Nation: "The success of the movie wasn't unexpected. All this publicity about the movie's rating and the queer community's issues helped to generate interest. But that was a trade-off we had to accept in order to make a point."

The first cut of *Basic Instinct* was ready by the end of January 1992, and it was sent to the MPAA to receive a rating. Jack Valenti declared it was one of the most powerful films he had ever seen. However, one person close to the board declared that the love scene in the film between Michael Douglas and Sharon Stone was "very graphic, very explicit, and beyond boundaries," and the rating board decided to give *Basic Instinct* an NC-17—meaning the film could be a financial disaster because the rating would severely restrict the number of theaters. Michael Douglas and Paul Verhoeven strongly argued in favor of retaining all the scenes of sex and violence, feeling essentially that the publicity surrounding the movie would attract audiences anyway. A Tri-Star executive said, "The MPAA is requesting things from the filmmaker that he has to decide whether to go along with or not. The changes are not substantive, and Mr. Verhoeven has a contractual obligation to create a film that carries, at the limit, the common R rating." After being submitted seven times, *Basic Instinct* finally received an R in February for strong violence and sensuality and for drug use and language. Four major scenes were cut down: the opening sequence (the murder of Johnny Boz); the so-called date-rape scene between Michael Douglas and Jeanne Tripplehorn; the sex scene between Douglas and Sharon Stone; and finally, the murder of George Dzundza, who played Gus.

Opening scene/Johnny Boz's murder:

In the uncut version, the camera pans down from a mirror placed on the ceiling above the bed, reflecting the image of a couple making love, to a woman on top of a man. In the U.S. version, the shot of the woman going up and down on the man is slightly shorter. The other changes involve the actual murder: In the uncut version, the scene is orchestrated as follows:

SHOT #1:   The woman raises her right arm holding an ice pick.

SHOT #2:   The woman stabs the man in the neck.

SHOT #3:   Medium shot of the woman stabbing the man.

SHOT #4:   The woman stabs the man in his left eye. The ice pick comes through his nose.

SHOT #5:   Medium shot of the woman stabbing the man; blood spurts on her breast.

SHOT #6:   Close-up of the woman's right arm as it goes up and down in the air.

SHOT #7:   Medium shot of the woman on top of the man, stabbing him repeatedly.

SHOT #8:   Long shot of the woman stabbing the man; there's blood all over his body.

The film you saw in the theater worked this way:

SHOT #1:   The woman raises her right arm holding an ice pick.

SHOT #2:   The woman stabs the man in the neck. (After this shot, we never see the man again.)

SHOT #3:   Head-and-shoulder shot of the woman stabbing the man.

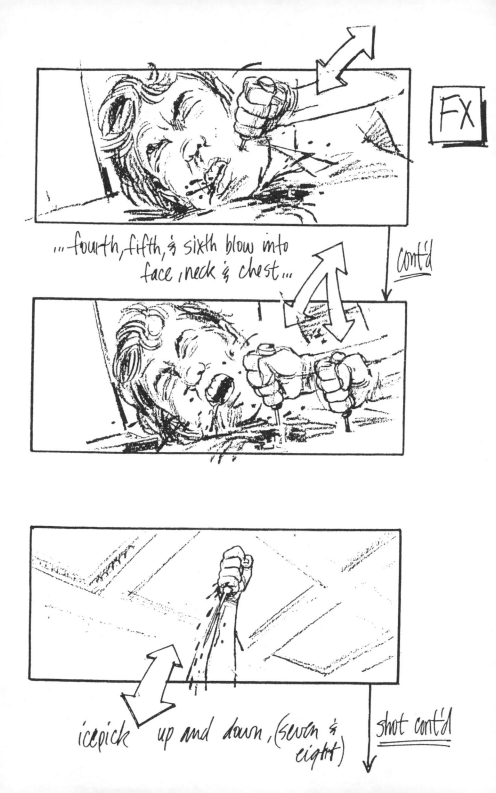

FX

...fourth, fifth, & sixth blow into
face, neck & chest...

cont'd

icepick up and down, (seven &
eight)

shot cont'd

SHOT #4:   Medium shot of the woman stabbing the man; blood spurts on her breast.

SHOT #5:   Close-up of the woman's right arm as it goes up and down in the air.

As to the date-rape sequence between Michael Douglas and Jeanne Tripplehorn:

In the film, Beth has been Nick's psychiatrist and is his former girlfriend. They're still attracted to one another. In this scene, Nick just had an unpleasant altercation with one of his colleagues. He goes home with Beth and. . . .

In the uncut version, Nick rips Beth's clothes. They start kissing and making love against the wall. He is facing her. They move violently against the wall. Nick is behind Beth. He then pushes her toward the edge of the couch. He forces her to bend over, rips her underwear. Long shot: Nick pulls down his pants and enters Beth from behind. Medium shot: Nick has an orgasm and then caresses Beth's face.

In the film that was released in the theaters, after Nick forced Beth over the edge of the couch and ripped her underwear, we immediately cut to him caressing her face.

After Nick seduced (or was seduced) by Catherine at a disco, they go back to her place, and we find them in bed:

At the beginning of the love scene, she is on the bed and he is lying on top of her. They kiss and he goes down on her, kisses her legs, and plunges between her legs. This scene is shot from three different angles: long shot from the side of the bed, a shot of Catherine from Nick's point of view, and a closer shot of him between her legs. In the theatrical version, the shots of Nick burying his face between Catherine's legs are gone. He then gets back on top of her. In the uncut version, the body movements are much longer, more explicit, and there's a shot of Catherine's head moving up and down toward Nick's, and another angle from behind the bars of the bed with the two of them moving frenetically. This is all gone in the U.S. version. Finally, in the third part of the love scene, Catherine attaches Nick to the bed's bars. Paul Verhoeven had to take out a shot from behind the bed's bars of Catherine beginning to move on top of Nick. He also had to trim her sensual moves and a long shot of her seen from the back.

Gus, Nick's partner, meets with a tragic end as he is stabbed to death with an ice pick in an elevator:

In the uncut version, we have two close shots of Gus being repeatedly stabbed, as well as a shot of the killer stabbing toward the camera with blood and pieces of flesh gushing out. In the cut version, these shots were replaced by a long shot outside the elevator, showing Gus being stabbed from a distance. Also, in the cut version, Gus disappears out of frame faster than in the uncut version.

Basic Instinct was shown uncut in Europe. This version was ultimately released on laserdisc and videotape, so it is possible to see the film as director Verhoeven had originally intended it. But a year after the film was released in America, *Basic Instinct* went through another transformation when Paul Verhoeven was asked by ABC to edit a network version. The following changes were applied by Verhoeven. The film could still be cut further by the network. This version is unique in the sense that it's basically a director's television cut, and was shown to me with the authorization of Paul Verhoeven and Carolco.

Opening sequence: Johnny Boz is making love to a blond woman. No nudity. All the long shots from the theatrical version in which we could see the woman's naked body have been substituted for close-ups of the woman and Johnny Boz. The scene is, of course, somewhat shorter (about ten seconds are missing), and the couple's bodies don't move as much. Another angle was chosen when the woman ties Johnny to the bedpost; we now have close-ups of the man's hands, and the scene is shown from the woman's point of view. Originally, this segment was shot from behind the bed's bars, giving us a view of the woman's naked body. The murder is even less graphic than it was in the U.S. version; all that remains is basically a medium shot of the woman stabbing Johnny in the neck. We immediately cut to a head-and-shoulder shot of the woman and then to a shot of her right arm going up and down.

Catherine
pulls scarf
extra-tight
- Nick's han[d]
snaps tigh[t]

PAN
w/
Catherine

cont'd

PAN

... as she
ties up oth[er]
hand...

Storyboards by David Lowery

Later, when the police are in the victim's room, the shot showing the nude body of Johnny Boz has been removed.

In the theatrical version of the film, when Nick and Gus pick
up Catherine to take her to the police station, she goes to her
bedroom to change. Nick watches her undressing in the background and putting on new clothes. In the TV version, we see
her naked, her back to us, only briefly. We then cut to a close-
up of Nick watching her as in the original, but when we catch
up with Catherine, she's already dressed. The notorious inter-
rogation scene in which Catherine uncrosses her legs, revealing to the men sitting in front of her that she is not wearing
underwear, has been trimmed quite a bit. There's now no way
of knowing anymore why these men look so intrigued.

Another scene that had to be edited for television is the
date-rape scene between Nick and Beth. All the long shots in
which we saw the actress's breasts exposed have been
replaced by close-ups of the couple kissing. We don't see Nick
ripping off Beth's bra or her underwear. Interestingly enough,
when Nick forces Beth to bend over the edge of the couch,
Verhoeven added a couple of lines, and we now hear Beth
screaming clearly, "Nick, no! Nick, no!" Obviously, in the theatrical version, the visuals conveyed the violence of the act,
but since most of the shots had to be removed, the impact of
the scene is gone. The director decided to add these lines in
order to convey the fact that Beth is not entirely consenting.
We then find Beth and Nick lying on the floor of the living
room. The shots of Beth sitting up and then standing with her
breasts exposed were replaced by close-ups of Michael Doug
las. We still hear her dialogue, but we don't see her half-naked,
arguing with Nick.

At one point, Nick goes to Catherine's house at night and
spies on her as she is undressing. The director trimmed the
long shots so that we barely get to see her body and removed
a closer shot of Catherine totally naked before she walks out of
the room.

The love sequence between Nick and Catherine was recut
in a similar way to the other sex scenes previously described.
All the long shots that revealed any nudity were removed and
replaced by close-ups of the two actors kissing. We still see

Nick holding Catherine's leg to his face and kissing, it but that's it. Also, in the original cut of the film, Catherine digs her fingernails deep into Nick's back, drawing blood. All we see now is Catherine sort of clawing her partner's back and Nick screaming in pain. All the shots that revealed Catherine's naked body when she is on top of him have been substituted for by medium shots showing the actress from the back only.

In the television version, the shot of Nick walking toward the bathroom completely naked is gone; instead, we stay longer on Catherine asleep. When Nick exits the bathroom after confronting Roxy, Catherine's girlfriend, half of the image that revealed Nick's rear end is gone, and we only see Roxy leaving the room.

In the second love sequence between Nick and Catherine, all the long shots revealing her breasts have been switched to close-ups of the couple kissing. There's also less moaning, especially on his part.

Gus's murder was dramatically changed for television. It's about four seconds long, whereas in the uncut version, that scene was at least three times longer. We see the killer from a distance, her back to the camera, striking Gus. (This shot is actually the same one that was used in the U.S. version of the film, only here it's a bit longer). Then comes a quick close-up of the killer's arm going up and down, followed by a repeat of the shot used at the beginning of this scene of Gus being stabbed in the neck.

Finally, the last sequence of the film, which shows Nick and Catherine making love, has been rearranged and pictures the action only in close-ups.

The language was changed in many places:

Theatrical version:	*Television version:*
CATHERINE: I wasn't dating him, I was fucking him.	CATHERINE: I wasn't dating him, I was having sex with him.
CATHERINE: Get the fuck out of here.	CATHERINE: Get the hell out of here.

NICK: The sex is actually pretty shitty. . . .

NICK: The sex is actually pretty shoddy. . . .

NICK: I'm just your average healthy totally fucked-up cop.

NICK: I'm just your average healthy totally screwed-up cop.

NICK: You're shittin' me.

NICK: You're kiddin' me.

NICK: She fucks fighters and rock'n'roll stars.

NICK: She does fighters and rock'n'roll stars.

GUS: Most times I can't tell shit from Shinola.

GUS: Most times I can't tell spit from Shinola.

CATHERINE: Have you ever fucked on cocaine, Nick?

CATHERINE: Have you ever had sex on cocaine, Nick?

NICK: . . . even though you were fucking him.

NICK: . . . even though you were having sex with him.

CATHERINE: Didn't you ever fuck anyone else when you were married, Nick?

CATHERINE: Didn't you ever sleep with anyone else when you were married, Nick?

LT. WALKER: I don't give a shit what else she published.

LT. WALKER: I don't give a damn what else she published.

GUS: Not unless she climbed into the ring and turned into one mean son of a bitch.

GUS: Not unless she climbed into the ring and turned into one mean son of a gun.

BETH: Just fuck off, Marty.

BETH: Just shut up, Marty.

NICK: I'll kick your fuckin' teeth in.

NICK: I'll kick your teeth in.

GUS: I came here to jack off the damn machine.

GUS: I came here to play with the damn machine.

NICK: Who has access to my goddamn files?"

NICK: Who has access to my damn files?

NICK: "Don't you fuckin' lie to me!"

NICK: Don't you dare lie to me!

NILSEN: You fucked yourself, shooter.

NILSEN: You screwed yourself, shooter!

LT. WALKER: Private joke, asshole.

LT. WALKER: Private joke, dum-dum.

LT. WALKER: Forget about it, for Christ's sake.

LT. WALKER: Forget about it, for Pete's sake.

NICK: What the fuck do you want from me, Catherine?

NICK: What the hell do you want from me, Catherine?

GUS: Why is it you've got your head so far up your own ass?

GUS: Why is it you've got head so far up your own butt?

NICK: I think she's the fuck of the century.

NICK: I think she's the bang of the century.

CATHERINE: She's seen me fuck plenty of guys.

CATHERINE: She's seen me with plenty of guys.

GUS: You fucked her, didn't you? Goddamn dumb son of a bitch, you fucked her! Goddamn, you are one dumb son of a bitch!

GUS: You had sex with her, didn't you? You damn dumb son of a buck, you did her, didn't you? Damn you. You are one damn son of a buck.

GUS: Sure I can get laid with damn blue-haired women.

GUS: Sure I can have sex with damn blue-haired women.

GUS: How could you fuck her?

GUS: How could you sleep with her?

GUS: Goddamn tourists.

GUS: Damn tourists.

GUS: That's her pussy talkin'.

GUS: That's her body talkin'.

GUS: Dickhead Nilsen.

GUS: Dorkhead Nilsen.

GUS: How the fuck do I know?

LT. WALKER: You signed your name to this crock of shit?"

LT. WALKER: Don't fuck with me!

LT. WALKER: Fuck you, Nick! Fuck you!

NICK: I don't remember how often I used to jack off, but it was a lot.

NICK: Why don't you two go fuck yourselves?

GUS: She's got that magnum-come-lawdy pussy on her that done fried-up your brain.

BETH: What am I supposed to say? Hey guys, I'm not gay but I did fuck your suspect.

CATHERINE: What do we do now?

NICK: Fuck like minks, raise rugrats.

GUS: How the hell do I know?

LT. WALKER: You signed your name to this piece of trash?

LT. WALKER: Don't mess with me!

LT. WALKER: The hell with you, Nick! The hell with you!

NICK: I don't remember how often I used to masturbate, but it was a lot.

NICK: Why don't you two go shoot yourselves?

GUS: She's got that magnum-come-lawdy body on her that done fried-up your brain.

BETH: What am I supposed to say? Hey guys, I'm not gay but I slept with your suspect.

CATHERINE: What do we do now?

NICK: Mate like minks, raise rugrats.

In this exclusive interview, director Paul Verhoeven exposed his views on censorship, the MPAA, preview audiences, cuts made for television, and how he perceives the controversy that surrounds most of his films.

LAURENT BOUZEREAU: You come from Europe and have directed several films in Holland. Even your early movies were quite explicit, and I was wondering if you ever encountered any form of censorship over there?

PAUL VERHOEVEN: I know that the producer of *Spetters* was a little bit concerned by my explicit images. He tried to influence me to tone it down. I was a partner in the production of *Spetters*; I directed the film, but I was also a producer on it and cowrote the script. So basically, I could outfight the other producer, but it never came to that point. I think he was a bit afraid about the homosexual violence, the homosexual rape, and also because you saw erections in the Dutch version.

LB: That's not in the American version I saw.

PV: No, that was all cut out. You know *Spetters* only came out in France for the first time after the success of *Basic Instinct*. They also released *The Fourth Man* in France a couple of months before *Basic Instinct* came out. It took *Spetters* about eleven years to come out, and I don't think it has anything to do with the fact that the film was not important enough, because they release everything over there in the theaters or directly on video. I think that the movie was not released earlier because, even for France, the directness of that film was too explicit.

LB: What was so explicit about it?

PV: You see an erection when the young boy, who is a bit unclear about his sexuality, follows two guys in the underground tunnel and sees one giving a blow job to the other. You have a close-up of the prick of one of the guys, and you see the other one actually giving the blow job. Later, you see a guy holding his prick and raping another guy. It was really hard, hard sex. I had never seen that in movies with perhaps the exception of a couple of films Pasolini did toward the end of his life. But still, *Spetters* was extremely harsh, and it was a big scandal in Holland. It was beyond what you normally saw in movies. I'm not even sure that the version of *Spetters* that was released in France contains the elements I mentioned. None of the reviews I've read said anything, so I'm not sure it's shown the way it was. It might have only been shown that way in Holland, where it was tolerated. Of course, it was on the edge of what people could accept, and there was an outrage over there about the movie.

LB: From whom?

PV: From people who said it was antihomosexuals, antiwomen, anti-invalids, that it was a fascist movie. In the film, an invalid kills himself, and people said it promoted the fact that invalids should commit suicide. There was a big committee created in Holland when the film was released called National Anti-*Spetters* Committee. The movie was received as being amoral and dirty and terrible. . .for months all the press on the film was 300 percent negative. I mean, there was no positive article about the movie. They all said the filmmakers were imbeciles and that no one should be allowed to do something like *Spetters.* After three months, there was an article in a film magazine that was sort of positive.

LB: What was the rating on the film in Holland?

PV: No one under sixteen admitted.

LB: When you shot the film, did you find it offensive?

PV: Oh yeah. Absolutely.

LB: Did you think you were being antigay, antiwomen, anti-invalids?

PV: No. But I thought it was extremely provocative. In fact, about two years ago there was an article in a film magazine readdressing the issues of *Spetters,* and now, after twelve years, people have a different opinion, and it's seen as an interesting portrayal of the eighties . . . but it took twelve years. Back when the film came out, people attacked it on the wrong issues, but if someone had asked me then if I wanted the movie to be provocative, I would have said yes. I wanted to go beyond what was normal, what you would normally see on the screen. I wanted to show things that are true and real but that are normally omitted. I wanted to say if it's true, then I'll shoot it, and I'll shoot it the way it's done. I'm not going to be elliptic or shoot it in a way you don't see it, in the dark or in the shadows, I'll shoot it straight. This is how people give a blow job, and this is how they rape, this is how they masturbate, this is how you jerk off somebody, and you see it all. That's just the reality of life. I wanted it to be provocative. My attitude was you think I'm not going to do it? Okay, then I'll do it.

LB: You're very much like Hitchcock. Studios always tried to stop him from being too explicit or too graphic, but he always found a way around it.

PV: Absolutely. I like to do that.

LB: Do you feel that, as an artist, you always have to go a step further?

PV: Yes, as an artist or as a person. You know, it's something I like to do. I like always to push the edges in every direction, in a moral way, in a sexual way, in a way of action and violence. I always feel that it's never enough. I always feel can we do more, can we be closer to reality. Because if you see someone who is wounded or loses an arm in battle, for instance, and what it does to somebody, well, that's never been portrayed on the screen; it has not, not even nearly. I mean, if you portrayed this as a reality of life, it would be intolerable probably. If you would shoot the act of sex in what is usually done only, in pornographic ways, which is, of course, without any dimension, but if you could use the ultimate power of reality in an artistic way, I would try to do that. If it's not in a context, if it's just for the sake of it, then I think it's useless, but it would always be my ambition to use the depth of reality, the scope of reality, as much as possible and still try to integrate it in what I would call a vision. . .that's the ultimate goal. Of course, alot of people immediately stop at a certain scope of reality. They say a lovemaking scene is softly lit, backlit mostly, moving bodies and fade-overs, dissolves. Basically, you never really see people fuck, but that's how these scenes are normally done in American movies.

They never really go for how these people really move.
I see love scenes basically like choreographed action
scenes. It's like *Scaramouche* [filmed in 1923 and remade
in 1952], for example, in which the sword fight is six
minutes long and everything is as precise as possible.
All the shots are really balanced. It was storyboarded
probably. I think a love scene should be done that way.

LB: So, you storyboard your love scenes?

PV: Yes I do.

LB: I must admit that the lovemaking sequences in
Basic Instinct are extremely well choreographed. You
create an interesting rhythm, and those scenes have very
interesting dynamics, not only in the way you shot the
scenes but also in the way you had the actors move.

PV: It's all extremely stylized, of course, and heavily
storyboarded and extremely precisely edited. It's kind of
a funny analogy, but if you look at the horse race in *Ben-
Hur*, it's done the same way. But in American movies,
lovemaking sequences are not scenes; they are what we
call a montage.

LB: Why do you think that is? Do you think American
directors are too self-conscious about what can happen
with the MPAA?

PV: No, I don't think so because even screenwriters
don't really write sex scenes. Joe Eszterhas at least gave
the different things that are happening, but what you
normally get is "They make passionate love" and that's it.
What you get is biology. It's seldom that sex scenes are
used in a nonbiological way [in American films.] We
should not intrude, we should not analyze, we should not
be precise, we should be distanced, we should be
revering, we should be. . . .

LB: Hypocrites?

PV: Well, not exactly. But it's almost like love scenes
are on the divine level and you should not be intruding
too much. It's like it's too personal. It's like a fear of
analyzing, a fear of destroying, a fear of even being

explicit about it. It's always shot in a way that you don't have to talk to the actors. That's my feeling.

LB: It's amazing how in Europe in commercials, for instance, you have male frontal nudity, and here it seems to be taboo. I was wondering if frontal nudity was an issue with Michael Douglas in *Basic Instinct*, since we only see him naked from the back? Did you want to show him completely naked?

PV: Well, he didn't want to. It was in his contract. But I don't think male frontal nudity would be a problem with the MPAA. But yes, *Spetters* would be intolerable because erections would not be acceptable. On the other hand, male frontal nudity without erection would be acceptable. If you wanted to go beyond that, you would get an NC-17. In *Basic Instinct,* there is male frontal nudity when you see the naked body of Johnny Boz on the bed after he's been murdered. It was essential to have that shot, and I asked my producer, Alan Marshall, to call the MPAA to see if we could shoot that scene as I wanted it. And the MPAA's comment was that as long as it's dead meat, it's fine. They didn't phrase it that way, but that's basically the idea. I want to be clear that I don't feel that the MPAA is crazy or something. I have done four movies in America, and I had to deal with the MPAA on all of them. *Flesh + Blood* got an X, *Robocop* got an X, *Total Recall* got an X, and *Basic Instinct* got an X, only now it's called NC-17.

LB: Why were these movies rated X?

PV: *Flesh + Blood* and *Basic Instinct* because of sex and violence, *Robocop* and *Total Recall* because of violence. On *Flesh + Blood* and *Total Recall*, I think I had to go back to the MPAA three or four times, on *Robocop* seven times, and on *Basic Instinct* ten times before they accepted it. Of course, I had protected myself with a lot of other shots. All the sex scenes in *Basic Instinct* were shot from a lot of different angles. We realized during the shooting that some of the angles, especially the one when Michael is between Sharon's legs and licking her vagina, would not be acceptable. Even when we looked at it in the replay because we were shooting simultaneously with video, we were all really laughing. . . .We knew we would never get away with that. But we went as far as we could, although each time I felt there could be a problem with the MPAA, I shot further away, from another angle, with a different light or whatever, so I had a lot of different possibilities. And so the MPAA could not force me to cut things out. I always offered them another solution that was less explicit without changing the scene. So if you compare the NC-17 to the R-rated version in terms of running time, they're not very different, but their intensity is different. The impact in the NC-17 version is much harsher, more powerful. You can really feel the difference in the so-called date-rape scene with Jeanne Tripplehorn. The original version of that sequence was much harsher, it was. . .WOW! He's really doing something to that girl. In the American version, it's kind of indicated, but then it's over. In the European version, it really hits it several times, WOW, WOW, WOW! Of course, in both versions I used different shots, but ultimately I had to take out about twenty seconds.

LB: In the European version, it's more obvious that she's consenting. . . . I noticed you said "the so-called date-rape scene." Do you not agree? What would you call it?

PV: I could call it that way too. It's not only that you know. A date rape would really be that she is raped and that at no moment is there any consent. I think this scene floats between consent and being angry or half angry. There is consent and there are moments when you feel it's going too far, and then she consents anyhow for whatever reason. I would certainly morally question the scene from the point of view of the guy who does it. Michael is behaving in a way that I would not behave. He is aggressively imposing himself and finds out that she is accepting it. But, of course, when he does it, he doesn't know this. The fact that she accepts is the second phase; he pushes her in to a situation that ultimately I don't know if she enjoys it, but she seems to accept it to a certain degree. But when he does it, there are clearly moments and seconds when you feel that she might not and he is pushing anyhow. So I would say that he is going into an unknown territory where he should be aware of her hesitations. I could never do that to a woman.

LB: I felt though that she was trying to seduce him by inviting him over to her apartment in the first place.

PV: I'm sure she wants to fuck him. There is no doubt that when she invites him she wants to fuck. Of course she wants to fuck, because she wants him back, you know. The question is that the way she fucks is not exactly the way that she imagined she would be fucked. She says that later. At several points in the scene, you definitely feel that there is a mutual understanding between the two of them that this isn't big fun. That's what I wanted, and his aggression has to do with the fact that he doesn't want to fuck her, he wants to fuck Sharon Stone. The sex with her would probably be on that level, and he is already imagining or playing out the fantasy on how it would be with that other woman. That's what this scene is about. From a moral point of view, the character played by Michael Douglas is to be accused, and I wanted him that way.

LB: I think that of all the scenes that you had to rearrange for the R-rated version, the opening sequence with the murder of Johnny Boz is the one that lost most of its initial impact.

PV: The murder in the European version is, I think, eight seconds. It's about seven seconds in the U.S. version. So time-wise, it's practically the same scene, but the impact of it is gone. The close-up of the ice pick going through his nose and the full body shot where you see the blood and her stabbing on top of him have all been taken out. The shock of the scene in the European version is. . .you're really like blown away. It's what I wanted. It's strange because it's so short. It's not twenty seconds, it's eight seconds! I mean, it's probably shorter than the shower sequence in *Psycho,* but it's so powerful. I wanted it to be that shocking because for a very long time after that scene, nothing really happens. And later, when we have a bed scene again and you see her, you should know that this might happen again and that it's horrible.

LB: What about Gus's murder in the elevator?

PV: If you compare the two versions, there is a difference. In the American version, there is a long shot from the back of the woman while she is stabbing. In the original version, it's a close-up, and you see the weapon going in and in and in, and we pumped all the blood out. It's like. . .ARRGHH! The cut is less important there. It's softer in the American version, but I think losing the impact in the opening scene is more important, because when you see Gus, you know he's going to die. And so it's less unexpected than in the opening love scene. There, it's love and then that complete reversion into death. Basically, it's like a black widow. . . . When the male starts to fuck the female, he's very careful. Genetically, he knows that's a dangerous thing, but he cannot resist so he fucks her anyhow. And then, slowly he wants to pull back. He seems to succeed, but at the moment he seems out of reach, she grabs him and sucks him to death, sucks all the blood out of him. That's basically the scene. That's the scene I wanted to make.

LB: I think you totally succeeded in conveying that parallel, at least in the European version.

PV: In the American version, it's a bit neutralized.

LB: I think that's a shame.

PV: Yes, it is.

LB: Is the first cut you showed the MPAA exactly the European version?

PV: Yes.

LB: What would you call the MPAA?

PV: Warning-system agents or something. It's a warning system basically. It has a certain impact that you could compare to censorship if you want to, but it's not an artistic censorship. If you want to use the term censorship, which I'm hesitant to use, I think you would have to call it more economic censorship. They don't censor your movie. They don't say you cannot release your movie. After showing the MPAA the first cut of *Basic Instinct*, they said this is great, it's a wonderful movie, please don't change it, it's an NC-17. The MPAA really wanted this film out as an NC-17. They wanted to protect children or warn parents, but also they felt that it was a powerful movie, done with artistic integrity, and they wanted a big audience movie to be NC-17 and still be a good movie, and not a work of exploitation. They wanted to legitimize the NC-17. Then, of course, the studio said we cannot release this film with an NC-17, and the MPAA knew that probably too, although they might have hoped that Tri-Star and Carolco might do the same as Universal Pictures that released *Henry and June*. So the studio wanted an R because in a lot of cases, and that's why I call it an economic censorship, theaters won't show NC-17 movies, especially in malls. Theaters in malls cannot play a film that's more than R. That's a contract that the theaters have with shopping centers.

LB: Do you think *Basic Instinct* would have been less successful if it had been released with an NC-17?

PV: Yes. It would have done half the business it did; sixty million [dollars] would be my guess, if that much. The studio thought it would make thirty or forty. I thought sixty or seventy. The studio said that with an NC-17 we would only get five hundred theaters at the maximum, probably four hundred. Ultimately, the R-rated version came out into sixteen or seventeen hundred theaters. We would have had 30 percent of the theaters only. In a certain way, you could expect the movie to recoup the money in a longer time, but then, of course, we were approaching the summer, many other movies and competition. The momentum of the movie would

have been lost after a couple of months, so I agreed with
Mike Medavoy [who was then the head of Tri-Star
Pictures], and, of course, Mario Kassar followed that.
Mike and I are really good friends, and he said, "Listen,
Paul, we'll never make the money with an NC-17, but we
could make $100 million with an R." The movie cost $45
million, you know, so you cannot say fuck you all. That's
not why you're in the industry because it is, of course,
an industry; it is an industry and it is artistic. It's both. If
you say it's only art, as they have for a long time in
Europe, I think you're wrong. If you say it's only an
industry, I think you're wrong too. But I think that you
have at a certain moment to look at both sides, and
especially when you make a movie of $45, $65 million,
you cannot say, well, you know, forget the money, I'm an
artist. It is a strange thing that this medium has two
values, an artistic one and a commercial one. If you want
to be in this business, you have to realize that people,
companies are investing money and are dependent on
the success of a movie in order to survive. I think you kill
the industry and good movies too if you consider film
only as art. If there's no industry, there can't be good
movies, you kill yourself, you kill your own babies, you
kill life. There is a tendancy here in America to see film
too much as economy. In Europe, and the results prove it,
there's only an art approach; film is killed over there
because of this art approach, I believe. We should be
somewhere in the middle. Making ten *Home Alones*, I
think that's cookie-making, but *Home Alone* one is not
cookie-making. *Home Alone 2* is dangerous, and *3* and *4*
and *5* will be cookie-making, unless a genius picks it up
somewhere. Otherwise, it will be cookie-making. If you
make only art movies like in Europe, you're killing what's
essential to this medium. As an artist, you have to be
aware of the economic values, or else you're better off
being a painter or a composer, although a composer
cannot always get as many musicians as he wants to
execute his work. We're always in a situation of an
economic environment. Take the example of Rembrandt

in Holland. In his time, art was something that was paid for by the middle class, by the merchants, and they wanted certain things. They wanted certain portraits, and they wanted the faces of the people who had ordered the portraits to be recognized in the paintings. Some of the problems with *The Nightwatch* when it was finished was that Rembrandt put so many people in the shadows that you couldn't recognize them. These were very important people in town who had ordered this canvas because they wanted to prove how great they were. Even da Vinci was paid by people who wanted to see themselves in paintings. So, you can't isolate art completely from its economic environment.

LB: But when you watch the two versions of *Basic Instinct*, do you feel betrayed in your artistic vision? Do you feel you're watching two different movies?

PV: No, it's not two different movies at all, but I think that the European version is stronger and more what I wanted, is more powerful, has more impact, is a better movie. I think the American version is watered down a little.

LB: How do you feel about the American versions of *Flesh + Blood*, *Robocop,* and *Total Recall*?

PV: Also that they were watered down for the American market.

LB: Were they released uncut outside the U.S.?

PV: No. *Basic Instinct* was the first time that I had the ability and the power or the support from the studio, in this case Carolco, to say okay, guys, let's do two versions, but normally, that's not the case. In *Total Recall*, the changes on violence were not so important to me really.

LB: What did you have to cut out?

PV: The shooting on the escalator, where Arnold [Schwarzenegger] holds a guy as a shield, was more explicit; it had more impact, more blood; it was longer. But I don't think anything essential was hit there. On *Robocop*, I feel that the original cut was better. The original was more violent, and I think that worked better. It was funnier. The scene, for example, when the young executive is killed [by a robot] in the boardroom was much more violent. We did not shoot the inserts until later; we rebuilt a little part of the set, and we did more stuff which was all in the first cut of the film. There were fountains of blood. The robot ED209 went on and on and on. The guy was already dead, but the robot was still shooting, and all that blood was spurting out. It was extremely, absolutely fascinating, I thought. After that, when the robot finally stops, one of the actors says, "Somebody call the paramedics." I have seen that version with a test audience, you know, and people were exploding with laughter after this tension. The whole thing was so interesting, so artistic, I would say. It was ultra violence and then ultra humor. It was like the same switch from the erotic to violence in *Basic Instinct*. Of course, by toning that down, people are still laughing, but they never laugh on the first line, they laugh on the second line when somebody says, "Nobody touches him," which is, of course, nonsense since he's been blown away. The killing of Murphy [Peter Weller] was also cut. This killing was absolutely agonizing the first time. It was unwatchable, I would say. I mean, it wasn't unwatchable, but that's probably how you would feel if you saw it. It was so powerful, it was so mean that I think it had more impact even for the rest of the movie. His death is memorable, and it's still agonizing in the film, but in the original cut, it threw a shadow over the whole movie that never left you. That's probably a cut that I regret, and I am hoping that we'll be able to restore that version one day. I'm really very glad that *Basic Instinct* is available in both drafts and that the American audience can now see the film uncut on video and laserdisc. Doing two versions is certainly something to consider from now on.

LB: What was taken out of *Flesh + Blood*?

PV: There was some violence. For example, at the end

of the film, Rutger Hauer shoots an arrow in the eye of a man. . . .

LB: You have a similar shot in *The Fourth Man*, which incidently was released unrated.

PV: Right. . .but in *Flesh + Blood* you see the arrow going in, and the MPAA found that unacceptable. In the bathtub sequence, Rutger Hauer brings Jennifer Jason Leigh toward him by her nipples. Of course, it was not possible to show this. When I shot this scene, I didn't even think I would have any problem because it was my first American movie. But by coincidence, there was one shot where you couldn't see exactly what he was doing, and you couldn't see how he got her close to him. So that's how I replaced that shot; it probably shortened it a little bit. Then there was a little bit taken out when they start to move and to make love. . . . The MPAA always has problems with sexual movements, not nudity. It's not the nudity that disturbs them, it's the sexual movement and if it's going on for a long time, if there's a lot of what they call grinding. You know, if one is sitting on top of the other and if we have this continuous back and forth.

LB: Is the MPAA very specific in their feedback?

PV: Sometimes they are, sometimes they're not. At the beginning, they didn't want to be very specific on *Basic Instinct*; they just said it's too long and too much.

LB: Do they call you? How does it work?

PV: No, you call them. In this case, the producer or sometimes a representative from the studio calls them and asks for their opinion. They have a spokesperson who gives you indications where the problems are. So in the case of *Basic Instinct,* they said we have problems with the violence in the first act and in the scene of the stabbing. Then we have a problem in the fifth reel, and we have a problem in reel seven, etc. I think they had problems in four or five reels altogether. With the big love scene between Sharon and Michael, they simply said it was too long and too strong. They didn't say that shot or this shot. In fact, we tried to get them to be more specific, but they said, "We won't tell you; we're not going to cut your movie. You cut your movie; you give us something we can accept. All we can tell you is that it's too long and too strong."

LB: How many people are on the board?

PV: I think about nine or ten.

LB: Are they anonymous?

PV: They're anonymous to me, yes. They're probably people who represent what the MPAA feels is the movie-going audience, people who have children, because kids is always the one issue that they bring up. It is supposed to be a system to warn parents about what their kids are going to see; that's the essence of it. To a certain degree, if it's not abused, there's nothing wrong with that. My youngest daughter saw at some point a book that I had called *Movie Monsters*. It has all these terrible photographs of Dracula and all that stuff. She opened that book and saw a photograph of a woman whose skin is kind of deteriorating. That was haunting her for weeks. She couldn't sleep. She was yelling and screaming every night, and ultimately, we could only solve the problem by buying her a pet and putting it next to her bed. The reality of that living being made it possible for her to sleep. So, of course, you do think about your kids. I say, tell the audience "You're going to see a lot of violence, you're going to see a lot of this, a lot of that." The system here is sort of strange because, if a kid is three, you can still take him to an R-rated film. Some R-rated films are real heavy and violent. I think you can do that, but you have to prepare your kids. I show my kids all my movies, always, even when they were nine or ten, but never without explaining to them what they are going to see and warning them and never without my wife and me sitting with them. We watch the films on video, and then we stop and explain how it is done. My wife will say, "It's going to be violent but only because Paul is throwing fake blood on the actors," and then we show them. I think you can show kids anything, but you really have to be aware under what circumstances you do that. I don't think preventing kids from seeing movies is a solution. I read an article recently in which they interviewed people about sex and violence, and somebody was explaining how embarrassing it was when his daughter asked him to explain love scenes from movies, and he didn't know how to respond. He said he shouldn't have to answer that kind of question, and that therefore, these films should not be shown on television. I think that's wrong; you should answer that question. You should tell what sexuality is. You should tell what a prick is and a vagina and how it works, and what homosexuality is. I think you should explain that to children when they're three, because I think a kid can accept everything. But I think that if they're exposed to these things without any warning, it could hurt them. That shock and being hurt can still lead later in life to being a wonderful artist. It can also lead you to seeing a psychiatrist every three days. For me, being exposed to violence when I was young and to very unpleasant things, especially in the war and later, in reading books that I shouldn't have read at that age, was and still is for me a source of inspiration for my work. But I have a way to filter it out because I can do it in my movies.

LB: Was *Basic Instinct* shown to a test audience?

PV: No.

LB: Why?

PV: Because there was no time. We didn't feel that it was necessary. Nobody asked, in fact. Nobody ever talked about it.

LB: What do you think in general of the concept of showing a film to a sneak-preview audience?

PV: I think it's nonsense. I think that you can know very well yourself what the situation is by looking at your movie and, if necessary, by showing it to a couple of friends. I think that for certain movies like comedies, having test screenings might be helpful. Mel Brooks, I know, always previews his movies and sets some microphones and records the laughing. Later, he looks at the movie with the laughter track to see where people laughed or didn't laugh. Sometimes, what he thought was funny doesn't work. Then he can change the joke or take it out. I think that serves a purpose, but for a movie like *Basic Instinct*, it would have been very bad to show it to a preview audience. I'm sure that all the cards would have come back saying the ending was too ambiguous. The studio would have read these cards and said people are confused. And everybody would have insisted to end it in a conventional way, like he kills her, she kills him, or whatever. But nobody would have dared to do what is there now; I think it would have been a disaster to have these cards for *Basic Instinct*. I think that no one at the studio could have read the cards and dared to say, "You know, everyone thinks it's ambiguous, and that's great." I wanted people to feel that ambiguity. With *Total Recall*, we had no time to preview the film either. I only previewed *Robocop*.

LB: Did you change anything based on the audience response?

PV: No, not at all. We only changed the film because of the MPAA. I know that Mike Medavoy found the movie extremely violent, but there wasn't much of a discussion since I had to tone it down anyhow for the MPAA. By the time they agreed, the studio had agreed as well.

LB: What do you think about the way your films were cut or are being cut for network television?

PV: It would be an extremely painful process if you had to do it immediately after the release of the film. In the case of *Total Recall,* for example, it happened four years after the film came out. You sit there and you say, "Okay, they want to make these couple of million bucks by selling the film to the network; how can I do that in the most elegant way." That's basically how I felt when I was doing it.

LB: What about *Robocop*?

PV: The producer Jon Davison supervised this one and showed me the result. I proposed a couple of changes, and they made them in fact. Ultimately, I felt the network version was as good as it could possibly be.

LB: What's happening with *Basic Instinct*?

PV: I worked with editor Penny Shaw on a television cut. [The theatrical release was edited by Frank J. Urioste.] We looked at all the different possibilities, we changed shots all the time. We made a version that, if the network accepts it, will still be kind of okay. We took all the notes from the network and Carolco, and we changed everything that they might dislike. You still have sex and violence, but it's all suggestive, much more abstract.

LB: Is it difficult for you to watch the TV versions of your films?

PV: I can work on them, but I would never watch them. I do it as good as possible because if I don't, someone else will recut my films. I know better solutions, I have the material in my head, I can propose other things, and if I work closely with my editor, I know I get the best and most elegant version that's possible. By doing it myself, I limit the damage. But I detest watching the results.

LB: During the shooting of *Basic Instinct*, you had to deal with the gay community, who tried to have you change the script and tried to stop the shooting. How do you view what happened retrospectively?

PV: I think they were completely wrong, and I always felt so. As you know, Joe Eszterhas switched sides and submitted thirty-seven changes, and I rejected them all. None of the things they said were right. I felt the film was not homophobic at all. I felt that it was just a story, and I felt that their approach was basically wrong. When people saw the movie, they realized that their whole approach was complete nonsense. They were militant, aggressive, and wrong. I think there is nothing wrong with them trying to get a better position for better rights for the gay community, but this was the wrong project. In a democracy, you should raise your voice; that's fine, and then the other people can say yes or no, and then ultimately, you should do what you want. There is nothing wrong with listening in the first place. I listened to them, I sat with them, but I thought they were wrong. But they wouldn't accept that. Fascism is not in raising your voice; the fascism is in not accepting the no.

LB: What changes did they exactly want in the story?

PV: They wanted to change a lot of things. First of all, they didn't want any of the gay characters to be a killer. They said that every killer in the film is a lesbian, which is not true. There's been a lot of talking about all this, but basically I felt that their position was completely wrong from the moment that they didn't accept no for an answer. Until then fine, but after evaluating their opinion, if you feel as an artist that what you're doing is the essence of your movie, and if you feel comfortable with that emotionally, personally, I think that to everybody else I would say fuck you. But there's nothing wrong with going through an interior process to reevaluate things, but after you've done that, it shouldn't be "You said no, so now we're going to punish you." That's clearly against the First Amendment in the first place.

LB: Do you think your film was used as a scapegoat because it was such a big Hollywood movie?

PV: Sure, but they failed. I'm glad they failed because they were wrong.

LB: What would be the ideal rating system for you?

PV: The only thing they should do is restore the X rating. When the NC-17 was announced, the X was abolished. In fact, everybody thought that we had an extra category, one between the R and the X. Nobody realized that NC-17 was not an extra category but exactly the same. What was supposedly a victory for filmmakers and what looked like the creation of a so-called adult category was merely renaming the X. So if you ask me what would be an advantage, I would say bring back the X, keep the NC-17, give *Basic Instinct* an NC-17, and give porno an X. In the meantime, it's not a perfect system, but it is an acceptable system. Taking it away would immediately lead to real censorship. If it would come down to the states, then it would be worse because each state would have different rules. It would be a big mess, and everybody would suffer, especially the filmmakers who are working on the edge. So in the non-perfect world, the rating system that Jack Valenti is defending is the best. Basically, I'm a supporter of the system and not really attacking it. I'm always displeased when my movies get an NC-17 because I feel that I have to make my movie into one that is not as good as the other but that's the world we're living in. I think that any other attempt to change the system would probably make it worse and give us less freedom.

AFTERWORD

As I'm finishing this book, I look back at the past several months, realizing it's been quite a year for movies, especially with Steven Spielberg's *Jurassic Park* becoming the biggest box-office champion of all time. The *Los Angeles Times* asked the question: despite the PG-13 rating, will *Jurassic Park* be dangerous to your child's mental health? Is it too intense? Can your child tell the difference between reality and fantasy? At $800 million worldwide so far, the answer is obviously no. . . .

What happened since this book got started . . .

Despite last-minute reshoots and many test screenings later, *Sliver* starring Sharon Stone was still a flop. And so was Arnold Schwarzenegger's *The Last Action Hero*; the film was rumored to have been tested a second time after a disappointing first test screening, generating a lot of heat over the fate of the film, later denied by Columbia Pictures, its distributor. Hong Kong action director John Woo made his U.S. directorial debut with *Hard Target*, which went through many transformations based on test audience reaction and in order to avoid an NC-17 for violence. Paul Verhoeven is preparing *Showgirls*, based on a script by Joe Eszterhas; the story is about a tap dancer in Las Vegas. The film supposedly has all the ingredients that constitute an NC-17 rating. Adrian Lyne was considering doing a remake of *Lolita*. James Brooks was testing his new film, *I'll Do Anything*, starring Nick Nolte, with and without musical numbers—it was finally released without any song and dance. Buena Vista Pictures had to remove a scene from *The Program,* in which drunken college football players tes their resolve by lying in the middle of a busy road, after the deaths of two men who were apparently trying to imitate the film.

Sex and violence on television is more than ever a controversial topic. How can we control what's shown on the small screen? Should it be controlled and by whom?

Meanwhile, the MPAA celebrated on November 1, 1993, its twenty-fifth anniversary. Since November 1, 1968, according to *The Hollywood Reporter,* the board has rated 11,400 movies, which represents 98 percent of the market. During that period, filmmakers, producers, and/or distributors have asked for appeals 251 times; 108 of the appeals were upheld. In 1968, there were more than forty local censorship boards across the U.S. The last one, in Dallas, closed in September 1993. Richard Heffner, who served as chairman of the MPAA's Classification and Rating Administration Board (CARA) since July 1, 1974, left the position at the end of June 1994 when he decided not to renew his contract. Heffner was replaced by Los Angeles attorney Richard Mosk.

And another thing: with the potential of interactive media entertainment, the possibilities are endless; we, as an audience, might have total control on the degree of violence or sex in a picture and be able to go as far as being able to decide the fate of a character. Is this a new beginning or the end? In Hollywood, it's just business as usual.

(BY CHAPTERS)

CHAPTER 1: CUT IT OUT!

Books:

Agel, Jerome, ed. *The Making of Kubrick's 2001*. Signet, 1970

Bach, Steven. *Final Cut*. William Morrow, 1985.

Biskind, Peter. *The Godfather Companion*. Harper Perennial, 1990.

Bouineau, Jean-Marc. *Le Petit Livre de Stanley Kubrick* SpartOrange, 1991.

Ciment, Michel. *Kubrick*. Calmann-Levy, 1980.

Donahue, Suzanne Mary. *American Film Distribution*. UMI Research Press Studies in Cinema, 1985–87

Leff, Leonard J., and Jerold L. Simmons. *The Dame in the Kimono*. Crovo Weidenfeld, 1990.

Mathews, Jack. *The Battle of Brazil*. Crown, 1987.

McClelland, Doug. *The Unkindest Cuts*. A. S. Barnes & Co., 1972.

Morris, Robert L., and Lawrence Raskin. *Lawrence of Arabia*. Anchor Books/Doubleday, 1992.

Robertson, Patrick. *Guinness Film Facts and Feats*. Edition 1 (French edition), 1980/85.

Schumach, Murray. *The Face on the Cutting Room Floor*. William Morrow, 1964.

Squire, Jason E. *The Movie Business Book*. Simon and Schuster, 1988.

Periodicals:

"Kubrick Trims *2001* by 19 minutes; Adds Titles to Frame Sequences." *Variety*, April 17, 1968.

"Kubrick Subs 30 Seconds of Film and *Clockwork* Sheds X, Gets R." *Daily Variety,* August 25, 1972.

"Kubrick Cuts *Orange* for R Rating." *New York Times*, August 26, 1972.

"Playing the End Game." *Time*, July 30, 1979.

"Shine It On." *Los Angeles Herald Examiner*, May 28, 1980.

"Two Endings for *Apocalypse Now*." *Daily Variety*, August 13, 1979.

Austin, Bruce A. "Movie Audience Research: The Focus Group." *Box Office*, October 1992.

Bailey, James. "*Fatal Attraction* Suicide Version Finds Takers at Japan Screen." *Variety*, November 16, 1988.

Bart, Peter. "This Guy, Not the Director, Often Has Final Cut." *Daily Variety,* May 3, 1993.

Bennett, Ray. "Adrian Lyne's Controversial *9 1/2 Weeks*." *Los Angeles Life Daily News*, March 2, 1986.

Broeske, Pat H. "The Cutting Edge." *Los Angeles Times*, February 16, 1986.

Bull, Peter. "The Ending You Never Saw in *Strangelove*." *New York Times*, January 9, 1966.

Caufield, Deborah. "Spielberg Is Upset." *Los Angeles Times*, May 7, 1982.

Cerone, Daniel. "Why Director Adrian Lyne Went for the Jugular." *Los Angeles Times*, February 18, 1992.

Champlin, Charles. "The Beginning of the End." *Los Angeles Times*, September 6, 1979.

Corliss, Richard. "No, but I Saw the Rough Cut." *Time*, August 18, 1980.

Dempsey, John. "MCA's TV Version of *Dune* Will Not Bear Lynch's Name." *Daily Variety*, May 26, 1988.

Dutka, Elaine. "The Man Who Makes You King." *Los Angeles Times*, July 12, 1992.

Farber, Stephen. "A Major Studio Plans to Test the Rating System." *New York Times*, September 4, 1990.

Fox, David J. "Ads for NC-17 Film Find Acceptance." *Los Angeles Times*, October 5, 1990.

Galbraith, Jane. Sam Peckinpah Meets *The Wild Bunch.*" *Los Angeles Times*, March 14, 1993.

Handel, Leo. "Hollywood Looks at Its Audience: A Report of Film Audience Research." 1950.

Harmetz, Aljean. "Is *Poltergeist* Too Violent for PG Tag?" *New York Times*, June 3, 1982.

————. "Rating of *Indiana Jones* Questioned." *New York Times*, May 21, 1984.

————. "*Fatal Attraction* Director Analyzes the Success of His Movie and Rejoices." *New York Times*, October 5, 1987.

Honeycutt, Kirk. "UA's *Midnight Cowboy* Returns." *Hollywood Reporter*, November 1, 1993.

Jonas, Gerald. "The Man Who Gave an X to Violence." *New York Times*, May 11, 1975.

Knight, Arthur. "A Few Cutting Remarks." *Hollywood Reporter*, June 24, 1977.

Kroll, Jack, with Andrew Murr and Ray Sawhill. "X Marks the Trouble Spot." *Newsweek*, September 17, 1990.

Landro, Laura. "Is It Too Late for Audiences to Ask for a Happier End to *Casablanca*?" *Wall Street Journal*, October 29, 1987.

Lydgate, William A. "Hollywood Listens to the Audience." *Reader's Digest*, April 1944.

McDonagh, Maitland. "In-flight films." *Premiere*, October 1991.

Pond, Steve. "Shot by Shot: *Fatal Attraction.*" *Premiere*, November 1987.

Pristin, Terry. "A Work Definitely in Progress." *Los Angeles Times*, September 19, 1993.

Valenti, Jack. "Valenti Rejects *Jones* Rating Criticism." *Hollywood Reporter*, May 31, 1984.

CHAPTER 2: HITCHCUTS

Books:

Behlmer, Rudy. *Memo From David O. Selznick.* Viking, 1972.

Haver, Ronald. *David O. Selznick's Hollywood.* Bonanza Books, 1980.

Leff, Leonard J. *Hitchcock and Selznick.* Widenfeld & Nicolson, 1977.

Spoto, Donald. *The Dark Side of Genius: The Life of Alfred Hitchcock*. Little, Brown, 1983.

Taylor, John Russell. *Hitch: The Life and Times of Alfred Hitchcock*. Pantheon Books, 1978.

Truffaut, François. *Hitchcock/Truffaut* revised edition, Simon & Schuster, 1983

Periodicals:

Suspicion. Hollywood Reporter, September 18, 1941.

"The New Hitchcock Thriller: *Suspicion.*" *Cue*, November 3, 1945.

Franklin, Richard. "Pistols at Dawn." Unpublished essay.

Grant, Jack D. *Hollywood Reporter*, October 31, 1945.

MacPherson, Virginia. "La Bergman's Back Gets a Workout." *Hollywood Citizen News*, October 11, 1944.

Othman, Frederick C. *PM*, August 27, 1944.

Scheuer, Philip K. "Dali Now Dreams for Movie." *Los Angeles Times*, September 10, 1944.

Twiggar, Beth. "Hitchcock, Master Maker of Mystery." *New York Herald Tribune*, December 7, 1941.

CHAPTER 3: CUTS BECOME YOUR FILMS

Periodicals:

"Death Reshoot." *Variety*, June 22, 1992.

Fox, David J. "*Death Becomes Her* and the Lost Ullman Ending." *Los Angeles Times*, August 9, 1992.

Martin, Kevin H. "Life Everlasting." *Cinefex*, November 1992.

CHAPTER 4: BLADES

BLADE RUNNER:

Periodicals:

Daly, Steve. "For a Few Seconds More." *Entertainment Weekly*, October 2, 1992.

Gader, Neil A. "The Return of *Blade Runner.*" *The Perfect Vision 3*, Winter 1991/92.

Gillogly, Jim. "*Blade Runner: The Director's Cut.*" *Usenet*, September 1991.

Kaas, David H. "The New Official *Blade Runner.*" *The Perfect Vision 5*, Spring 1993.

Kael, Pauline. "Baby, the Rain Must Fall." *New Yorker*, July 12, 1982.

Kilday, Gregg. "The Cutting Edge of Hollywood Gossip." *Los Angeles Herald Examiner*, July 2, 1982.

Knight, David B. "*Blade Runner*—The Director's Cut." *Usenet*, May 9, 1991.

Loud, Lance. "*Blade Runner.*" *Details*, October 1992.

Osborne, Robert. "*Blade Runner* Re-cut Is a Delicate Operation." *Hollywood Reporter*, October 7, 1992.

Salisbury, Mark. "Back to the Future." *Empire* [UK], December 1992.

Sammon, Paul M. "Do Androids Dream of Unicorns? The 7 Faces of *Blade Runner.*" *Video Watchdog*, (Nov/Dec/93).

Solman, Gregg. "Uncertain Glory." *Film Comment*, (May–June 1993).

Sragow, Michael. "*Blade Runner*: Stalking the Alienated Android." *Rolling Stone*, August 5, 1982.

Strick, Philip. "*Blade Runner*: Telling the Difference." *Sight & Sound 2*, December 1992.

Turan, Kenneth. "*Blade Runner* II." *Los Angeles Times Magazine*, September 13, 1992.

LEGEND:

Periodicals:

Broeske, Pat H. "Outtakes: Tuning-up *Legend.*" *Los Angeles Times*, November 3, 1985.

Desowitz, Bill. "*Brazil, Legend* Stay on the Shelf." *Hollywood Reporter*, September 3, 1985.

———— "Good vs. Evil Topic of Scott's *Legend.*" *Hollywood Reporter*, April 11, 1986.

MacLean, Paul Andrew. Liner notes on *Legend* CD. 1992.

Ressner, Jeffrey. "Goldsmith Outlines his Upcoming Plans." *Hollywood Reporter*, April 25, 1985.

Smith, Steven L. "Tangerine Dream Knows the Score." *Los Angeles Times*, July 4, 1986.

CHAPTER 5: SPECIAL EDITIONS

Books:

Cameron, James, and William Wisher. *Terminator 2: Judgment Day: The Book of the Film: An Illustrated Screenplay.* (Annotations by Van Ling.) Applause Books, 1991.

Periodicals:

Cameron, James. "*The Abyss* Special Edition." Liner notes/laserdisc. Supplement by Van Ling. 1993.

Fein, David C. "*Aliens*/Special Laserdisc Edition." Liner notes. Supplement also by Van Ling. 1992.

Ling, Van. "*The Abyss* Special Edition." *Widescreen Review*, May/June 1993.

Reber, Gary. "On Screen: James Cameron." *Widescreen Review*, May/June 1993.

Welkos, Robert W. "Back into *The Abyss.*" *Los Angeles Times*, February 22, 1993.

CHAPTER 6: ADDED SUBTRACTIONS

CLOSE ENCOUNTERS OF THE THIRD KIND
AND *CLOSE ENCOUNTERS OF THE THIRD KIND: SPECIAL EDITION*

Periodicals:

"*Close Encounters'* Future as Told by (1) Levy and (2) Spielberg." *Variety*, October 31, 1979.

"Columbia *Encounters* Plans News to Steven Spielberg." *Daily Variety*, October 24, 1979.

"New *Encounters* a Refinement of Original Version." *Daily Variety*, August 1, 1980.

Beller, Miles. "The High Cost of Going Inside the Alien Spaceship." *Los Angeles Herald Examiner Weekend*, August 1, 1980.

Fivelson, Scott. "Another *Close* Call." *Los Angeles Times*, August 24, 1980.

Harmetz, Aljean. "*Close Encounters* to Get Even Closer." *New York Times*, December 6, 1978.

Knight, Arthur. "Special Edition of *CE3K*." *Hollywood Reporter*, August 1, 1980.

Schriger, Charles. *Close Encounters. Los Angeles Times*, February 10, 1979.

Shay, Don. "A Close Encounter with Steven Spielberg." *Cinefex*, (February 1993).

1941:

Pollock, Dale. "Spielberg Cuts *1941* 17 Minutes." *Variety*, December 19, 1979.

————. "*1941* Cancelled as Pic Undergoes Surgery." *Daily Variety*, January 24, 1979.

CHAPTER 7: THE DEVIL IN THE CAN

Books:

Ciment, Michel. *John Boorman*. Faber & Faber, 1986.

Pallenberg, Barbara. *The Making of Exorcist II: The Heretic*. Warner Books, 1977.

Periodicals:

Exorciste II: L'Hérétique. L'Avant-Scène Cinéma, February 1978.

"Warner Bros. Not Happy With the Last *Heretic* Laugh." *Daily Variety*, June 22, 1977.

Grover, Stephen. "*Exorcist II*, Bedeviled by Audience Laughs, Undergoes Surgery." *Wall Street Journal*, June 30, 1977.

Harmetz, Aljean. "The Movies That Draw Hatred." *New York Times*, May 4, 1981.

McBride, Joseph. "Boorman Shoulders Responsibility for *Heretic*, Which He's Recutting." *Daily Variety*, June 24, 1977.

———. "Recut *Exorcist II* Test Gets Favorable Audience Response." *Daily Variety*, June 28, 1977.

CHAPTER 8: THE DE PALMA CUTS

DRESSED TO KILL:

Periodicals:

Deeb, Gary. "NBC-TV Censors Sharpen Their Knives for *Dressed to Kill*." *Los Angeles Herald Examiner*, November 26, 1981.

Grant, Lee. "Women Vs. *Dressed To Kill*: Is Film Admirable or Deplorable?" *Los Angeles Times*, September 12, 1980.

Wood, Peter. "*Dressed To Kill*: How a Film Changes From X to R." *New York Times*, July 20, 1980.

SCARFACE:

Periodicals:

"Pacino's *Scarface* Outrage." *Photoplay* [UK], March 1984.

"Rating *Scarface*: a Postmortem." *Motion Picture Product Digest*, February 15, 1984.

"*Scarface* Gets X, Appeal Next Week." *Hollywood Reporter*, November 4, 1983.

"*Scarface* Wins R After MPAA Plea Over Violent Content." *Hollywood Reporter*, November 9, 1983.

"*Scarface* Wins R Tag on Appeal." *Daily Variety*, November 9, 1983.

"*Scarface* Still Bleeding." *Los Angeles Herald Examiner*, March 6, 1984.

"20 Questions: Brian De Palma." *Playboy*, December 1983.

Darton, Nina. "On Brian De Palma—Crossing the Line Between Art and Pornography." *New York Times*, November 18, 1984.

Farber, Stephen. "*Scarface* and the Onus of the X Rating." *New York Daily News* November 20, 1983.

Fernandez, Enrique. "*Scarface* Died for My Sins." *Village Voice*, December 20, 1983.

Gritten, David. "The Battle to Avoid the X Rating." *Los Angeles Herald Examiner*, December 9, 1983.

Harmetz, Aljean. "Movie *Scarface* Receives X Rating." *New York Times*, October 30, 1983.

Heffner, Richard D. "X Marks the Film Parents Would Balk at." *Wall Street Journal*, December 19, 1983.

Hirschberg, Lynn. "Brian De Palma's Doath Wish." *Esquire*, January 1984.

McCarthy, Todd. "*Scarface* Gets an X Rating; Appeal Planned." *Daily Variety*, November 4, 1983.

McGuidan, Cathleen, with Janet Huck. "Should X Mark the Violence?" *Newsweek*, December 5, 1983.

Pollock, Dale. "X excised From New *Scarface*." *Los Angeles Times*, November 10, 1983.

———. "De Palma Takes a Shot at Defending *Scarface*." *Los Angeles Times*, December 5, 1983.

Salamon, Julie. "X-ploiting the Ratings System." *Wall Street Journal*, September 21, 1983.

Swertlow, Frank. "Ratings War." *Los Angeles Herald Examiner*, October 25, 1983.

———. "Scar Wars." *Los Angeles Herald Examiner*, November 9, 1983.

Weinstein, Dan "Martin Bregman on *Scarface*." *America Ink*, January/February 1984.

CHAPTER 9: THE FRIEDKIN CONNECTION

Books:

Blatty, William Peter. *The Exorcist*. Harper & Row, 1971.

Blatty, William Peter. *The Exorcist: From Novel to Film*. Bantam Books, 1974.

Segaloff, Nat. *Hurricane Billy: The Stormy Life and Films of William Friedkin*. William Morrow, 1990.

Travers, Peter, and Stephanie Reiff. *The Story Behind The Exorcist*. Crown, 1974.

Walker, Gerald. *Cruising*. Stein and Day, 1970.

CRUISING:

Periodicals:

"Gays Denounce *Cruising*." *New York*, July 23, 1979.

"GCC Still Won't Play *Cruising* After Rescreening." *Hollywood Reporter*, February 6, 1980.

"General Cinema Cancels Restored *Cruising* Dates; Fear Gay Tactics." *Variety*, February 6, 1980.

"Gotham Vows *Cruising* Assistance." *Daily Variety*, July 30, 1979.

"UA Theater Chain Slaps Its Own X Tag on the R-rated *Cruising*." *Daily Variety*, February 21, 1980.

Denby, David. "Movie Bashing." *New York*, August 6, 1979.

Devere, John. "On the Set." *Mandate*, February 1980.

Ginsberg, Steven. "General Cinema Screens Won't Be *Cruising*." *Daily Variety*, February 1, 1980.

————. "Friedkin and Weintraub Defend *Cruising* Against MPAA's Rating Changes." *Daily Variety*, June 18, 1980.

Goldstein, Richard. "Why the Village Went Wild." *Village Voice*, July 30, 1979.

Gould, Martin. "New York Meeting Held With Gays on *Cruising* Film." *Hollywood Reporter*, July 26, 1979.

————. "New York Gays Plan Rallies, Disruption of *Cruising* Film." *Hollywood Reporter*, February 5, 1980.

————. "*Cruising* to Be Rescreened by General Cinema." *Hollywood Reporter*, February 5, 1980.

Haddad-Garcia, George. "A Controversial New Film Has Al Pacino *Cruising* for a Bruising From Gays." *US*, March 9, 1980.

Harmetz, Aljean. "How *Cruising* Received Its R Rating." *New York Times*, February 16, 1980.

Klain, Stephen. "UA Mum re Lorimar's *Cruising*, Greenwich Village Battle Goes On." *Variety*, August 1, 1979.

Maslin, Janet. "Friedkin Defends his *Cruising*." *New York Times*, September 18, 1979.

Merritt, Jay. "Coming Attractions." *Rolling Stone*, September 6, 1979.

Pollock, Dale. "*Cruising* in War Zone; Finished on Sched, Bow Set." *Variety*, September 12, 1979.

————. "R-rated *Cruising* the MPAA Seal of Disapproval." *Los Angeles Times*, May 4, 1980.

————. "*Cruising* Fails the *Times* Stopwatch Test." *Los Angeles Times*, May 4, 1980.

————. "R-rated *Cruising* Reclassified R." *Los Angeles Times*, June 11, 1980.

Rechy, John. "A Case for *Cruising*." *Village Voice*, August 8, 1979.

Richman, Alan. "Homosexuals Ask City to Bar Filming of *Cruising*." *New York Times*, July 26, 1979.

Russo, Vito. "*Cruising*: the Controversy Continues." *New York*, August 13-20, 1979.

THE EXORCIST:

"Blatty's *Exorcist* Target of Censorship Attempt." *Hollywood Reporter*, November 14, 1972.

"Catholic Conference Slaps MPAA for Giving *Exorcist* R Tag Rather Than X Rating." *Daily Variety*, January 29, 1974.

Meacham, Roy. "How Did *The Exorcist* Escape an X Rating?" *New York Times*, February 3, 1974.

"Jack Valenti, President of the MPAA, Argues That His Rating Board Was Fully Justified in Giving an R Rating—Instead of an X—to *The Exorcist*." *New York Times*, February 25, 1974.

RAMPAGE:

Cohn, Lawrence. "Miramax Gets Friedkin Pic." *Variety*, March 2, 1992.

Kermode, Mark. "Friedkin Vs. Friedkin, *Rampage* Revisited." *Video Watchdog*, September/October 1992.

Kimmel, Daniel M. "*Rampage* Not 'Restored,' Says Helmer Friedkin." *Variety*, November 2, 1992.

Ullmer, James. "William Friedkin Stages *Rampage* in Montreal." *Hollywood Reporter*, September 8, 1992.

CHAPTER 10: BASIC CUTTING

Periodicals:

"Censors on the Street." *Time*, May 13, 1991.

"Director Trims *Basic Instinct* to Get R Rating." *Los Angeles Times*, February 11, 1992.

Berman, Marc. "Carolco Gets Only Partial Legal Relief in *Basic* Flap." *Daily Variety*, April 25, 1991.

———. "Queer Nation to Protest *Instinct* at Carolco H.Q." *Daily Variety*, June 7, 1991.

———. "Eszterhas Proclaims Support for Gay Rights." *Daily Variety*, March 17, 1992.

Brennan, Judy. "Verhoeven Addresses *Instinct* Flap at AFM." *Daily Variety*, February 28, 1992.

Easton, Nina J. "Eszterhas Vs. Verhoeven." *Los Angeles Times*, August 23, 1990.

———. "Verhoeven, Eszterhas Make Amends." *Los Angeles Times*, April 1, 1991.

Eller, Claudia. "New Hollywood Chapter Unfolds." *Daily Variety*, June 25, 1990.

———. "*Basic* Buyout for Eszterhas." *Daily Variety*, August 22, 1990.

———. "Verhoeven Trusts *Instinct*; Eszterhas Back." *Daily Variety*, April 1, 1991.

———. Verhoeven Nixes *Basic* Changes." *Daily Variety*, April 30, 1991.

Fox, David J. "San Francisco Gays Defy Court, March on Movie Location." *Los Angeles Times*, April 25, 1991.

———. "Activists 'Dis-invited' to *Basic* Screening." *Los Angeles Times*, March 11, 1992.

———. "*Instinct* Sizzles at the B.O." *Los Angeles Times*, March 23, 1992.

———. "Eszterhas Presses for *Basic Instinct* Script Changes." *Los Angeles Times*, May 1, 1991.

Fox, David J., and Donna Rosenthal. "Gays Bashing *Basic Instinct*." *Los Angeles Times*, April 29, 1991.

Frook, John Evan. "NOW Attacks 'Negative *Instinct.*'" *Daily Variety*, March 19, 1992.

Greig, Geordie. "Too Hot to Handle." *London Sunday Times*, January 26, 1992.

Grove, Martin A. *Hollywood Reporter*, August 24, 1990.

Guttman, Edward. "Latest Plans to Upset Oscars." *San Francisco Chronicle*, March 19, 1992.

Harris, Scott, and Miles Corwin. "Opposition to Film *Basic Instinct* Rises." *Los Angeles Times*, March 21, 1992.

Harwood, Jim. "*Basic* Fear: That Lensers May *Instinct*ively Avoid San Francisco." *Daily Variety*, April 26, 1991.

Harwood, Jim, and Claudia Eller. "Citizen's Arrest on *Basic Instinct* set." *Daily Variety*, June 6, 1991.

Hirschberg, Lynn. "Say It Ain't So, Joe!" *Vanity Fair*, August 1991.

Lew, Julie. "Gay Groups Protest a Film Script." *New York Times*, May 5, 1991.

Marx, Andy. "We Thought About It (Really) and Decided That Movie Endings Are Special." *Los Angeles Times*, February 16, 1992.

Weintraub, Bernard. "Violent Melodrama of a Sizzling Movie Brings Rating Battle." *New York Times*, January 30, 1992.

AFTERWORD

Periodicals:

Cagle, Jess. "Chopped *Sliver.*" *Entertainment Weekly*, May 21, 1993.

Frook, John Evan. "Accident Prompts BV to Cut *Program* Scene." *Daily Variety*, October 20, 1993.

Galbraith, Jane. "Even Showgirls Get the Blue (Treatment)." *Los Angeles Times*, October 10, 1993.

Honeycutt, Kirk, and Brooks Boliek. "At Age Twenty-five, MPAA System Is Rated a Survivor." *Hollywood Reporter*, November 1, 1993.

Wells, Jeffrey. "Phantom Screening: You Haven't Heard the Last About *Action Hero.*" *Los Angeles Times*, June 6, 1993.

INDEX

ABOUT THE AUTHOR

Born in France but now a California resident, Laurent Bouzereau is the author of *The Alfred Hitchcock Quote Book* (Citadel Press) and *The DePalma Cut*. He wrote essays for the special laserdisc editions of Brian DePalma's *Carrie* and Alfred Hitchcock's *Blackmail* and also made the new English subtitle adaptations for eight films by Francois Truffaut.